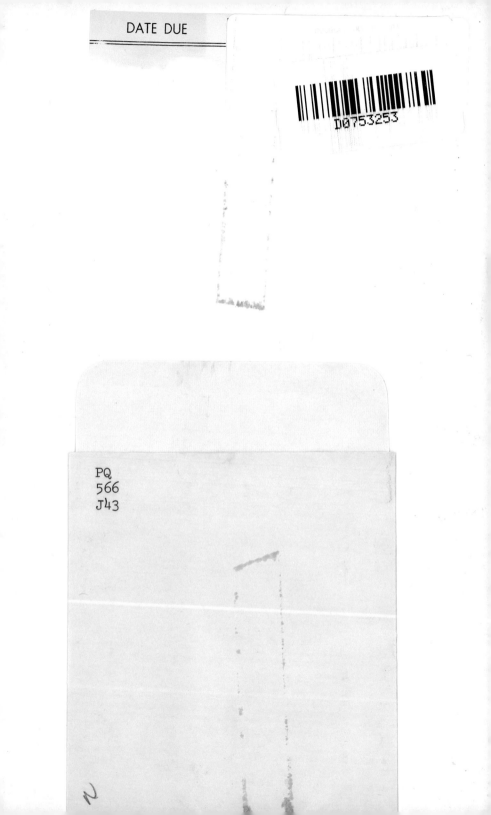

FRENCH
RENAISSANCE COMEDY
1552-1630

FRENCH RENAISSANCE COMEDY

1552–1630

BY

BRIAN JEFFERY

OXFORD
AT THE CLARENDON PRESS
1969

Oxford University Press, Ely House, London W. 1

GLASGOW NEW YORK TORONTO MELBOURNE WELLINGTON
CAPE TOWN SALISBURY IBADAN NAIROBI LUSAKA ADDIS ABABA
BOMBAY CALCUTTA MADRAS KARACHI LAHORE DACCA
KUALA LUMPUR SINGAPORE HONG KONG TOKYO

PRINTED IN GREAT BRITAIN

PREFACE

I T is just over a hundred years since Émile Chasles published his perceptive and thorough *La Comédie en France au seizième siècle*. In that time, both the live theatre and dramatic criticism have adopted new approaches to Renaissance drama, and new facts have been made available. In the light of these new approaches and facts, my aim here has been to re-examine the texts and to offer new perspectives on French Renaissance comedy. The field is a small one, on the face of it. But it is large enough to support valid conclusions; moreover, I have cast my net wide.

My thanks are due to Professor I. D. McFarlane for his encouragement and advice over a period of years; to Professor H. W. Lawton; to the Sir Ernest Cassel Fund for making possible a stay in Paris; to the University of St. Andrews, in particular for grants from the Travel Fund and Research Fund; to the Committee on Research of the University of California at Berkeley; to the Mermaid Dramatic Society of the University of St. Andrews for allowing me to produce Ben Jonson's *Alchemist* for them; and to numerous friends who have read parts of the manuscript and made their suggestions.

Berkeley, California
June 1968

CONTENTS

LIST OF PLATES

Illustrations are reproduced by courtesy of: the British Museum; the Bibliothèque Nationale, Paris; the Bibliothèque de l'Arsenal, Paris; Drottningholms Teatermuseum; the Nationalmuseum, Stockholm; the Department of Rare Books and Special Collections, University of California, Berkeley; Photographie Giraudon; and the Centre National de la Recherche Scientifique.

TEXT-FIGURES

INTRODUCTION

THIS book is about a neglected part of French Renaissance drama: about comedy and the conventions of comedy, seen not only in a comparatively small number of regular comedies, but also in translations and adaptations, dialogues, and hybrid farce-comedies, and in aspects of other genres such as tragi-comedy. It is a neglected genre today, and has been so for the past half-century. For England, we have a number of studies, editions of separate authors, and an established series, the Revels Plays, which includes a full complement of comedies of the late sixteenth and early seventeenth centuries; whereas in France, the excellent editions of Jodelle's *L'Eugène* by Professor Balmas, of Turnèbe's *Les Contents* by Dr. Spector, of the anonymous *Les Ramoneurs* by Professor Gill, are isolated, and I know of no recent over-all study.

For this reason, I begin with a survey of comedy in France from 1552 to 1630. The various genres that are concerned, different as they may be, and scattered as the evidence is, show a continuity in certain conventions from the Pléiade to the plays of the 1620s: to Corneille's *Mélite* as well as to the frankly traditional *Les Ramoneurs*. Moreover, throughout the period certain influences, in particular the importance of the study of Terence in schools and universities, remained constant. So a certain pattern may be observed in the relationship between dramatist and audience; and this first part of the study should begin to illuminate that pattern. Most of the facts in this first part are already known, and I claim no great originality for it. It may appear somewhat allusive in parts, but its purpose is to set the scene for a discussion of the conventions, not primarily to be a history of the genre. That is ground that has already been covered. In Appendix A, the reader will find information about the plots of the plays.

It has been much argued whether or not these plays were

produced in their own time. It is my belief that they were, and
I hope to have produced some new evidence that this is so. But
by now this is something of a dead horse. And for the present
purpose it is a red herring. If a reader regards the plays only as
literature, the question is irrelevant. If they are regarded as
texts for stage production, it is certain from the texts themselves
that the authors at least had in mind an idea of the stage which,
taken in conjunction with other known sources (prints, archives,
etc.), can certainly help to tell us something about staging in the
Renaissance. Finally, in the last analysis, on purely theoretical
grounds, the fact that a work is written in dramatic form is
certainly justification enough for treating it as a work of the
theatre. The second part of the book is therefore given to the
question of staging.

The third and principal part of the book studies the conventions in the plays: that is, the constant features in a relationship
between author and audience. First the comic theory of the
French Renaissance is examined, because it was certainly
known to every educated man in the Renaissance. In 1577 Gérard
de Vivre could write: 'Amis Lecteurs, chascun sçait desja bien que
c'est que la Comedie, pourtant ne m'amuseray à la vous deschiffrer en ce lieu ci, à cause, qu'il y en a tant d'autres qui en ont
faict mention.'[1] This knowledge of comic theory, gained primarily but not only through the study of Terence in schools
and universities, will affect both the attitude of writers towards
their plays and the reactions of audiences (and readers) to the
plays they saw (and read). Plays, even more than other forms of
literature, depend for their effect by their very nature upon a
two-way relationship between author and audience. To understand how a play works, you cannot afford to ignore either the
audience (as literary critics may be tempted to do) or the
dramatist (as theatrical producers may be tempted to do).
Comic theory therefore has its importance for the actual stage
presentation of these plays, and so I have given a separate

[1] Gérard de Vivre, *Comédie de la Fidélité nuptiale* (Antwerp, 1577), preface 'Aux
Lecteurs'.

chapter to it. It may be pointed out here that dramatic theory in the Renaissance is not as isolated a form of criticism as dramatic theory could be in later times, from the seventeenth century to today: in the sixteenth century a play was a 'poème' like other forms of literature, and much criticism not specifically dramatic was applicable to it. Indeed, specifically dramatic criticism in the Renaissance consisted only of a kind of appendix to what the writer had probably already said about literature in general and therefore about drama as well.

Then the plays themselves are examined under different aspects in turn: plot, character, and speech. This division is purely for critical convenience. In terms of production, it makes no sense, because for an audience a play can succeed or fail only as a totality, but for the purpose of studying the conventions it should be valid. 'Plot' includes the divisions of the play (prologues and epilogues, acts and scenes), the parts of the plot (exposition, dénouement, and what lies in between), and their arrangement. The other two divisions cover the use made of character and of verbal conventions respectively. Then I have attempted to sum up the use of conventions in general in these plays, their relation to dramatic and general literary theory of the time, and their function in terms of actual performance.

The books in which the external history of French Renaissance comedy may be found are today long out of print or deal only with isolated aspects. In the sixteenth century itself, tragedies were the more often written and published, while in theory the genre of comedy took second place to its more elevated counterpart. Since the sixteenth century, critical attention has been focused rather on tragedy, considered as a more serious and worthwhile genre, and Renaissance comedy has seldom emerged into the limelight of criticism, let alone into that of the modern stage. In the encyclopedic theatre histories of the seventeenth and eighteenth centuries—by the Frères Parfaict, La Vallière, Léris, etc.—the relevant entries are generally quite brief. The nineteenth century saw the reprinting of most of the comedies, and two general surveys: Émile Chasles's

La Comédie en France au seizième siècle (Paris, 1862), and P. Toldo's
'La comédie française de la Renaissance', published in instal-
ments in the *Revue d'histoire littéraire de la France*, iv–vii (1897–
1900). The reprints are variable in quality. Chasles's perceptive
and encyclopedic mind produced a work typical of the best of
nineteenth-century criticism, full of insight, clear and forthright.
But he is too accepting of the critical notions of his time; the
central idea behind his book is an evolutionary one: from the
enthusiastic but naïve gropings of the Pléiade we traverse a
dimly perceived region before emerging into the full light of
day with Corneille. We are reminded, I think, of similar notions
about the lyric poetry of the turn of the century. Toldo covers the
same ground, in greater detail, generally with Chasles's faults
but without his qualities. In 1905, Eugène Lintilhac once more
surveyed the field in his *La Comédie: Moyen Âge et Renaissance*,
but added little new. P. Kohler, in his *L'Esprit classique et la
comédie* of 1925, took us on an unhurried stroll over familiar
territory. Since then, as we shall see, excellent but isolated
editions and studies have appeared. One play (the only one that
I have heard of) has even reached the modern professional stage:
Larivey's *Les Esprits*, in an adaptation by Albert Camus made in
1940, acted in 1946, and remodelled for the 1953 Festival d'art
dramatique at Angers.[1]

But since Chasles and Toldo, much has been discovered in
related fields, and new approaches in criticism adopted. Even
Camus's comments on Larivey's play are seen to be quite mis-
guided in the light of recent work: 'L'ancien français, les lon-
gueurs d'un texte qui se ressent de ses origines improvisées
[*Les Esprits* is translated from a *commedia erudita*, not a *commedia
dell'arte*], deux ou trois situations gratuites [only in terms of
twentieth-century drama] risquaient de faire oublier la richesse
et les inventions de cette jolie comédie',[2] while the way in which
he uses Larivey in the first part of *L'État de siège* (as 'Pedro de
Lariba') shows his incorrect (though certainly fertile) conception

[1] Albert Camus, *Les Esprits, comédie, adaptation en trois actes* (Paris, 1953).
[2] Ibid., Avant-propos.

of that author in terms of improvised comedy. Among the more important works in related fields are Professor Duckworth's study of Roman comedy; Jacques Scherer's exhaustive study of the conventions of French seventeenth-century drama; Scherer's study of Beaumarchais's comic technique and J. B. Ratermanis and W. R. Irwin's equally close study of the same author; Miss M. C. Bradbrook's study of the conventions of Elizabethan comedy; the work of P. Duchartre, Professor Allardyce Nicoll, and others on the *commedia dell'arte*; and B. L. Joseph on Elizabethan acting.[1] These, to name only a few, have shown that the time is ripe for a fresh approach.

The conventions of French Renaissance comedy, it may be stated now, are seldom original creations by the French authors concerned. They derive from Roman comedy, from the farces, from the *commedia erudita* of Ariosto and his successors, and from the *commedia dell'arte*, but they are not identical with the conventions in those sources. For the moment, I am less interested in the sources of the French plays and of their conventions than in trying to establish what conventions were in use in French Renaissance comedy, and to judge their function and success in terms both of the practical stage and of literary theory. When this is done, we may better appreciate the genre as a whole—and, more important, individual plays. My own respect for *L'Eugène* and *Les Contents*, for example, has gone up considerably in writing this study. Also, I have refrained from discussing very much the influence of Plautus and Terence on these comedies, because I understand that a work on Terentian influence and imitation is being prepared by Professor H. W. Lawton.

Certainly the fact that the conventions are 'unoriginal' should not affect any evaluative judgement we may care to

---

[1] G. E. Duckworth, *The Nature of Roman Comedy. A Study in Popular Entertainment* (Princeton, 1952); J. Scherer, *La Dramaturgie classique en France* (Paris, 1950); id., *La Dramaturgie de Beaumarchais* (Paris, 1954); J. B. Ratermanis and W. R. Irwin, *The Comic Style of Beaumarchais* (Seattle, 1961); M. C. Bradbrook, *The Growth and Structure of Elizabethan Comedy* (London, 1955); P. Duchartre, *La Comédie italienne* (Paris, 1924); Allardyce Nicoll, *The World of Harlequin* (Cambridge, 1963); B. L. Joseph, *Elizabethan Acting* (Oxford, 1951), and a second edition, considerably altered (Oxford, 1964).

make. The conventions, whether derivative or not, on the one hand enabled writers to produce variations on an accepted framework in exactly the same way as lyric poets wrote variations on the accepted Petrarchan frameworks of the time, and on the other hand in terms of stage technique enabled them to achieve a particular kind of audience-relationship which would otherwise have been impossible. In the Renaissance, too, I do not believe that there is any such thing as an utterly conventional character or form of speech; in every play, however good or bad the play may appear, the function of the conventions is to provide a basis for variation. A parallel could be drawn with the popular music of the Renaissance in France or in England; we never, or hardly ever, find simple unelaborated versions of *L'Homme armé*, or *Faulte d'argent*, or *Go from my window*, or *Walsingham*, because everybody knew these tunes; instead we find a number of different, more or less elaborate uses made of these tunes in newly written compositions.

French Renaissance comedies are today neglected. Yet they are not such inferior productions as the space given to them in literary histories would suggest: they are certainly as good as much of the lyric poetry which is today the object of critical attention, and they have the added interest, perhaps, of the dramatic form. The reason seems to be, to a great extent, the unrefuted accusation that the plays are derivative. On this charge, who in the Renaissance shall 'scape whipping? Du Bellay's sonnets, as is well known, are often translations, more or less straightforward, from the Italian. Why should drama suffer an accusation no longer levelled against lyric poetry? Weber, Saulnier, and others have shown how often specific sixteenth-century lyric poems, including some of the most widely acclaimed, are adaptations or even translations of Italian models. Grahame Castor has analysed the whole question in the light of ideas of Pléiade theorists[1]—ideas which are in fact concerned with literature in general and not merely with lyric poetry. So if we are able today to keep our appreciation of a lyric poem

[1] Grahame Castor, *Pléiade Poetics* (Cambridge, 1964).

independent of our knowledge of its sources, then we ought
to be able to keep our appreciation of a play similarly independent.

Let us see what kind of debt is owed to their models by two
plays generally held to be imitative: Turnèbe's *Les Contents*
and d'Amboise's *Les Néapolitaines*. Édouard Fournier, in his 1871
edition of *Les Contents*, writes: 'nulle part l'imitation n'est
précise ni directe. Elle tourne autour de la comédie de Turnèbe,
l'imprègne et la colore, mais ne la pénètre pas.'[1] In his edition of
1964, Norman Spector analyses a number of analogues, of which
the following is a typical example:

> RODOMONT. Que me conseilles-tu, Nivelet? Dois-je endurer
> une telle bravade?   (*Les Contents*, I. iv)

> Che il capitan Trasilogo patirà che gli sia fatta cotanta ingiuria?
>   (G. B. della Porta, *L'Olimpia*, III. iv)

It may be a question of direct borrowing; but quite possibly
another Italian play, or some other source entirely, may be the
creditor. They are braggart soldiers speaking; and the braggart
soldier is one of the most widespread of Renaissance comic
figures. Short of a close examination of the hundreds of extant
sixteenth-century Italian comedies, the question cannot be
resolved, so that it is sensible in this as in most cases to speak
only of 'analogues' and not of 'sources'. Even where specific
borrowing can be established, it is clear that Turnèbe has recast
the borrowed material for his own play, as indeed one would
hope and expect. Slavish borrowing simply does not come into
the question with this play. *Les Néapolitaines*, too, by its very
title, seems to owe much to Italy. Its nineteenth-century editor
Fournier again writes: 'elle doit être au moins une imitation
assez peu déguisée de la comédie qui nous échappe, et qui se
retrouvera quelque jour.'[2] But although we cannot exclude the
possibility that a single close source may one day turn up—

---

[1] É. Fournier (ed.), *Le Théâtre français au XVIe et au XVIIe siècle* (Paris, 1871),
p. 91.
[2] Ibid., p. 132.

that *Les Néapolitaines* may even be a translation—it seems most likely that the play, like *Les Contents*, is a transmutation of borrowed elements into a new individual creation. It is certain that native French elements exist in it: the character of Gaster is not the only reminiscence of Rabelais; the proverbs draw on a rich native store; while the praise of Paris in the fifth Act is enthusiastic indeed.

There are, then, a number of different kinds of imitation. Larivey, apart from writing a good idiomatic French, was content with little more than altering Italian proper names to French ones. Turnèbe and d'Amboise use a process one stage further, whereby a number of different details are adopted from different Italian (and classical) sources. This can be readily done in comedy, a form which begins with a wider perspective than does the lyric poetry that Du Bellay was mainly concerned with.[1] Lyric poetry achieves its effect primarily through concentration upon a small area; a play is longer, has a different structure (different types of language put into the mouths of a variety of characters for dramatic purposes), and moreover has to stand up to stage presentation. That is to say that numerically speaking a lyric poem is likely to have a smaller number of sources than a play. In a play, a certain character may come from one source, the structure of a scene from another, a particular tirade from another, and so on. The possibility of combination is greater. And in fact we find that there are often a great number of sources used in this way; for Turnèbe's *Les Contents*, Dr. Spector finds reminiscences and borrowings from twelve Italian plays and a large number of French and other ones.

The study was begun on the basis of those texts only which are strictly comedies and which are not close translations, namely: Jodelle's *L'Eugène*; Grévin's *La Trésorière* and *Les Ébahis*; Belleau's *La Reconnue*; La Taille's *Les Corrivaux*; Larivey's *Les Esprits* (and his eight other plays, although strictly, all nine

[1] In his *Deffence et illustration de la langue françoyse* (1549), Du Bellay makes only one reference to the theatre. Cf. H. W. Lawton, *Handbook of French Renaissance Dramatic Theory* (Manchester, 1949), pp. xvi and 44.

are close adaptations); Turnèbe's *Les Contents*; d'Amboise's *Les Néapolitaines*; Perrin's *Les Écoliers*; Godard's *Les Déguisés*; Troterel's *Les Corrivaux*; the anonymous *Les Ramoneurs*; and Corneille's *Mélite*.[1] These are comparatively few in number. But they still do not exhaust the list of comedies written or performed in France in the Renaissance. Italian plays written, published, or performed there are surely part of the tradition, and we should be as wrong to ignore them as we should be if we ignored, say, Pirandello in the modern theatre outside Italy. Also, some plays are lost: thus, François d'Amboise is said to have written three comedies besides *Les Néapolitaines*, but they do not survive.[2] It was found, too, that a study of conventions (as opposed to a mere historical examination of the plays listed above) simply could not leave aside certain other works: certain translations, dialogues, or tragi-comedies, foreign plays in France, Marc de Papillon's curious *Nouvelle tragicomique*, plays bordering on farce, iconographical evidence, and so on. All these imply certain kinds of knowledge on the part of the audience or reader, so I have not hesitated to refer to them when it seemed desirable to do so. On the other hand, there are certain comedies to which I seldom refer: Pierre Le Loyer's *Néphélococugie* because it is isolated from the tradition, the only French translation from Aristophanes in the century; or Jean-Antoine de Baïf's *Eunuque* because (unlike his *Brave*) it is so close a translation that French theatre tradition hardly comes into the question. Larivey's nine plays would have overbalanced the study if all had been dealt with in detail, so in general *Les Esprits*—which critical opinion since the sixteenth century seems to have decided, I think rightly, to be the best of them—has been made to stand as typical of the nine plays. Larivey's reputation should in any case not be allowed, as it sometimes is, to obscure the real merits of, say, *L'Eugène* or *Les Ramoneurs*. I use the term 'Italianate comedy' when speaking of the plays of the central period

[1] Full details of the dates of these plays will be found in the Bibliography below.

[2] See Bibliography, sections 3 and 4, for a list of comedies supposed to have been written but now lost.

not because there was no Italian influence before or after, but because that influence is much more obvious in the plays of this time.

I chose *Mélite* as the *terminus ad quem* because it marks the first significant change in the comedy of the seventeenth century. Audiences saw and acclaimed a new variety of comedy in it, and its success even established a new troupe in Paris. It does indeed contain new elements as well as traditional ones, as we shall see. But all the same, it is not entirely typical of Corneille's later comedies like *La Galerie du Palais* or *Le Menteur*, nor does it mark the end of traditional characters like the braggart soldier, of traditional forms of speech, of traditional plots. The different types of comedy from *Mélite* onwards are another story.

Existing bibliographies turned out to be inadequate. In particular, there were frequent disagreements on points of detail, especially dates and bibliographical niceties: François d'Amboise's *Les Néapolitaines*, for example, exists in two different *tirages*, a fact which one would not gather from modern bibliographical sources. Location of copies, too, was a thorny problem. So the Bibliography at the end is a detailed one and should be a reliable source of reference on such points of detail.

The plays themselves have been reprinted in a variety of modern editions, some now in print and some out of print, which I list in my Bibliography, section 5. In addition I am preparing an edition of some of them, to be published by the Athlone Press, London.

CHAPTER ONE

The Plays

I. PLÉIADE COMEDY: 1552–1574

WHEN Étienne Jodelle wrote *L'Eugène*, and when his contemporaries hailed it as the first native French comedy, three forms of the comic theatre were already well known in France: the native farces, the plays of Terence, and Italian comedies. The farces were still firmly alive, though they had passed their heyday fifty years before, at the end of the fifteenth century: reprints of the old farces still appeared, some new ones were still written, and performances of them were certainly known both in Paris and in the provinces, both in Court circles and to the populace. Sébillet in 1548 writes of farce as a flourishing genre:

> Car le vray suget de la Farce ou Sottie Françoise sont badinages, nigauderies, et toutes sotties esmouvantes à ris et plaisir. . . . Toute licence et lascivie y [dans les Mimes ou Priapées] estoit admise, comme elle est aujourd'huy en nos Farces.[1]

In short, the farce was one of the most tenacious of theatrical forms and was to flourish continuously side by side with French Renaissance comedy. We shall see how nearly all the Renaissance comedies show one or other of its features: its characters, its particular kind of indecency, its octosyllabic metre; though not its shortness or its almost complete disregard for considerations of time or place.[2] By a piece of conscious

---

[1] *Art poétique françois*, ed. F. Gaiffe (Paris, 1932), p. 165.

[2] On farces in France, cf. Ian Maxwell, *French Farce and John Heywood* (Melbourne, 1946), and its bibliography; H. Lewicka, 'Note sur un schéma de farce au XVe et au XVIe siècle', *Bibliothèque d'Humanisme et Renaissance*, xx (1958), 569–77; B. Cannings, 'Towards a Definition of Farce as a Literary Genre', *Modern Language Review*, lvi (1961), 558–60; B. C. Bowen, *Les caractéristiques essentielles de la farce française et leur survivance dans les années 1550–1620* (Illinois Studies in Language and Literature, 53) (Urbana, 1964).

antiquarianism, and by the sheer merit of the piece, Pasquier's enjoyment of *Pathelin* even in the time of the Pléiade was like Sir Philip Sidney's enjoyment of *Chevy Chase*:

Le semblable [comparing Virgil's reading of Ennius] m'est advenu n'agueres aux champs, où estant destitué de la compaignie, je trouvé sans y penser la farce de maistre Pierre Patelin, que je leu et releu avecq' tel contentement que j'oppose maintenant cet eschantillon à toutes les Comedies Grecques, Latines, et Italiennes.[1]

In 1583 *Pathelin* was still on a reading list in French and other literatures drawn up by Gabriel Chappuys.[2]

The plays of Terence, and Italian comedies, provided two further models at the time of Jodelle, one more literary than theatrical, the other only intermittent. Professor Lawton has listed the remarkable number of editions of Terence in France in the sixteenth century, a number due mainly to his use as a set book in schools and universities: his excellent Latinity as well as his lively dramatic style made him especially suitable for the study of rhetoric as well as of other aspects of the dramatic art.[3] Again, in French Renaissance comedies elements of his plays are constantly used although his dramatic technique as a whole is never slavishly imitated; while as a background to sixteenth-century dramatic productions the commentaries on Terence—by both Donatus and his sixteenth-century followers—provide a remarkably constant body of theory and of conventions.[4] As for the Italian comedies, their performances in France at this time, such as that of Bibbiena's *La Calandria* in 1548 at Lyon, or of Alamanni's *Flora* in 1555 at Fontainebleau, were isolated,

[1] E. Pasquier, *Les Recherches de la France* (Paris, 1617), p. 925.
[2] In *L'Avare cornu*; cf. I. 2 below.
[3] H. W. Lawton, *Térence en France au XVIe siècle* (Paris, 1926).
[4] M. T. Herrick's *Comic Theory in the Sixteenth Century* (Illinois Studies in Language and Literature, 34) (Urbana, 1950) is a study largely based on the numerous and important sixteenth-century commentaries on Terence's plays; while E. W. Robbins's *Dramatic Characterization in Printed Commentaries on Terence* (ibid. 35) (Urbana, 1951) studies one chosen aspect of Terence's work as reflected in those same commentaries.

and we shall see how their influence does not become properly significant until the establishment of Italian troupes in France in the early 1570s.

Jodelle's *L'Eugène* bears the marks of farce and of Terentian comedy. From the farce it takes its octosyllabic metre, its satire on the clergy in the person of the self-indulgent Eugène, the characters of the *mari complaisant* and his wife with her easy morals; from Terence, its five acts, the rather larger number of characters, the serious nature of some of the speeches (such as Arnault's on the professions of scholar and soldier), and the developed characterization. From the Italians, as yet, nothing. In the last analysis, the essence of a play lies in what it is *about*: and there can be no doubt that this play is about the relationship of Alix the wife and Eugène her lover; about a peril that threatens that relationship and how the peril is avoided. This kind of immoral situation is not Terentian; but it is so typical of farce that we are certainly justified in regarding this play as essentially a farce elaborated by certain formal elements from Latin comedy.[1] Why should this be so? In the serious theatre, Jodelle was certainly an innovator, writing in the new form of classical tragedy, which was utterly different from the non-comic forms of his day. But here he has accepted much more, discarded less. A reason may be that the farces were successful with all social classes in the theatre of his day and so offered something of a guarantee of success if Jodelle used them and simply added certain classical elements. Again, theoretically, comedy is a picture of the life of ordinary people: the figures of, for instance, Guillaume the simpleton or Arnault the enthusiastic soldier-scholar were doubtless considered sufficiently close to contemporary society, without any attempt

---

[1] M. Balmas, in his edition of *L'Eugène* (Milan, 1955), gives greater importance to the formal elements such as the use of acts and scenes and the observation of the unities, and states: 'Il serait injuste d'en faire tout simplement une farce affublée à l'antique' (p. 16). It is true that the observation of the unities represents a clear break from the extraordinary looseness of the farces in matters of time and place. But these formal elements cannot be said to outweigh the basic subject of the play—what it is about—which is certainly farcical.

to adapt Terentian characters. As M. Chamard says, the play shows 'un curieux [!] effort pour créer une comédie nationale, inspirée essentiellement de la réalité contemporaine'.[1]

Marty-Laveaux, writing in his 1868 edition of Jodelle's works, calls *L'Eugène* 'un des meilleurs ouvrages de Jodelle'.[2] He points out 'des vers heureux' and 'quelques traits de caractère', saying, though, that it does not show 'le moindre talent de composition'. Certainly the play is no masterpiece of comic structure like, say, Jonson's *Alchemist* with its carefully interwoven strands; but it has at least a perfectly unified structure and in three ways shows a definite 'talent de composition'. First, the unity lies, as I have said, in the appearance of a peril and in its successful deflection, without any irrelevant action at all. Another virtue is in the character of Eugène: he is the only character in French Renaissance comedy who develops in the course of the play, from recklessness to authoritative resourcefulness. And finally, the play is one of the few in French Renaissance comedy in which there is no *deus ex machina* and in which the whole action stems from the nature of the characters. Given the arrival of Florimond in Act II (at the beginning of the action) and given the characters of the others, the action follows naturally.

L'Eugène is the only surviving comedy out of two by Jodelle, the other being *La Rencontre*. M. Balmas, in his edition of *L'Eugène*, dates that play at September 1552, and *La Rencontre*, together with the tragedy *Cléopâtre*, at 1553.[3] The text of *La Rencontre* does not survive, but we know a little about its plot: that its dénouement consisted of a group of characters finding themselves within a single 'maison' or compartment; and that either in this play or in *Cléopâtre* or in both, parts were played by Belleau and by Jean de la Péruse.[4] The resounding success of the performance of these plays is well known.

The next comedies after Jodelle's, Grévin's *La Trésorière* and

---

[1] H. Chamard, *Histoire de la Pléiade*, vol. ii (Paris, 1939), p. 19.
[2] *Les Œuvres et meslanges poetiques d'Estienne Jodelle*, ed. Ch. Marty-Laveaux, vol. i (Paris, 1868), p. 311.
[3] Ed. cit., pp. 6–12.
[4] Cf. Chapter II, section 5, below.

PLATE I

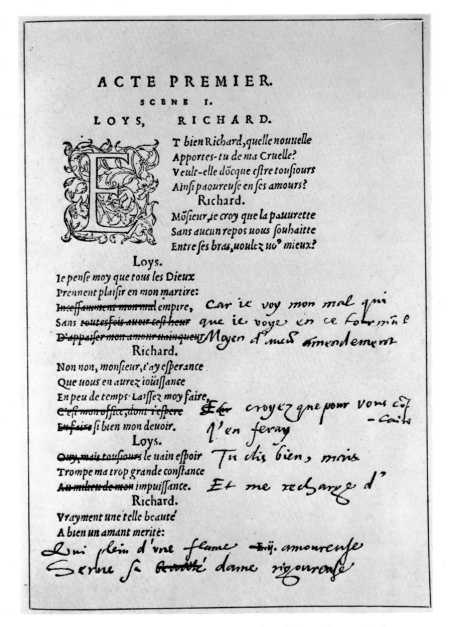

The beginning of Jacques Grévin's *La Trésorière* in his *Théâtre*, Paris, 1561, in the copy of the Musée Plantin-Moretus, Antwerp, showing corrections in Grévin's own hand, perhaps for a projected new edition by Plantin

Les Ébahis, resemble *L'Eugène* in their metre, still the octo-syllable; in their small scale and restricted number of scenes; and in their immorality. Grévin, like Jodelle a student at the Collège de Boncourt,[1] had his plays acted in university circles, at the Collège de Beauvais, in 1559 (*La Trésorière*) and 1561 (*Les Ébahis*). *La Maubertine* is probably a third comedy by him, now lost.[2] Both plays were published in *Le Theatre de Jaques Grevin* in 1561; and it seems that in 1567 he still thought highly enough of them to prepare a new edition, for a copy of the 1561 edition exists with manuscript changes in his hand, probably dating from that year and apparently made for a new edition by the printer Plantin which never appeared.[3]

Grévin's interest in the theatre was wide. Each of the two comedies was performed together with other plays, *La Tré-sorière* preceded by the so-called 'satyre' or 'jeux satyriques' *Les Veaux*, *Les Ébahis* by *Les Veaux* and Grévin's tragedy *César* —a deliberate attempt to reproduce something of the dramatic performances of the ancients. And side by side with this neo-classical endeavour, he shows a knowledge of the theatre in his own time, telling us in his *Brief discours* of the plays staged on moving carts in Flanders in his day. Finally, theatre imagery is used in a number of his poems, especially in one sonnet of his *Gélodacrye*:

> Qu'est-ce de ceste vie? un public eschafault,
> Où celuy qui sçait mieux jouer son personnage,
> Selon ses passions eschangeant le visage,
> Est toujours bien venu et rien ne luy défault.
>
> . . . Ainsi souventes fois l'on voit sur un theatre
> Un conte, un duc, un roy à mille jeux s'esbatre,
> Et puis en un instant un savetier nouveau . . .[4]

It may be partly because of this theatrical interest that it is the plots that are the most attractive feature of his two comedies:

[1] Cf. H. Chamard, *Histoire de la Pléiade*, ii. 5.
[2] Cf. Appendix B below.
[3] Cf. Bibliography, section 1, below, and Plate I.
[4] *Théâtre complet et poésies choisies*, ed. L. Pinvert (Paris, 1922), p. 316.

they are restless, skilfully built up and unified, especially in *La Trésorière* with its financial complications, as though he were most aware of this side of dramatic writing. His characters, on the other hand, are less full than Jodelle's, and his language less colourful than Belleau's. Both his plays are about the progress of rather complicated *amours*.

Rémy Belleau, as we saw, acted in the first performances of Jodelle's *Cléopâtre* and *La Rencontre*; he was also to write verses for Baïf's *Le Brave*. His own comedy, *La Reconnue*, was first published in the posthumous collection of 1578, but in an apparently incomplete form, in that a number of lines lack a rhyme. There are eleven such lines in the play; four of them are lines ending a scene and one of them is the closing line of the whole play:

> . . . on souppe, je le sens.
> Je vous prirois d'entrer ceans
> Si la salle estoit assez grande.
> Mais adieu, je me recommande,
> Ce sera pour une autre fois.[1]

It may indeed be, as the preface 'Au lecteur' of the 1578 edition says, that the play was left unfinished; but it seems an odd process of composition whereby Belleau should intend to add extra lines for the sake of rhyme at a later date, so I am inclined to accept the imperfection as it stands.

The play is set in 1563, the year of the siege of Le Havre and a year after the siege of Poitiers, both of which are mentioned in the text. We may suppose that the date of composition, and perhaps of performance, is the same as the date of the action. In any case, the play must already have been old by the time of its first publication in 1578.

La Reconnue is again like a farce, in its metre and in its subject, an old man in love. It has a classical model, Plautus' *Casina*: but that is a play which though gay and hilarious is certainly not

---

[1] Text from *Ancien Théâtre français*, ed. Viollet-le-Duc, vol. iv (Paris, 1855), p. 438.

one of the more developed of classical comedies, and is indeed described by Professor Duckworth as a 'musical farce'.[1] Belleau has taken from it the figure of the old man and his discomfiture, and his shrew of a wife and her gossip the neighbour. However, the character of L'Amoureux, the speeches about the law-courts, and the whole plot-structure are Belleau's rather than Plautus', and it is in a more general way that his play resembles Terence's or Plautus': in that it gives us a much more unified picture of a bourgeois society. Jodelle's main characters, for example, are a *mari complaisant* and his wife, a churchman whose pleasures are music and hunting, and two soldiers fresh from the wars, a varied collection who give a piecemeal picture of their society. With *La Reconnue* we are much more clearly in a single unified milieu: that of bourgeois men of law and their families. Monsieur is an advocate; Maistre Jehan is his clerk; the young lover is also in the legal world. The young woman around whom the action revolves is, plausibly, Monsieur's ward; Madame, the neighbour, and the servants discuss the problems of marriage and family life completely within the context of a closed social circle. So closed is it, in fact, that the whole atmosphere is most success-fully a claustrophobic one, of sour discontent at one's profes-sional or marital status, of selfishness, of determination to use other people to gain one's own ends: an atmosphere entirely different from the gaiety of nearly all other French Renaissance comedies.

Of those of the Pléiade who dreamed of resuscitating the classical theatre, the first was not Jodelle, but Jean-Antoine de Baïf. It even appears that Baïf had chosen the subject of Cleo-patra before Jodelle:

> Jodelle moy present, fist voir sa Cleopatre,
> En France des premiers au Tragique theatre,
> Encor que de Baïf, un si brave argument
> Entre nous eust esté choisi premierement.[2]

---

[1] Duckworth, *The Nature of Roman Comedy*, p. 165.
[2] Jean Vauquelin de la Fresnaye, *Art poétique*, II. ii. 1035-8, ed. G. Pellissier (Paris, 1885), p. 119.

But he tells us himself that other subjects and other forms of literature, in particular lyric poetry, tempted him away from the theatre:

> Encor, Jodelle, en voix humble je chante,
> N'osant pousser d'aleine qui soit forte
> Mes petis vers rampans d'alure basse,
> Bien que Ronsard pour tragique me vante:
> Mais celle ardeur que j'eu premier est morte,
> Depuis qu'Amour me rompit mon audace.[1]

Only later did he return to it, with three plays that survive, and perhaps a further four, reported by Du Verdier in 1585,[2] but now lost. Even so, despite the example of original plays in French from 1552 on, all Baïf's seven plays are translations or adaptations from classical models. They are *L'Eunuque* from Terence, *Le Brave* from Plautus' *Miles gloriosus*, *Antigone* from Sophocles; and versions of Aristophanes' *Plutus*, Terence's *Heauton Timorumenos*, Euripides' *Medea*, and Sophocles' *Trachiniae*.

Of the two surviving comedies, *L'Eunuque* is an almost literal translation, *Le Brave* an adaptation. *L'Eunuque* makes only small changes for stylistic purposes, and the proper names are only modified and not changed: for example Phaedria in the *Eunuchus* becomes 'Fedri jouvenceau'. It seems likely that it was performed, perhaps at Court, for the manuscript now in the Bibliothèque Nationale bears the words 'Achevée Lendemain de Noël devant jour 1565', as though it were written for some Christmas festivity. *Le Brave* certainly was so performed, as its title-page tells us: 'Le Brave, comedie de Jan Antoine de Baïf, jouee devant le Roy en l'hostel de Guise, à Paris, le XXVIII de janvier M.D. LXVII.'[3] Preceding or following the acts were five 'chantz recitez entre les actes de la comedie', verses perhaps sung, and in honour of the Royal Family and without connection with the subject-matter of the play. As interludes, they may be

---

[1] *Œuvres*, ed. Ch. Marty-Laveaux, vol. iv (Paris, 1881), p. 394.
[2] Antoine du Verdier, *Bibliothèque* (Lyons, 1585), p. 641.
[3] J.-A. de Baïf, *Le Brave* (Paris, 1567).

considered a variant on the classical instrumental music referred
to, but rejected, by Jodelle:

> Mesme le son qui les actes separe,
> Comme je croy, vous eust semblé barbare,
> Si l'on eust eu la curiosité
> De remouller du tout l'antiquité.[1]

Le Brave is more of an adaptation than *L'Eunuque*, though the
plot-structure remains the same, down to the placing of the
prologue at the beginning of Act II. Place-names and personal
names are naturalized: the action occurs at Orléans, Plautus'
Pyrgopolynices becoming Taillebras and Periplectomenus
Bontams. The speeches are sometimes cut, sometimes amplified:
in the last scene of the play, for instance, Taillebras has a speech
of fourteen lines in which he pulls himself together ('Ay-je au
moins toute ma personne?') which is not in Plautus and is a
deliberate amplification of the braggart captain's part. Indeed,
in view of the favour enjoyed by the braggart in France, from
the *Franc-archer de Bagnolet* on, perhaps it is not a coincidence
that Baïf should have chosen to translate the *Eunuchus* and
Miles gloriosus, which of all Terence and Plautus are precisely
the two plays that feature that character most. Both Baïf's
plays are in octosyllables, like the farces, like the Pléiade
comedies (and like the *Franc-archer*)—but unlike Terence and
Plautus, both of whom use a majority of comparatively long
lines.[2]

Jean de la Taille is a figure of transition between the Pléiade
and the more Italianate generation which was to follow. One
of his two comedies, *Le Négromant*, is a translation from Ariosto,
while the other, *Les Corrivaux*, borrows its plot from Boccaccio.
T. A. Daley believed[3] that it was based mainly on Parabosco's *Il*

---

[1] *L'Eugène*, ed. Balmas, prologue, ll. 69–72. On Baïf's 'chantz', cf. Helen Purkis,
'Les intermèdes à la cour de France au XVIᵉ siècle', *Bibliothèque d'Humanisme et
Renaissance*, xx (1958), 296–309.

[2] Baïf's plays are discussed, and comparisons with their originals made, in
M. Augé-Chiquet, *Jean-Antoine de Baif* (Paris, 1909), ch. v.

[3] T. A. Daley, *Jean de la Taille (1533–1608), étude historique et littéraire* (Paris,
1934), pp. 193–5.

Viluppo (1547), to which it certainly shows strong resemblances. It is also very similar to Nardi's *I due felici rivali* (1513). But both the Italian plays are certainly based on the fifth story of the fifth day of Boccaccio's *Decameron*. And La Taille's play is much simpler than either of the Italian plays, so that it appears to be derived not from them, but from Boccaccio, either from the original or from a French translation. Two factors confirm this. First, in La Taille, the heroine is recognized by a mark under her left ear. Neither *Il Viluppo* nor *I due felici rivali* has this, but it is the device used by Boccaccio. And second, in La Taille the heroine bears the unusual name of Restitue, a name not used either in *Il Viluppo* or in *I due felici rivali*. This name, admittedly, is not Boccaccio's heroine's name either; but in the form Restituta, it appears in the *succeeding* story of the *Decameron*, the sixth story of the fifth day. The play itself may be dated 1562: for in Act II, scene i Fleurdelys is called 'une fille jeune d'un quinze ans', and in Act IV, scene v we learn that she was five years old when the French army entered Metz (in 1552). *Le Négromant* probably dates from the same period, when La Taille and his brother Jacques were at the University of Paris and when we know that they both wrote tragedies and comedies.[1]

Le Négromant takes its place in the number of translations of Italian comedies into French which had begun already in the 1540s; but *Les Corrivaux* is the first original French comedy to be inspired by an Italian source. In this, and especially in that it is a non-dramatic source, La Taille shows his originality, just as he did in his *Saül le furieux*, in showing an individual variation on tradition.[2] But despite its Italian debt, *Les Corrivaux* (like *Saül*) is *only* a variation on an established tradition, not a breaking away from it like Le Loyer's *Néphélococugie* later. In its formal structure, it remains close to *L'Eugène*, *La Trésorière*, *Les Ébahis*, and *La Reconnue*. It is short; it has few scenes; its characters are

---

[1] Jean de la Taille states that his brother wrote 'comme moy (selon le vray art, et la façon antique) Poëmes entiers, Tragedies et Comedies, en l'âge de 16, 17 et 18 ans' (*Saül le furieux* (Paris, 1572), f. 70).

[2] Cf. Daley, op. cit.; A. Werner, *Jean de la Taille und sein Saül le furieux* (Leipzig, 1908), pp. lvi–lviii.

few. It uses a farcical situation whereby two servants find themselves at the same place at the same time to give secret signals to the two young lovers who have bribed them; but the situation is less developed than it might have been in one of the later Italianate plays of the kind of Turnèbe's *Les Contents*. A major novelty is that it is in prose.

To these various comedies we may add three translations from the Italian in this early period. Charles Estienne's *Comédie du Sacrifice* (Lyon, 1543) has the distinction of being the first translation of an Italian comedy into French, and is taken from *Gl'Ingannati* of the Intronati of Siena. It proved popular enough to be printed in two futher editions, in 1548 and 1556, though under the new title of *Les Abusés*.[1] Jacques Bourgeois's *Comedie tres elegante, en laquelle sont contenues les Amours recreatives d'Erostrate . . . et de la belle Polimneste . . .* (Paris, 1545), from Ariosto's *I Suppositi*, unfortunately does not survive, though the very precision of the title, given by La Vallière in 1768,[2] seems to show that it did in fact exist. Jean-Pierre de Mesmes's *Comédie des supposés*, too, seems to have been a good deal less popular than Estienne's play, in that the first edition (Paris, 1551) exists in a reissue of 1585, some thirty years later, consisting of unsold copies of the first edition provided only with a new title-page.

It is surely remarkable that two of these three translations, and La Taille's *Le Négromant* as well as Godard's *Les Déguisés* later in the century, should all be from Ariosto, when very large numbers of other Italian comedies were by this time in existence and in print. It is yet another example of Ariosto's great popularity in France in the sixteenth century in various literary fields, including the related one of French tragi-comedy.[3]

[1] The first edition is rare; a copy in the Bibliothèque de l'Arsenal is cited by Mme Horn-Monval, *Traductions et adaptations françaises du théâtre étranger*, vol. iii (Paris, 1960), p. 70. Cf. H. W. Lawton, 'Charles Estienne et le théâtre', *Revue du seizième siècle*, xiv (1927), 336–47.

[2] *Bibliothèque*, vol. iii (Dresden, 1768), p. 243.

[3] Garnier's *Bradamante*, the first surviving tragi-comedy, is from Ariosto; so, presumably, was the lost *La Belle Genièvre*, performed at Fontainebleau in 1564 (cf. G. Cohen, 'Ronsard et le théâtre', *Mélanges offerts à Henri Chamard* (Paris, 1951), p. 124). Cf. A. Cioranescu, *L'Arioste en France* (Paris, 1939).

The whole question of translation and imitation, of course, has a particular significance when it is considered in the context of the literary theories of the time, according to which translation was a highly acceptable form of literary endeavour.[1] Thomas Sébillet could write in 1548: 'La Version ou Traduction est aujourd'huy le Pöéme plus frequent et mieus receu des estimés Pöétes et des doctes lecteurs',[2] and the example of, say, Amyot and countless others throughout the century confirms this. The less direct form of imitation was by so much the more acceptable. Du Bellay's idea is well known, that the writer should take over elements from his models (who might be Greek or Roman or Italian), should assimilate them to become as it were part of his own flesh and blood, and then out of them, once assimilated, should produce his own works. Actual literal translation found less favour in his eyes, though some of his own poems are in fact almost direct translations from the Italian. Sébillet, his opponent, on these grounds was able to accuse him of hypocrisy:

> Si je fay moins pour moy en traduisant anciens auteurs qu'en cérchant inventions nouvelles, je ne suy toutefois tant a reprendre que celuy qui se vante d'avoir trouvé, ce qu'il ha mot a mot traduit dés autres.[3]

But it remained a fact that translations and imitations from the Latin and from the Italian found sufficient favour in Renaissance eyes for there to have been a constant stream of them throughout our period. For comedy perhaps more than for other literary genres, the point is an important one, and we shall return to it.

The genre of comedy, then, has its place in the Pléiade's literary activity. Ronsard himself seems to have taken part in it, for his biographer Claude Binet tells us that he translated Aristophanes' *Plutus* while at the Collège de Coqueret. If this

---

[1] Cf. esp. Grahame Castor, *Pléiade Poetics* (Cambridge, 1964), in particular chapter 6, 'Imitation of Model Authors', pp. 63–76.

[2] *Art poétique françois*, ed. F. Gaiffe (Paris, 1932), p. 28.

[3] Preface to his translation of Euripides' *Iphigenia at Aulis*, quoted from H. Chamard, *Joachim du Bellay* (Lille, 1900), p. 147.

were so, it and Le Loyer's *Néphélococugie* of 1578 would be the only known translations of Aristophanes into French in the sixteenth century. But it has not survived; and a *Plutus* is also attributed to Baïf, who, as we know, translated or adapted two Latin comedies and may well have translated this also. Without further evidence, we cannot do better than adopt M. Lebègue's ingenious suggestion that the translation was a joint undertaking of the two while at the Collège de Coqueret.[1] There are also other marginal connections of Ronsard with the theatre: the 'chant' which he wrote for Baïf's *Le Brave*, or the liking for farce which he shows in the *Élégie à la Reine* of 1564:

> Quand voirrons nous sur le haut d'une scene
> Quelque Janin, ayant la jouë pleine
> Ou de farine ou d'ancre, qui dira
> Quelque bon mot qui vous resjouyra?[2]

In the time of the Pléiade, ten comedies at least were written; two were performed at Court, which was no small achievement; Belleau and Jean de la Péruse acted in the performance of *La Rencontre* with *Cléopâtre*; Étienne Pasquier, Jean Vauquelin de la Fresnaye, and Turnèbe (father of the author of *Les Contents*) saw the performance. The verses between the acts of *Le Brave* were written by Vasquin Philieul, Ronsard, Belleau, Desportes, and Baïf himself. It is no exaggeration to say that at this early period, comedy was a genre that owed its existence almost entirely to the students of the Collège de Boncourt: first Jodelle, with his fellow-students Belleau and La Péruse as actors; then Belleau himself; while La Taille and Grévin both studied there.[3] Muret and Buchanan, both teaching at the Collège de Boncourt in the early 1550s, may perhaps have encouraged this production, though they themselves wrote tragedies only and not comedies.

---

[1] 'Tableau de la comédie française de la Renaissance', *Bibliothèque d'Humanisme et Renaissance*, viii (1946), 301. Gustave Cohen, in his 'Ronsard et le théâtre', p. 123, suggests that the translation was neither by Ronsard nor by Baïf, but by Dorat.

[2] *Œuvres complètes*, ed. P. Laumonier, vol. xiii (Paris, 1948), p. 148.

[3] Cf. H. Chamard, *Histoire de la Pléiade*, ii. 5–8.

Ten plays are not many, in a period of twenty years. Italy was producing far larger numbers of comedies at this time; so was England, fifty years later. The number of the comedies is not so important as their qualities; but still, we may ask why there were so few. First, it is certain that the comic genre was less highly rated than the tragic, as we shall see when we come to examine comic theory in the Renaissance: it dealt with bourgeois rather than nobles, it showed comparatively trivial matters for entertainment rather than high moral ones for edification. Certainly Terence was admired; but it was for his rhetoric and his abundant moral *sententiae*, not for the morality of his plots. Second, on practical grounds: of all literary works, plays cannot exist only on the printed page; they need theatres and a whole theatrical tradition. Italy and England had at different periods such a tradition, but the Pléiade generation in France had only fellow-students to use as actors, necessarily amateurs without any established tradition. The non-academic theatre of the time had only trivial farces as a comic genre. These authors of the first generation, then—Jodelle, Grévin, Belleau, La Taille— were faced with a choice of using a living theatrical tradition in the farces, or working within a university milieu without permanence or experience; and all of them seem to have tried to create, and to have succeeded in creating, a fusion of the two. But they still lacked theatres and actors; and practical reasons of this kind doubtless partly explain the small number of comedies written at the time of the Pléiade.

2. ITALIANATE COMEDY: 1575–1588

In the late 1570s, a new period begins not only in the history of comedy but in the literary scene as a whole. The Italianism of the time of the Pléiade, that by reaction had for a time become less evident in France, now returns in a different way, and in strength. Translations and adaptations of Italian works appear; Italian music and literature become talking-points; and in the theatre particularly, the situation is completely changed by the enormous success, hitherto only sporadic, of the travelling troupes of Italian actors.

The translations and adaptations are legion. One of the most prolific writers was Gabriel Chappuis, who by the sheer volume of his work and the kaleidoscope of his interests resembles the other writers of comedies, Pierre de Larivey and François d'Amboise. The full stream of his literary production is around the late 1570s and early 1580s. Italian literature concerns him most of all. One book in particular interests us here: the 1580 edition of his translation from Antonfrancesco Doni's *I Mondi*: *Les Mondes celestes, terrestres et infernaux . . . Tirez des œuvres de Doni Florentin, par Gabriel Chappuis Tourangeau. Depuis reveuz, corrigez et augmentez du Monde des Cornuz . . . par F. C. T.* (Lyons, Estienne Michel, 1580). *I Mondi*, first published in 1552, was a collection of dialogues, Lucianic in form but without Lucian's trenchant wit, adopting a variant of Lucian's *Vera Historia*: a satire on this world by a supposed description of another. Chappuis first published his translation at Lyons in 1578. A second edition, of 1580, says on the title-page that the *Mondes* are here 'reveuz, corrigez et augmentez du Monde des Cornuz par F. C. T.'. The *Monde des Cornuz* also reappears in the 1583 edition, and it includes a short but interesting comedy, *L'Avare cornu*.[1] We are to imagine the situation of the prologue to *The Beggar's Opera*; to prove a point (in this case about cuckolds), Le Poëte takes Le Curieux aside and has a play acted before him:

Je vous feray sortir maintenant quelques personnages qui vous demonstreront par la Scene Comique une autre maniere de cornuz que vous ne pensiez et vous feront toucher au doigt ce que je

---

[1] The first French edition is entitled *Les Mondes celestes, terrestres et infernaux . . . Tirez des œuvres de Doni Florentin, par Gabriel Chappuis Tourangeau* (Lyons, Barthelemy Honorati, 1578). Both the 1580 and the 1583 editions attribute the *Monde des Cornuz* to 'F. C. T.' These letters have been interpreted as 'François Chappuis Tourangeau', but there are reasons for supposing that 'F. C. T.' is either a misprint or a pseudonym for 'G. C. T.', i.e. 'Gabriel Chappuis Tourangeau'. Cf. the clear article 'Chappuis' in Michaud's *Biographie universelle*, vii (Paris, 1880), 503.

vous nye [*sic*; 'dye'?]: car la chose representée au vif ainsi qu'elle ha esté faite, ha plus d'energie et d'efficace, que ce qui se declare par parolles.[1]

In between the five acts, and after the play, there are discussions between the two onlookers. This play, *L'Avare cornu*, appears to be an original creation by Chappuis—so, indeed, does the whole of the *Monde des Cornuz*—a point which I have never seen sufficiently made clear.[2] No edition of Doni that I have seen includes an Italian original of this section, so that Chappuis in fact appears to have appended his own original contribution to his translation. The title-page of the 1580 edition is in fact ambiguous: 'reveuz, corrigez et augmentez du Monde des Cornuz' could mean that Chappuis was the author of the additions, or merely that he was adding more translations to this 1580 edition. But in view of the absence of an original by Doni, and the very traditionally French nature of the play, it is most likely that the play is by Chappuis.

The play itself reminds us of the earlier generation in its combination of farce elements with modern ideas of the comic ideal. The *avant-jeu* repeats some of Jodelle's claims:

> Vous orrez l'antique sujet
> Et non le stile trop abject
> Des basteleurs qui veulent plaire
> Tant seulement au populaire.[3]

The play itself, like *L'Eugène*, has five acts. But there are few other classical elements: like *L'Eugène*, its simple plot derives from the farces (a *vieillard amoureux* and his amorous adventures) and its metre is octosyllabic like the farces. Only by its inclusion

---

[1] 1580 edn., pp. 190–1.

[2] In his article '*L'Avare* de Doni et *L'Avare* de Molière', *Revue d'histoire littéraire de la France*, i (1894), 38–48, Émile Roy bases literary judgements on the unfortunate assumption that Chappuis's play is necessarily a translation of a play by Doni, existing but not found by Roy. Toldo, five years later, in a footnote to his 'La comédie française de la Renaissance', ibid. vi (1899), p. 571, attributes 'une certaine originalité' to Chappuis in the section '*Le Monde des Cornuz*'.

[3] 1580 edn., p. 193.

in a translation from the Italian does it provide a link with the new generation.

One of the more interesting figures—though his comedy is unfortunately lost—is Hierosme d'Avost. In 1583 he published his *Essais de Hierosme d'Avost, de Laval, sur les sonets du divin Petrarque*, a slim book elegantly produced: *essais* not in Montaigne's sense or in ours, but experiments or attempts in translation. The sonnets are few in number but thoughtful in technique and presentation. D'Avost has a more than academic interest in translation and its problems: the dedication discusses the ways in which he is naturalizing Petrarch, while at the end of the book, for comparison with his own versions of the same poems, he prints four translations of Petrarch sonnets by other poets: two by Vasquin Philieul of Carpentras, and two versions of *Hor che 'l ciel*, one by Peletier and one by Étienne du Tronchet. D'Avost's interest in the Italians extended to comedy. La Croix du Maine reports in 1584 that he has made a translation (which might mean an adaptation) from Loys Domenichi, called *Les Deux Courtisanes*, which is now ready for publication.[1] As far as we know, it never appeared, and La Croix du Maine's is the only evidence that we have about it. That should be reliable evidence, however, for d'Avost's book actually contains a sonnet 'A Monsieur de La Croix du Maine, sur sa Bibliotheque'.[2]

The pattern of Chappuis's and d'Avost's achievement—an interest in literary creation, largely based on Italian models, with a bias towards translation, and an interest in comedy as one part of that creative activity—is on a small scale a pattern typical of Pierre de Larivey and François d'Amboise. It seems likely that Odet de Turnèbe, too, had he lived, might have written in the same pattern, for his one play, *Les Contents*, shows him to have had a closer knowledge of Italian literature than a mere passing interest could account for. The philosopher

---

[1] La Croix du Maine, *Bibliothèque* (Paris, 1584), p. 488.

[2] In the *Poesies* appended to the *Essais* (but dated 1583), f. 11. The poem by Philieul provides a link with the earlier generation of comic writers, for as we saw Philieul was the author of one of the 'chantz recitez entre les actes de la comedie' of Baïf's *Le Brave* in 1567.

Giordano Bruno, visiting Paris in 1581–3, published his comedy *Il Candelaio* there; it may well have been French influences of this kind that inspired him too to produce this side-product of his other very different works.

Pierre de Larivey fits the pattern closely. His plays are not the isolated products of a single enthusiast for the Italian theatre, but rather fit into the variegated literary production, of many different kinds but always Italianate, of a circle interested in the same kinds of models and literary techniques, producing the same kinds (and the same volume) of works. Larivey's interests were as wide as any: his *Nuits facetieuses* are translated from Straparola, the *Filosofie fabuleuse* from Firenzuola and Doni, the *Philosophie et Institution morale* from Piccolomini, the *Humanité de Jesus-Christ* from Aretino, the *Veilles* from Arnigio. His nineteenth-century editor Édouard Fournier saw him as a Renaissance Jekyll and Hyde, turning now to sacred works, now to profane ones:

> Après cette débauche de traductions comiques, où la décence avait eu fort à souffrir, notre chanoine trouva bon de se purifier par un peu de philosophie et de piété . . . lui-même vivait, malgré le contraste de ces écrits si mêlés, avec toute l'édification d'un chanoine honnête et pratiquant.[1]

Certainly a glance at Larivey's comedies will show that they might well represent one of the two sides, in moral terms, of such a characterization. For us, we need only regard him, I think, as a man of wide interests; and if we place him in the context of the group in which he moved, we can see that these wide interests are in fact typical of the whole group: Larivey, d'Amboise, Chappuis, d'Avost, Gabriel Le Breton, and others connected with the group, even if not authors of comedies, such as François de Belleforest or Béroalde de Verville: a literary coterie who unlike the Cinq Auteurs left no collective works, and who unlike Madame de Rambouillet's friends left little

---

[1] *Le Théâtre français*, p. 56.

direct evidence of actual meetings, but whose friendship is shown by a whole series of liminary verses (to be found in numbers in the pages of Lachèvre), by dedications, even sometimes by 'L'Imprimeur au Lecteur'.[1] The most constant of their preoccupations was an interest in the literature of Italy.

All nine of Larivey's comedies—indeed, all twelve, if we include the three that were not eventually published—are translations from the Italian, and all are dedicated to François d'Amboise. The friendship between these two was a long one. As early as 1573 a sonnet by Larivey was included in a work by the young d'Amboise, *La Pologne*,[2] while the dedication of his second collection of plays, in 1611, is nearly forty years later. It is difficult to discover precisely what their relations were. Larivey, though a canon of Troyes who at least towards the end of his life is known to have performed his duties in residence at Troyes, implies in a publication of 1580 that he has served M. de Pardessus, 'conseiller du Roy en la cour de Parlement de Paris', in some capacity for twenty years: this, presumably, in Paris. D'Amboise, though from 1581 to 1585 and again in 1589 a member of the Parlement at Rennes, does not appear to have exercised his office there,[3] and to judge from his many publications in Paris remained largely in that city. Something of a clue is provided by the same publication of Larivey—Piccolomini's *Philosophie et Institution morale*—in whose dedication Larivey writes to Pardessus, 'ce grand politique Piccolomini ayant apprins la langue françoise en vostre maison et à vos despens'. This seems to mean that the translation was made in Pardessus's house, presumably while Larivey was in his service in some

[1] For instance, the intriguing note by the printer of d'Amboise's translation from Orazio Landi, *Regrets facetieux et plaisantes harengues funebres sur la mort de divers animaux* (Paris, Nicolas Bonfons, 1583), that the translation was originally to be made by François de Belleforest, who, however, passed the task on to d'Amboise; that d'Amboise had accepted it as an honour, although extremely occupied with journeys to Germany and Italy.

[2] *La Pologne de François d'Amboyse Parisien. Au tres-victorieux roy Henry, sur les occurrences de l'election, et observations des choses plus dignes de memoire veües par l'autheur en son voyage. En diverses langues* (Paris, Denis Du Pré, 1573), f. 10ᵛ.

[3] Cf. F. Saulnier, *Le Parlement de Bretagne 1554-1790* (Rennes, 1909), p. 26.

capacity, and at a time when d'Amboise and Pardessus were professional colleagues. It should be noted that not the least of Piccolomini's many works is the comedy *L'Alessandro*; there is more than the ordinary family likeness of any two Renaissance braggarts between Piccolomini's Captain Malagigi and d'Amboise's Dom Dieghos, while Dr. Spector sees a number of resemblances between the play and Turnèbe's *Les Contents*.[1] The connection with d'Amboise is strengthened by a translation which d'Amboise made from yet another of Piccolomini's works: the *Dialogues et devis des damoiselles*, which went through at least four editions by 1583.[2]

A colleague of d'Amboise, though younger than he, was Odet de Turnèbe. Turnèbe died in 1581 at the age of 29, and only one major work of his survives: the comedy *Les Contents*. The play was published in the same year (1584) as d'Amboise's *Les Néapolitaines* (though both plays are earlier); the Italianate nature of both plays, the reading which both presuppose, the use of the comic are so strikingly similar, that some connection between the two men seems likely. One would expect it in any case from the professional links. And the society in which both men moved—legalistic, intellectual, Italianate—was a small one. Pardessus's house may well have entertained these two as well as Larivey. Piccolomini's comedy *L'Alessandro*, as we saw above, appears to have been known to Turnèbe, which would fit in with the translations from that author made by both d'Amboise and Larivey. *Les Contents* itself has been amply studied by Dr. Spector in his edition of it. It is a lively play, with memorable characters, and the interesting counterpoint between hypocrisy and actual disguise gives it an unusual depth. Although strongly Italianate in every way, it nevertheless does not discard the earlier French tradition: its staging is only an elaboration of that

[1] Odet de Turnèbe, *Les Contents*, ed. N. B. Spector (Paris, 1964), pp. 146–67.

[2] I have seen two editions: Paris, Vincent Normand, 1581, and Paris, Robert le Magnier, 1583; two Lyons editions, one without date and one of 1583, both Benoist Rigaud, are cited by Baudrier, *Bibliographie lyonnaise*, iii, 188 and 378; and a Lyons edition of 1577 is cited in the *Biographie universelle*, vol. ii (Paris, 1811), p. 25.

used before, its master–servant relationships use the same techniques and contrasts, its language often derives in detail (as Dr. Spector has shown) from the earlier comedy. There is one feature that makes the play unique in France, although it is found in Italy: Turnèbe's attempt to mitigate the great artificiality of certain dramatic conventions of his time. This he does on several fronts, making the gap between what happens in life and what happens on stage yawn less widely. We shall see later how he does this—we shall see, too, that his example was not followed.

D'Amboise's play, *Les Néapolitaines*, is the only surviving comedy of his out of several which he says were acted: 'veuës et receuës avec un indicible plaisir'.[1] La Croix du Maine says that he wrote four comedies in all.[2] This one is lively and entertaining; Professor Lawton calls it 'undoubtedly one of the best of the century'.[3] It is about two Neapolitan ladies of reasonable respectability, who have come to Paris, and their gallants. The parasite Gaster and the Spanish-Neapolitan braggart Dom Dieghos, the students at the University of Paris, and the continual references to Parisian inns, colleges, gardens, and churches, give the play a colouring which the lively colloquial style reinforces. It borrows from two main plays: Terence's *Eunuch* and either the *Olimpia* of della Porta or the *Angelica* of Fornaris (the *Angelica*, as we shall see, is a reworking of the *Olimpia*).[4] Neither of these two last plays, however, was published before *Les Néapolitaines*, so we must assume either that d'Amboise knew a manuscript copy of one of them or that he saw a performance, whether in Italy or in France. Moreover, he must have

---

[1] François d'Amboise, *Les Néapolitaines* (Paris, 1584), f. 2.
[2] *Bibliothèque* (Paris, 1584), p. 87.
[3] *Handbook of French Renaissance Dramatic Theory*, p. 83.
[4] Bayle called *Les Néapolitaines* 'la Traduction d'une Comédie Italienne' (*Dictionnaire historique et critique*, 3rd ed. (Rotterdam, Michael Bohm, 1720), i. 175); its nineteenth-century editor, Fournier, wrote that it might indeed be a translation, like Larivey's plays, and that an Italian original for it might one day turn up (*Le Théâtre français*, p. 132). As yet, none has. I hope to examine the question of sources more closely in a new edition of the play which I am preparing.

gained his knowledge of one or other play well before 2 December
1583, the date of the privilege of his own comedy. We know that
the *Angelica* was acted in France in 1584, before its publication
in 1585 (Fornaris refers to this in his dedication, as we shall see),
so that it may well be that it was in fact also acted there even
earlier, that d'Amboise saw it and used it for his play. Fornaris
tells us that he has had the model for his play—that is to say,
the *Olimpia*—in his hands for some years, so he may well have
used it for acting purposes before 1584.

Les *Néapolitaines* is today one of the rarest of sixteenth-century
books. I have traced only two copies, both in the Bibliothèque
de l'Arsenal in Paris. A slight bibliographical point arises: the
two copies, although both of 1584, are not identical. The title-
page of one describes the play as 'facecieuse', the other as 'fort
facecieuse', an alteration which has necessitated changing the
setting of the type; and the privileges differ.[1] Possibly two
impressions are concerned, or possibly the differences were
introduced by L'Angelier, the printer, in the course of printing.

In precisely this period—in 1582—one of the masterpieces
of Italian comedy was published in Paris: Giordano Bruno's
Il Candelaio.[2] Critics are unanimous about the excellence of this
play, which is nevertheless the philosopher's only dramatic
work, for its liveliness and wit and for its use of the dramatic
possibilities that the genre of comedy offers. We know that
Bruno was in Paris from late in 1581 to (at latest) June 1583;[3] the
activity of the French literary circle there which we have just
discussed, as well as the popularity of the Italian actors and
Italian theatre there may have prompted him to publish—indeed,
perhaps even to compose—in Paris rather than in Italy.

Within our period, two translations of *Il Candelaio* were
made into French. One was printed in 1633 as *Boniface et le*

---

[1] Cf. Plate II.

[2] *Candelaio comedia del Bruno Nolano Achademico di nulla Achademia; detto il
fastidito. In Tristitia hilaris; in Hilaritate tristis.* (In Pariggi, Appresso Guglelmo
Giuliano [Guillaume Julien], 1582. No privilege.)

[3] Cf. Frances Yates, *Giordano Bruno and the Hermetic Tradition* (London, 1964),
pp. 190, 202–4.

PLATE II

LES
NEAPOLITAINES,
COMEDIE FRANÇOISE
FACECIEVSE.

Sur le ſubieſt d'vne Hiſtoire d'vn
Pariſien, vn Eſpagnol, & vn
Italien.

par françois d'Amboiſe Pariſien
Advocat à la Cour du Parlement.

A PARIS,

Pour Abel l'ANGELIER, au
premier Pillier de la grand
Salle du Palais.

AVEC PRIVILEGE DV ROY.

1584.

The title-page of François d'Amboise's *Les Néapolitaines*, Paris, 1584

Pédant;[1] one is still in manuscript, in what is probably an early seventeenth-century hand;[2] both are anonymous. The first is a poor effort indeed. Its author writes, in the preface 'Au lecteur':

> Ceux qui l'auront leue [*Il Candelaio*] en son original, recognoistreront aisément combien de choses il m'a falu retrancher, et ceux qui la regarderont de prez, telle qu'elle sort de mes mains, se douteront bien combien il en a falu changer. Les Autheurs qui s'attachent aux naivetez de leur langue, et aux particularitez de leur nation, comme font principalement les Comiques, sont plus à imiter, qu'à traduire; une trop grande fidelité m'eut rendu ridicule, et c'eut esté proprement en cette occasion qu'il se fut fait des vices François, de vertus estrangeres: Tu ne trouveras donc pas tousjours icy les mesmes choses, quoy que tu trouves le mesme subjet, non les mesmes rencontres, quoy que de semblables, mais plus modestes: en un mot, si quelque liberté, du moins point de libertinage. Adieu.

This is no proud statement of confidence in one's native language and in the consequent necessary techniques of imitation, such as we might have found at the time of the Pléiade; rather, principally, a statement of purification of offending passages, which in the case of a play like *Il Candelaio* is as absurd as Dr. Bowdler's enterprise, and as unsuccessful. If we examine the text, as we are invited to do, we find that it is a cut rather than an altered version of the original, and we also find two other curious facts: first, not all the passages which might be considered offensive have really been removed; and second, certain passages, which seem to us today theatrically lively and morally inoffensive, have gone. Thus, the play on *asini* and *animi* in I. iii remains. Bruno's text reads:

> BARTHOLOMEO. In questo tempo s'inamoró il Petrarcha, et gl'asini anch'essi cominciano a'rizzar la coda.
>
> BONIFACIO. Come havete detto?

---

[1] *Boniface et le pedant comedie en prose, imitee de l'Italien de Bruno Nolano* (Paris, Pierre Menard, 1633).

[2] Bibliothèque Nationale, MS. Fr. n.a. 2879, ff. 226–48ᵛ.

BARTH. Ho detto che in questo tempo se inamoró il Petrarcha, et gl'animi anch'essi si drizzano alla contemplatione.[1]

And *Boniface et le Pédant*:

BARTHOLOMEE. Ce fut justement en ce temps-là que Petrarque devint amoureux, et c'est aussi en ce temps-là que les asnes commencent à dresser la queüe.

BONIFACE. Que dis tu?

BARTH. Je dy que ce fut justement en ce temps-là que Petrarque devint amoureux, et que c'est aussi en ce temps-là que les ames se dressent à la contemplation.[2]

A lively passage in I. ii, where the character Boniface refers to, and indeed quotes, a poem by the 'Achademico di nulla Achademia'—who is, of course, Bruno himself—disappears. So does the amusing note in the *Argumento* on the three principal elements in the play.[3]

The manuscript version, in the Bibliothèque Nationale, probably of the early seventeenth century, is a different translation from the one printed in 1633. For example, the play on *asini* and *animi* referred to above is translated as follows:

BARTHOLOMEO. Dans ce temps la petrarque devint amoureux et les âsnes aussy commencent a dresser la queuë.

BONIFACE. Comment aves vous dit?

BARTH. Jay dit que dans ce temps la petrarque devint amoureux et que les ['esprits' struck out and 'âmes' substituted] âmes aussy ['se dressent' struck out and 's'elevent' substituted] s'elevent a la contemplation.[4]

But it seems to be a more or less close translation of Bruno's play, and although it is interesting that it should have been made, this straightforward translation need not concern us here. There appears to be no evidence which might connect it with any specific person or troupe.

---

[1] 1582 ed., f. 4v.   [2] p. 6.
[3] Cf. Ch. III, section 3, below.   [4] B.N., MS. Fr. n.a. 2879, f. 226v.

With the *Angelica* of Fabrizio de Fornaris, we return to strictly stage history: the Italian troupes in Paris. A very full collection of documents published by Armand Baschet in 1882 still remains the essential reference work; little new evidence has been discovered since then.[1] From his book, and from a study of the French theatre as a whole, it is clear that the success of the Italians in Paris from 1571 onwards was of capital importance. The Gelosi, the Confidenti, the Raccolti: their success and their influence are undoubted even if our knowledge of their repertory and even of their names is limited. One important text in that repertory is Fornaris's *Angelica*.[2]

Fornaris was the leader of the Confidenti and a specialist in the role of the braggart soldier, that sure success on the Renaissance stage. As the braggart soldier, he called himself 'Il Capitano Coccodrillo'. John Eliot probably saw him in Paris, and he included him in one of the dialogues in his *Ortho-epia gallica* (London, 1593).[3] We even have two contemporary prints, and paintings derived from them, showing him in his role of Coccodrillo, living up to the thunderous captain of his play.[4] *Angelica*, in which the captain is called Coccodrillo, is a reworking of the comedy *Olimpia* by Giambattista della Porta (in which the captain is called Trasilogo). Fornaris says in the dedication to the Duc de Joyeuse, in whose house he says it was acted, that it is based on a comedy given him by a Neapolitan gentleman in Venice—'mi fu da un gentil-homo Napolitano virtuosissimo spirto, donata questa comedia'—quite possibly della Porta himself, who was, like Fornaris, a Neapolitan

[1] *Les Comédiens italiens à la cour de France sous Charles IX, Henri III, Henri IV et Louis XIII* (Paris, 1882). The influence of the Italians on French comedy has been discussed in three recent articles: R. Lebègue, 'La comédie italienne en France au XVIe siècle', *Revue de littérature comparée*, xxiv (1950), 5–24; R. C. D. Perman, 'The Influence of the Commedia dell'arte on the French Theatre before 1640', *French Studies*, ix (1955), 293–303; N. B. Spector, 'Odet de Turnèbe's *Les Contens* and the Italian Comedy', *French Studies*, xiii (1959), 304–13.

[2] *Angelica, comedia de Fabritio de Fornaris Napolitano detto il Capitano Coccodrillo Comico Confidente* (Paris, Abel l'Angelier, 1585).

[3] Cf. Frances Yates, *A Study of 'Love's Labour's Lost'* (Cambridge, 1936), pp. 50–72, 163, 177–8.

[4] Cf. Plates VIII and IX

and who spent a considerable time in Venice at this period. The theory that Fornaris constructed his play on a *commedia dell'arte* scenario by della Porta (rather than on a full-length *commedia erudita* by him) appears to rest on an unsupported statement by the eighteenth-century scholar Francesco Bartoli.[1] In fact the play is so similar to *Olimpia* that no other source comes into the question.

Angelica was acted, according to the dedication, in the house of the Duc de Joyeuse. As a vehicle for Fornaris in his role of Coccodrillo, as we see him in the painting, it is excellent; but we should not assume that the changes from his model were directed exclusively towards the development and expansion of this role. He says that his model was 'da me vista, et in qualche parte imbellita, ó fiorita, per quanto con la Comica prattica sapevo intraducendoli il Capitano Coccodrillo con alcune sue rodamontate'.[2] In fact, Coccodrillo's role is by no means disproportionate (IV. ii is the last scene, by no means near the end, in which he appears). *Olimpia* has been changed according to Fornaris's taste ('imbellita, ó fiorita') as a totality, in many details outside the captain's part, doubtless to suit the troupe as a whole of which Fornaris was leader.

Angelica, then, is an example of the *commedia erudita*, not of the *commedia dell'arte*, acted by the Confidenti in Paris. It can hardly have been the only one of its kind. A professional troupe does not develop the technique necessary for such a performance for the sake of a single play. Moreover, the little we know of the sixteenth-century Italian troupes tells us that they performed both *commedie erudite* and *commedie dell'arte*: two genres, and techniques, related but certainly different. When we add to this the scraps of evidence that we have about the performance of comedies in France at this time (such as d'Amboise's plays

---

[1] *Notizie istoriche de' comici italiani* (Padua, 1781), i. 230. M. T. Herrick mentions this theory in his *Italian Comedy in the Renaissance* (Urbana, 1960), pp. 216–22, but wisely concentrates his attention on *Olimpia*. The question is fully dealt with by Louise G. Clubb in her *Giambattista Della Porta Dramatist* (Princeton, 1965), pp. 250, 305–6.

[2] Dedication, f. a ii[v].

'veuës et receuës avec un plaisir indicible'), it seems quite clear that the dramatic production of France, at least in the 1570s and 1580s, was set within the context of active and frequent stage performances.

One such stage performance is that at the Château de Pougy in 1585. As it very probably concerned either Larivey or d'Amboise, it is worth recalling it here. It was a performance of a comedy at the baptism of Henri, duc de Luxembourg, on 16 January 1585 [N.S. 1586] at Pougy. The festivities included a banquet, 'et apres souper force Musique, un grand Bal, une Comedie, et toute autre sorte d'esbatements et recreations honnestes, qui durerent l'espace de trois jours'.[1] The words are from the description of the *Discours sur le baptesme de Henry de Luxembourg Prince de Tingry, Dressé par Maistre Guillaume de Taix Doyen en l'Eglise de Troyes*; that is, by a colleague of Larivey. The baptism was administered by the Bishop of Troyes. That the comedy was one of Larivey's seems at least possible; it would be confirmed by Larivey's dedication of his *Divers Discours* (from Cappelloni) to Charles, Henri's cousin, another member of the house of Luxembourg. Charles, too, was the dedicatee of d'Amboise's *Les Néapolitaines*. The connections seem to be too many to be fortuitous.

In 1599, fourteen years after publishing *Angelica*, Abel L'Angelier published a translation of it into French: *Angelique Comedie, de Fabrice de Fournaris Napolitain, dit le Capitaine Cocodrille Comique Confidant. Mis* [sic] *en François, des langues Italienne et Espagnolle, par le sieur L. C.* The gap in time is surprising. 'Le sieur L. C.' may well be 'Larivey Champenois', since the adjective appears on the title-page on all Larivey's acknowledged works ('Pierre de Larivey Champenois'); if so, the gap in time would be paralleled by the equally surprising gap in Larivey's acknowledged dramatic publications, between the 1579 edition and the three subsequent plays thirty years later, in 1611. The attribution is by no means certain, however. In all Larivey's nine acknowledged plays, the action is modified so that the

[1] N. Vignier, *Histoire de la maison de Luxembourg* (Paris, 1617), p. 392.

plays may be 'representées comme advenues en France': the
place-names are changed, the savour of French colloquial speech
replaces the Italian. But *Angélique* takes place in Venice, like
its original; even though its prose style is lively enough. The
preface 'L'Imprimeur au Lecteur' tells us only that some small
changes have been made in the translation. There appears
to be no evidence other than the initials 'L. C.' connecting this
translation with any specific troupe or literary circle.[1]

When Montaigne travelled to Italy in 1580–1, he bought
in Florence 'un paquet d'onze comédies'.[2] He can hardly have
been alone in this, and in fact many of the copies of Italian plays
now in French libraries have probably been in France since the
sixteenth century. Larivey, to translate his nine plays, must have
had access to his nine originals, and Turnèbe and d'Amboise, too,
unless they saw their various models acted by Italian troupes,
must have known copies of them. D'Amboise, who certainly
travelled in Italy, may well have done as Montaigne did. But
some supplement to these imported copies was feasible, and
two Paris printers saw a commercial opening in the mode for
Italian things: Jerome de Marnef and the widow of Guillaume
Cavellat, who published in 1585 a reprint of the old facing-page
translation of Ariosto's *I Suppositi* by Jean-Pierre de Mesmes.[3]
It is something of a bibliographical curiosity. Thirty-eight years
had elapsed since the last edition of this translation, yet the
type is identical. Either the type had been left set up for thirty-
eight years (which is unlikely), or this edition represents a
number of unsold copies of the earlier edition, provided with
new title-pages and sold off. In any case, the translator's name

[1] The printer is Abel L'Angelier, the same who printed Larivey's other plays
and d'Amboise's *Les Néapolitaines*; but in view of L'Angelier's considerable other
productions, this is scanty evidence. The Italian version was once more reprinted,
in Venice in 1607; the dedication of this edition refers to 'L'Angelica Comedia
del Capitan Coccodrillo, stampata già in Pariggi'. This new edition is perhaps
curious, since the play's close original *Olimpia* had already been reprinted in
Venice in 1597, after the first Naples edition of 1589 (cf. Clubb, *Giambattista
Della Porta*, p. 318).

[2] *Journal de voyage en Italie*, ed. M. Rat (Paris, 1955), p. 192.

[3] First published by Estienne Groulleau in 1552; cf. Ch. I, section 1, above.

is not mentioned, and the new edition, unlike the old, is explicitly aimed at the teach-yourself market: 'Pour l'utilité de ceux qui desirent sçavoir la langue Italienne.'

Montaigne comments on the Italian plays that he knew, and his comment, as one would expect, is to the point. His taste in some matters was for simplicity—in the cannibals' songs of love and war, for example, which he paraphrases in *Des cannibales* —and in comedy he preferred Terence and Plautus to what he considered the excessive complexity of the Italians:

> Pour l'estimation et preference de Terence, il m'est souvent tombé en fantasie, comme en nostre temps, ceux qui se meslent de faire des comedies (ainsi que les Italiens, qui y sont assez heureux) employent trois ou quatre argumens de celles de Terence ou de Plaute pour en faire une des leurs. Ils entassent en une seule Comedie cinq ou six contes de Boccace. . . . N'ayant pas du leur assez dequoy nous arrester, ils veulent que le conte nous amuse.[1]

He is telling us here about his own taste, as so often in the *Essais*, and the comment is hardly intended to be an absolute judgement; after all, Bibbiena's *Calandria* or Bruno's *Il Candelaio* are not intrinsically less likely to succeed than Terence or Plautus, and Montaigne must have known that the *Calandria* had in fact succeeded on stage in France in his own century. In the theatre, a stage success counts for more than any abstract evaluative judgement. But in one point he seems to exaggerate: Italian comedies are not as a rule built up on the plots of 'cinq ou six contes de Boccace' or indeed of any other *conteur*. M. T. Herrick's *Italian Comedy in the Renaissance*, which covers all the most important plays in some detail, mentions several based on *one* story of Boccaccio, none based on more than one. They do, however, often borrow a variety of different elements, such as characters, forms of speech, or types of disguise, from different *contes*. In France, as we saw, the only comedy based on Boccaccio is Jean de la Taille's *Les Corrivaux*, and that is based on a single story, borrowing only a proper name from another story.

[1] *Essais*, ed. A. Thibaudet (Bibl. de la Pléiade, 1956), p. 452.

One product of the new Italianism, in 1580, was Robert Garnier's *Bradamante*. It may appear odd to introduce this tragi-comedy into a discussion of comedy; but certain features of the play can best be understood in the context of specifically *comic* theory and practice of the time. First, the name of the genre: a tragi-comedy may be so called because of certain character elements, as Plautus applied the term *tragicomoedia* to his *Amphitryon*: a play not only about gods and heroes (like a tragedy) or about ordinary citizens (like a comedy), but a play mixing the two. In *Bradamante*, the comic character element is in the couple Aymon and Beatrix. Aymon is a paladin of Charlemagne's court, and might be expected to behave accordingly; yet he and his wife Beatrix discuss the future of their daughter Brada-mante as any bourgeois couple would in any out-and-out comedy; anxious concern that her marriage shall be socially acceptable, complaints that children no longer obey their parents, and so on. The result is a deliberately comic incongruity. Another feature related to comedy is in the character of Leon. This braggart goes through all the standard paces of any braggart in any Renaissance comedy, though not as violently: he boasts, he threatens, he is faced with the need to fight, he is deflated. Turnèbe's Rodomont, Hardy's Scanderbec do nothing different. This point, it is true, should not be exaggerated, because although this is primarily a situation of comedy, it is one of tragi-comedy and of non-theatrical genres as well: Garnier's braggart has a model, indeed, in the Rodomont of the *Orlando furioso*, which is the main source for the play as a whole.

The history of comedy at this time is not tidy. We are faced with gaps like the fourteen years between *Angelica* and its translation; and too many facts, like the precise repertory of the Italian troupes, are unknown to us. We come now to two writers within our period who are isolated both geographically and aesthetically from the society we have just discussed. The first is Pierre Le Loyer, Angevin. Better known than his plays today are his volumes on witchcraft, which passed through three editions in 1586, 1605, and 1608, as well as a 1605 translation

into English. His two plays, *Le Muet insensé* and *Néphélococugie,
ou la Nuée des cocus*, are quite isolated in their day. The 1869
editor of the comedy *Néphélococugie* called it 'une œuvre qui
n'a pas, ce nous semble, son pendant dans quelque langue que
ce soit': in fact, it is an adapted version of Aristophanes' *Birds*;
with the lost *Plutus* of Ronsard (or Baïf, or Dorat) it is the only
comedy from Aristophanes within our period.

The second is Gérard de Vivre, a Ghent schoolmaster. His
three plays are all written 'pour l'utilité de la jeunesse et usage
des escoles françoises', and to judge from the number of editions,
enjoyed some success in their time. All three are called 'comedies',
but all three are in fact hybrids. One of them, *La Fidélité nuptiale*,
was first published in 1577 and already in part imitates the
techniques of the Italian troupes of the 1570s.[1] La Vallière
rightly speaks of *lazzi* in this play: in the second Act Charès,
'jeune gentilhomme avec la cappe et l'espée', sings to his lute, as
a serenade to his beloved's window above, no fewer than five
popular tunes of the day, but is interrupted by a servant empty-
ing a bucket of water from the window. In the third Act his valet
tries to imitate him, and a whole series of stage directions
describe the *lazzi* of the scene, for example:

> Cependant qu'il chantera, sortira un autre accoustré legiere-
> ment ayant un masque devant la face, lequel se mectra devant la
> porte tout debout en un coin, là ou l'autre ira chanter, et se tiendra
> là coy, comme si c'estoit une colomne à soustenir les fenestrages.

Vivre's concern for stage business is seen, too, in specific signs
that he uses throughout his plays; the full table will be found in
the chapter on staging below. *La Fidélité nuptiale* and the other
two plays are as far as I know the only French plays of the
century where stage directions and signs are used in any
number. The *lazzi*, the mask, and certain names (Achantio,
Pardalisca) in particular show Italian influence.

[1] *Comédie de la Fidélité nuptiale* (Anvers, 1577).

3. TO CORNEILLE'S *MÉLITE*: 1589–1630

It may be imagined that Émile Chasles, with his Darwinian theory of the evolution of literature, found this an unprofitable period. To him, it seemed a period of silence through which French comedy somehow had to pass before the new comedy of the seventeenth century could be reached: 'La comédie grandit en silence, dans le secret, pour ainsi dire; et, lorsqu'elle reparaît au XVIIᵉ siècle, on la trouve mûrie et déjà forte' (*La Comédie en France au seizième siècle*, p. 114). In fact, the silence is in part an absence of documents; if we cannot 'see' comedy at this time, then, to continue the Darwinian metaphor, it is partly because the fossils have been destroyed. But we are slightly better off today than Chasles was. In particular, Mme Deierkauf-Holsboer in her life of Alexandre Hardy (unfortunately published in a non-literary periodical), and Professor Gill in the introduction to his edition of *Les Ramoneurs*, have demonstrated that a whole comic genre existed at this time, whose plays were very probably similar to the one surviving example *Les Ramoneurs*: that is, complex, vigorous, and designed as entertainment, never published, and standing firmly in a long theatre tradition.[1] Professor Gill has shown conclusively that *Les Ramoneurs* cannot be earlier than 1623 (probably 1624); so that if we may judge from this one play (and it seems that we may), then Corneille's scorn for the plays before *Mélite*—'Je n'avois pour guide qu'un peu de sens commun, avec les exemples de feu Mr Hardy'[2]—seems to derive from a prejudice against a form of drama he considered out of date, and not from the degeneration of the genre itself. Renaissance comedy was out of date, just as Marot, Saint-Gelais, and Sébillet were out of date and condemned by the Pléiade despite any merits that may be apparent to us today. In any case, no special pleading is necessary

---

[1] S. Wilma Deierkauf-Holsboer, 'La vie d'Alexandre Hardy, Poète du Roi', *Proceedings of the American Philosophical Society*, 91 (1947), 328–404; *Les Ramoneurs*, ed. A. Gill (Paris, 1957).

[2] 'Examen' to *Mélite*, ed. Mario Roques and Marion Lièvre (Lille and Geneva, 1950), p. 135.

to show that *Les Ramoneurs* is as lively a play, as capable of achieving stage success, as any of the sixteenth-century comedies.

But how deep is the silence that Chasles refers to? It seems improbable in historical terms, not to speak of evolutionist ones, that the genre of comedy should disappear from the scene at the end of the sixteenth century, produce one excellent play around 1624, and then take a different turn with Corneille. Let us look at the evidence. The following table reproduces everything I have found that is relevant to the texts of actual comedies in France from 1588 to 1629, excluding only farces pure and simple and references to performance:

1589 François Perrin: *Sichem ravisseur*, containing *Les Écoliers* (possibly written earlier).

1589 Gérard de Vivre: new edition of plays first published in 1577.

1594 Jean Godard: *Œuvres*, containing *Les Déguisés*.

1595 Gérard de Vivre: new edition.

1597 Pierre de Laudun d'Aigaliers: a comedy (text does not survive).

1597 Pierre de Larivey: new edition of plays first published in 1579.

1597 Étienne Jodelle: new edition of *Œuvres poétiques*, including *L'Eugène*.

1597 Marc de Papillon (Le Capitaine Lasphrise): *Premieres Œuvres poétiques*, including *La Nouvelle Tragicomique*.

1598 Jacques de Lavardin: new edition of translation of the *Celestina*.

1599 Marc de Papillon: new edition.

1599 Translation of Fornaris's *Angelica* (first published in Paris in 1585) into French as *Angélique*, possibly by Larivey.

1600 Pierre de Larivey: new edition.

1602 Jean de la Taille: new edition of plays first published in 1573.

1602   Gérard de Vivre: new edition.

1604   Rémy Belleau: new edition of *Œuvres poétiques*, including *La Reconnue*.

1608   *Les Bravacheries du capitaine Spavente*, a translation of the first six of fifty-five dialogues by the actor Francesco Andreini, made by Jacques de Fonteny.

1611   Pierre de Larivey: three new comedies published (but probably composed much earlier) and a new edition of the six earlier ones.

1612   Pierre Troterel: *Les Corrivaux*.

c. 1620? Manuscript translation of Giordano Bruno's *Il Candelaio*.

1620   Pierre Troterel: *Gillette* (written summer 1619).

1624   (between 1624 and 1626) anon. (Alexandre Hardy?): *Les Ramoneurs*.

1624   Jean Godard: new edition.

1625   Alexandre Hardy: *Le Jaloux* (text does not survive).

1626   Odet de Turnèbe: *Les Contents*, new edition (first published 1584), under the title *Les Déguisés*.

1629   Pierre Corneille: *Mélite* (acted in the season 1629–30).

In a way, the table is unfair, because it includes new editions and reprints; but even reprints show the interest of an age in what is being reprinted. Booksellers then as now were in the trade to stay in business. There are one or two other scraps of evidence: in the 1626 edition of Turnèbe's *Les Contents* (now entitled *Les Déguisés*), the editor Charles Maupas writes that many people have admired the play so much that they have been making copies of it by hand.[1] And besides *Le Jaloux*, Alexandre Hardy almost certainly wrote other comedies that do not survive.[2] In general, we have a picture of an age from which very few texts survive to us but where activity is apparent. We see Pierre de Laudun d'Aigaliers writing his comedy in 1597, *Les Ramoneurs* in 1624, Hardy's *Le Jaloux* in 1625, Pierre Troterel

---

[1] Cf. Odet de Turnèbe, *Les Contents*, ed. Spector, p. xiv.
[2] Cf. *Les Ramoneurs*, ed. Gill, pp. lviii–lxii.

parodying the genre (as we shall see) in 1612 and 1620 (and you do not parody a genre if your audience is not familiar with the real thing). It looks very much as though essential texts are missing, possibly a large number of them. Why? The answer may well lie in the financial and administrative arrangements of the theatre and of the equivalent of copyright at the turn of the century. Paradoxically, it seems that when the theatre became established enough in France for regular troupes to appear and for the theatre to become a profession, publication immediately and as a direct result became less easy. Mme Deierkauf-Holsboer has shown how Hardy was specifically legally debarred, in his contracts with the troupes, from publishing his plays, while the troupes themselves (who would hold the manuscript) would have little interest in publishing a play after its first stage success was past. As for the manuscript copies, these are notoriously ephemeral and may quite easily all have disappeared, like the composing copies, supposed to have existed, of medieval and Renaissance music.

However that may be, let us look at the comedies that do survive. François Perrin and Jean Godard, isolated from the circle of d'Amboise and his friends, need not concern us long here. Structural elements in their plays will be dealt with in greater detail below. Briefly, Perrin's curious *Les Écoliers* is the work of a provincial churchman, with wide interests like his fellow-churchman Larivey, but without Larivey's zest. Besides *Les Écoliers*, he wrote a collection of sonnets; a tragedy *Sichem ravisseur*; a tragedy *Jephté* which may have been a translation from Buchanan but is now lost;[1] and a history of his own city of Autun, 'anciene capitale des Gaules', never published, and also now lost. The volume containing his plays[2] is an inelegant piece of printing by Guillaume Chaudière, in which the dedications, liminary verse, title-pages, and text are haphazardly arranged. Only one copy of the first edition of 1589 survives today. *Les Écoliers*

---

[1] One of the poems printed in *Sichem ravisseur*, by J. B. Dardault, is headed 'Sur la tragedie de Jephte traduitte par Monsieur Perrin'.

[2] *Sichem ravisseur, tragedie extraite du Genese trente quatriesme Chapitre. Par François Perrin Autunois* (Paris, Guillaume Chaudière, 1589).

itself is a slight piece of writing, an elaborated, somewhat humourless farce with elements of the Italianate conventions of Perrin's predecessors. It may date from earlier than 1589, as Perrin says that he searched it out from 'un grand fatras de vieux papiers'. There seems to be no internal evidence of date.

Les Déguisés, published in 1594 in Godard's Œuvres,[1] may also date from earlier than its publication: there seems to be no internal evidence which would date it more precisely. It is a product of the Midi: Godard, though a Parisian by birth, lived in the South, published his book in Lyons, dedicated it to a Lyons worthy, and set his comedy in Toulouse.[2] He adapts from Ariosto's I Suppositi, the third French writer to do so in the sixteenth century; and in some ways he deserves more credit for his adaptation than he has sometimes received. According to Cioranescu, the play is dull. But, for instance, Prouventard the braggart captain and Maudolé the braggart valet have scenes which are good theatre, as we shall see, and which are Godard's creation, not Ariosto's.

The interest in Italianate comedy that we discussed in the preceding section—a tradition from which Godard curiously seems to stand aside in many ways, despite his adaptation from Ariosto—continues into the seventeenth century with three new comedies by Larivey and a number of translations, dialogues, pictures, and other accessory works. The Larivey comedies, published in 1611,[3] are in some ways a curious survival from the sixteenth century, rather than a living product of the early years of the seventeenth. Larivey says that the plays are ones which he has found, dusty after many years, in his study; he dedicates them to François d'Amboise, to whom

---

[1] Les Œuvres de Jean Godard, Parisien, two vols. (Lyons, Pierre Landry, 1594). Les Déguisés, ii. 91–208.

[2] Not 'Valence', as A. Cioranescu states (L'Arioste en France, vol. i (Paris, 1939), p. 302).

[3] Trois Comedies des six dernieres de Pierre de Larivey Champenois. A l'imitation des ançiens [sic] Grecs Latins et Modernes Italiens. A sçavoir: La Constance. Le Fidelle. Et les Tromperies (Troyes, Pierre Chevillot, 1611).

he had also dedicated the 1579 collection; and as far as can be judged, the style gives no evidence of a date of composition later than that earlier collection. They are not, however, incongruous in 1611: new editions of the 1579 collection had continuously appeared since then and presumably found a market: in 1597, in 1600, and again to accompany the new plays in 1611. The new ones are as closely adapted from the Italian as the old had been.

A continuing interest in Italianate comedy is shown, too, by the three translations which we discussed in the preceding chapter: *Angélique*, in 1599, from Fornaris's *Angelica*, possibly made by Larivey; and two translations from Giordano Bruno's *Il Candelaio*, one printed in 1633, the other manuscript and possibly earlier.

Les Bravacheries du capitaine Spavente[1] gives us another glimpse, following Fornaris's *Angelica*, of the Italian troupes in Paris. The author of this is another stage captain, Francesco Andreini of the Gelosi, whose stage name was 'Il Capitano Spavento' and who tells us in his book that it is 'una raccolta di tutti le Hiperboli, ch'io soleva dire nella Parte del Capitano Spavento, recitando nelle Publiche, e nelle Private Comedie'—just as the part of Coccodrillo in *Angelica* probably tells us something about Fornaris's stage delivery. The original of the *Bravacheries* was published in Venice in 1607,[2] a long series of 55 dialogues, of 406 pages. The translation, by Jacques de Fonteny, gives us only the first six dialogues, but the shortening is probably rather a good thing. The six include things that a French audience would certainly know: the famous *Miles gloriosus* opening about polishing the Captain's armour, which is in *Les Ramoneurs*: 'Va de ce pas vers Vulcan mon Armurier, et luy

[1] *Le bravure del capitano Spavento. Divise in molti ragionamenti In forma di Dialogo. Di Francesco Andreini da Pistoia, Comico geloso. Les Bravacheries du capitaine Spavente, divisees en plusieurs discours en forme de Dialogue. De François Andreini de Pistoie, Comedien de la Compagnie des jaloux, Traduictes par I. D. F. P.* [Jacques de Fonteny Parisien] (Paris, David le Clerc, 1608).

[2] *Le bravure del capitano Spavento; divise in molti ragionamenti In Forma di Dialogo, di Francesco Andreini da Pistoia Comico Geloso* (Venice, Giacomo Antonio Somasco, 1607).

48 THE PLAYS

di de ma part qu'il face mes armes, plus claires que n'est le
Soleil quand il est le plus clair, afin que la splendeur d'icelles
oste la veuë aux regardans' (*Bravacheries*, f. 2); the proverbial
hunger of the valet: 'Mon maistre resouvenez vous que l'heure
de disner est quasi passee' (ibid., f. 21); or the reference to the
old French war-horse Bayard (whom Adam de la Halle had
already put out to graze[1]): '[Order my *trompette* (trumpeter) to
rise early on the day of the parade] et que galoppant son cheval
Bayard, il s'en aille par la cité sonnant boutte-selle, boutte-
selle, tous à cheval, tous à cheval, tous à cheval' (ibid., f. 9),
or to the old *clericus–miles* dispute: 'Mon maistre changez d'advis,
ne mettez à vostre table des docteurs, et des Capitaines, parce
que par entre eux ils se rompront la teste, seulement pour la
preference qui se recherche entre les gend'armes, et les lettrez'
(ibid., f. 27). Jacques de Fonteny dedicated the book to a real-
life captain, Charles d'Angenes, 'Capitaine des cent Gentils-
hommes de la maison du Roy, et Colonnel general de l'infanterie
Italienne'.

Another real-life captain, 'Le Capitaine Lasphrise', otherwise
Marc de Papillon, produced a by-product of our comic tradition
in 1597: *La Nouvelle Tragicomique*.[2] It is a work without parallel,
as far as I know, in its time—indeed, possibly in any time.
Papillon was a man who, in an age when the *gab* of the stage
braggart was known to every educated person, and to a good
many who were not, could write such a *gab* about himself:

Vous m'en estes tesmoings, Rencontre de Dormant,
Où je fus veu tuant, en pourpoinct, pesle-mesle,
Le Vernay, Vymory, fossé de la Rochelle,
Vous monde d'escarmouche, assaults de Lusignan,
Danfront, Sainct Lo, Broüage, et Fontenay, Maran,
Sainctes, Mesle, La Meure et villes Daulphinoises . . .[3]

---

[1] 'Or est Bayard en la pâture': *Rondeaux*, ed. J. Chailley (Paris, 1942), no. 8.
[2] *Les Premieres Œuvres poetiques du Capitaine Lasphrise* (Paris, Jean Gesselin,
1597; privilege, 31 January 1597). *La Nouvelle Tragicomique*, pp. 565–91. Second
edition, 1599. Reprinted in *Ancien Théâtre français*, vii. 463–91.
[3] *Les Premieres Œuvres poetiques* (1597), pp. 537–8.

or this Cartel:

> Cartel envoyé aux ennemis de Boutteville par
> des Capitaines mes compagnons et moy.

> . . . Nous sommes six soldats au Service du Roy
> Qui vous irons trouver vous donnant nostre foy,
> Pour vous combatre hardis avec espée et cappe.
> Six de vous soyent donc prests pour acquerir honneur.
> « C'est toujours au danger que reluist la valeur
> « Mais il est bien-heureux qui de nos mains eschappe.[1]

The braggart in his play, however, Furcifer, is hardly one at all. People call him a 'vaillant gendarme', an 'asseuré brigand si plein d'artifice', but he has no *gab*, none of the usual attributes. The play itself has an extraordinary, quite possibly a unique, structure. Papillon says at the beginning: 'Je n'ensuy en cette œuvre icy la facon de l'ardeur antique', and indeed he does not. But nor does he simply imitate the farces. We are given a lament on a friend and servant's death, with ideas on vengeance typical of the most Senecan of tragedies ('Par vengeance on connoist le cœur d'amour parfait'); the consultation of a magician in a remote valley; an action which moves from a house outside Paris to the valley, to the gates of Paris, to an inn in Paris, to a prison; and although there is no prologue, on four occasions different characters turn and speak to the audience, commenting on the action:

HOSPES
> Si jamais on a veu une ame perturbée,
> Il fallait voir Griffon . . .

> Griffon, luy, n'est plus luy, par l'estrange spectacle;
> Il ne dict ni ne faict, car ce triste miracle
> Cloisoit la bouche à tous qui sont sortis de là:
> Puis enfin, souspirant, au traistre ainsi parla.
> *(La Nouvelle Tragicomique)*[2]

---

[1] Ibid., p. 447. The original has 'nous donnant vostre foy'.
[2] *Ancien Théâtre français*, vii. 486–7.

There is no act-division—indeed, no division at all—and the play is shorter than most five-act plays and longer than most farces. Papillon seems to use his title as a blanket term to cover as varied a collection of dramatic whims as the Renaissance ever produced. One amusing idea of Papillon's is to call the watch by the name of Rabelais's Chicanoux, that is, people who are paid to receive blows and who never deal them.

With the two 'comedies' of Pierre Troterel, Sieur d'Aves, *Les Corrivaux* of 1612 and *Gillette* of 1620, we come to a different kind of theatre.[1] By their subject-matter, they are farces; they are certainly indecent and make little demand on the intellect. But they are structurally rather more than farces. H. C. Lancaster saw merit enough in them to regret their immorality.[2] And if we are interested in the kinds of theatrical convention current in France in the opening years of the seventeenth century, the two plays take on a new interest. They appear to take for granted the conventions of comedy to such an extent that they become parodies of the genre. A knowledge of those conventions is assumed in the audience (or reader). *Les Corrivaux*, for example, has an 'Advertissement au Lecteur' mocking that part of comic theory which claims a moral function for comedy:

> Lecteur sçaches que je n'ay pas composé ceste folastre comedie, pour t'apprendre à suivre le vice: car il n'y a rien au monde que j'abhorre tant. Et te jure de bonne ame que je hay plus que la peste ceux qui le suivent. Le subject donc, pour lequel je l'ay composée, est à fin qu'en y voyant sa noirceur si bien depeinte, tu t'animes à suivre la vertu. Ainsi les anciens Romains faisoyent ivrer leurs serviteurs et esclaves, devant leurs enfants, à fin qu'en contemplant leurs vilaines actions, ils apprinssent à fuir la brutalle yvrongnerie, et les autres vices qui la suyvent.

Troterel's tongue-in-cheek claim for the uplifting nature of his play can best be savoured only if you know the piece of theory behind it.

---

[1] *Les Corrivaux* (Rouen, Raphaël du Petit Val, 1612); reprinted in *Ancien Théâtre français*, viii. 227–96. *Gillette* (Rouen, David du Petit Val, 1620).

[2] H. C. Lancaster, *French Dramatic Literature in the Seventeenth Century*, part I, vol. i (Baltimore, 1929), pp. 144, 217.

A prologue, spoken by a braggart, begins the play. But this standard piece of comic structure is interrupted by someone (Le Caché) behind the curtain of the stage: this is surely aimed at an audience familiar with the usual uninterrupted prologue. And again, once the play starts, we find that there is not just one braggart, but two or even three. And so on. Whether we consider these things as variations on the conventions, as in the earlier comedies, or as parodies making fun of them, it seems that familiarity with those conventions can still, in 1612 and 1620, be assumed.

With *Les Ramoneurs* we are back in the main stream of comedy, with a play which, as we saw above, is probably typical of a number that no longer survive. Whereas Troterel had parodied the conventions and had been heavily influenced by the farces, this play merely assumes the conventions and in many ways is as different from the farces as any comedy of the 1570s or 1580s. Professor Gill has discussed it in some detail in his edition, and we shall examine a number of features later; but perhaps one point should be made here. *Les Ramoneurs* dates at the earliest from the 1623–4 season. Corneille's *Mélite* dates from the 1629–30 season, at most six years later. Corneille claimed that his play was written in a kind of dramatic wilderness; but *Les Ramoneurs* shows that this is simply untrue. It is a lively play, as Professor Gill has shown probably written for the professional theatre of the time, and one whose features are clearly traditional: the characters, the prose form, performance by the traditional farce-actors at the Hôtel de Bourgogne, the immorality, the structure of its plot. It is a consciously French play, not an Italian one: thus in v. vii Scanderbec refuses to be addressed as a *capitan*: 'Ah Ventre, je ne veux pas qu'on me traitte à l'Italienne. Dites Capitaine Scanderbec, et vous parlerez bien.' Its language is particularly vivacious and rich in imagery. Only in this play do we approach in any degree the comedy of Jonson.

The anonymous *Comédie de proverbes* is related to *Les Ramoneurs*, probably written for the same troupe. Its list of *dramatis personae* resembles that of *Les Ramoneurs*: a pedant, a braggart, two valets, a pair of lovers, a woman servant called Alizon. Nevertheless, the lovers are called Lidias and Florinde, and gipsies are important in the plot, both of which features show a certain pastoral influence. It has only three acts. It is inferior to *Les Ramoneurs* in that structure, characterization, and dialogue are all sacrificed for the sake of making a play out of some 500 or more proverbs. H. C. Lancaster has shown[1] that it probably dates from about 1632: not 1609 as Beauchamps suggested, nor 1616 as the Frères Parfaict did. But in any case, it belongs to a similar tradition to that of *Les Ramoneurs*: the tradition against which, surely, the audiences of 1629–30 saw Corneille's new comedy *Mélite*.

There can be no doubt that *Mélite* did in fact inaugurate a new type of comedy in France; the fact is, though, that the novelty does not lie where Corneille claimed that it did, in his 'Examen' of the play:

On n'avoit jamais veu jusques-là que la Comedie fist rire sans Personnages ridicules comme les valets boufons, les Parasites, les Capitans, les Docteurs, etc. Celle-cy faisoit son effet par l'humeur enjoüée de gens d'une condition au dessus de ceux qu'on voit dans les Comedies de Plaute et de Terence, qui n'estoient que des Marchands.[2]

Mélite does not aim to make us laugh; nor does it avoid conventional characters, since the nurse is utterly traditional, Philandre has more than a touch of the braggart soldier about him, and Corneille admits that Eraste's madness is a traditional theatrical device in France (though not of comedy).

The novelty lies in a new ethic of love. Before Corneille, the love-affairs that formed the core of the plot (when the plays were not frankly immoral like *L'Eugène* and *La Trésorière* especially) were so bound up with Renaissance social structure that the parents of the young people themselves played an important

---

[1] *History of French Dramatic Literature*, vol. i/2 (Baltimore, 1929), pp. 650–3.
[2] 'Examen' to *Mélite*, ed. cit., p. 136.

part in the plays. Here, that social structure has been relegated to the background. Mélite's mother does not appear, though her approval is still necessary for a marriage; and the action concerns only the young people and is conducted according to the *précieux* love-ethic familiar in the salons of Madame de Rambouillet and her successors. Consequently, there can be no peril of the old familiar kind; no relation or friend of the family can appear as a *deus ex machina*. The emphasis has changed, from dealing with external perils to examining the affections of the characters. Hence the unified, even claustrophobic plot, hence the dignified alexandrines, hence too the emphasis on individuality in the different kinds of affections. Some characteristics survive from earlier, such as the nurse and the braggart parts of Philandre's character, the convention of staging with *décor simultané*, the epilogue spoken by the nurse. But they are externals, and it is clear that a new type of comedy has begun— new, but not in the ways that Corneille claimed.

CHAPTER TWO

The Stage

THE stages that were used for French Renaissance comedies are very much a matter for deduction from indirect evidence. The iconographical sources that survive are only partly relevant, because they refer only to other, though related, genres: to Terence's plays as illustrated in Renaissance editions, to farces, and to Italian comedies. Something can be gained from medieval illustrations, even though they are before our period, and from the *Mémoire de Mahelot*, even though it is after it. The rise of the professional troupes provides information in archives mainly from the end of the sixteenth century onwards. And finally the plays themselves, if we look at them in detail, consistently imply certain kinds of staging. All this evidence taken together, scattered though it is, does eventually provide a coherent picture of the comic stage within our period.

I. THE ILLUSTRATED EDITIONS OF TERENCE

The woodcuts in Renaissance editions of Terence have recently been exhaustively discussed by T. E. Lawrenson and Helen Purkis.[1] Their work shows above all that as the woodcut in Renaissance printed books is an art-form of its own, these illustrations too must be regarded in the first place as examples of that art-form. Renaissance woodcuts were decorations, integrated into the design of the printed page, often copied or combined or used again as the output of printed books increased in the late fifteenth and early sixteenth centuries. So these

[1] T. E. Lawrenson and Helen Purkis, 'Les éditions illustrées de Térence dans l'histoire du théâtre', *Le Lieu théâtral à la Renaissance*, ed. J. Jacquot (Paris, 1964), pp. 1–23 and plates I–VIII.

illustrations of Terence's plays were copied and adapted from edition to edition, the 1545 Venice edition, for example, still using variants of woodcuts found in the 1493 Lyons one. They are decorations, examples of an art-form and not necessarily representative of the actual stage conditions of the Renaissance.

Professor Lawrenson and Miss Purkis distinguish three kinds of stage shown in these illustrations to the early editions: an entire *theatrum* shown in a certain number of frontispieces; a straight row of compartments; and a group of compartments projecting forward into the centre of the picture.[1] All three represent something theatrically simple: a platform with, at the back, up to five compartments. There is no elaboration of what the compartments are meant to be; there are no windows, no balconies, or the like, nothing to indicate a difference between one kind of building and another.

Upon this pattern is imposed, towards the middle of the sixteenth century, the Serlian design of a neutral space surrounded by stage elements on three sides: a city street, with representations of houses and city buildings. Such a design first appears in the Terentian illustrations in the 1545 Venice edition, while woodcuts showing the older pattern still continue to appear, and by 1614 we have the first edition of Terence using *only* the Serlian type of design.[2] Serlio's work was first published in France in 1545; we shall return to it later.

How far, then, *are* these woodcuts sources of information about sixteenth-century theatre design, in particular for comedy? It is apparent that a too literal interpretation of them is dangerous. But there are two ways at least in which they are relevant to the sixteenth-century stage, and in particular to comedy.

First, an artist, even if interested primarily in the design of a printed book, does not produce a picture from nothing. We

---

[1] Cf. Plate III.

[2] The woodcuts in this 1614 edition by Jean de Tournes are curious in that they had already existed a half-century earlier, since 1556. It is possible that they were even then intended for an edition of Terence, but this is unproven. Cf. Lawrenson and Purkis, op. cit., p. 17, n. 32.

shall be quite justified in looking to the theatre for *some* inspiration. Professor Lawrenson elsewhere rightly looks to the
medieval mystery play for some of the inspiration:

> Firstly, the period of Terentian illustration is that of the
> mystery play. Secondly, the concept of house in the comedies of
> Terence and the *mansion* would easily be allied in the mind of the
> illustrator. Thirdly, whenever the houses in the Terence illustra-
> tions jut forward they are virtually identical with the baldaquin
> type of mystery compartment. Fourthly, the labelled houses in
> the illustrations resemble the *écriteaux* of the mystery; and fifthly
> [rows of mystery *mansions* can resemble an arcade such as those
> in the Terentian illustrations].[1]

The complex medieval mystery and passion play sets, though,
used much more than mere curtains for their compartments;
some, such as Hell and the Sea of Galilee in the Valenciennes
set, are very complex. Why, then, were these Terentian woodcuts so simplified? Partly, certainly, as a kind of systematization
of the action of the play (Badius wrote, for Trechsel's 1493
edition, 'Effecimus ut etiam illiterati ex imaginibus quas cuilibet
scenae praeposuimus, legere atque accipere possint comica argu-
menta'); but also, I would suggest, because the theatre of
the time which may have influenced them included not only
mystery and passion plays but also farces and *sotties*, whose
stages were much simpler.[2] The late fifteenth century, when the
early illustrated editions of Terence were produced, was, after
all, the golden age of the farce. Whether as isolated pieces or as
parts of a more extended play, farces were at the time of the
Trechsel edition the only flourishing *comic* theatrical form in
France; and they were, of course, much simpler than mystery
and passion plays and, as we shall see, performed on more
primitive stages. It may well be that the simplicity of the
farce stages had some influence on the illustrations to the new

---

[1] T. E. Lawrenson, *The French Stage in the Seventeenth Century* (Manchester,
1957), p. 52.

[2] The distinction between farce and *sottie* need not detain us here, where we
are discussing only the question of staging. Cf. Maxwell, *French Farce and John
Heywood*, pp. 18–20.

PLATE III

Scenes from Terence's *Eunuchus* and *Adelphi*, from the editions of Lyons, 1493 (Trechsel) and Strasbourg, 1496 (Grüninger) respectively, showing different arrangements of compartments

PLATE IV

A farce stage of c. 1540, from a set of part-books (MS. 126) in the Bibliothèque Municipale, Cambrai

editions of Terentian comedy, and that therefore we are justified in looking cautiously to these illustrations for information about the staging of comic plays in the sixteenth century.

The early editions, and Trechsel's in particular, were humanist productions with a pedagogical aim. The stages they show, as we saw, are in the first place systematizations of Terence's comedies; secondly they derive (loosely) from contemporary stages; and thirdly they correspond (in an even looser fashion) to humanist ideas of the classical stage (ideas about five entrances, etc.). The parallel with the nature of the first native French comedies is remarkable: Jodelle and his immediate successors are also humanists, with serious aims, even if not pedagogues; they imitate above all the contemporary stage, that is the farces; and only very loosely imitate the classical models for which they enthuse. In the stage practice of the humanists of the 1550s, as with the humanists' illustrated editions of Terence sixty years earlier, the attraction of the farces does seem to have been stronger than the attraction of classical models.

Secondly, whatever stages may have actually been used for Renaissance comedies, any cultivated member of the audience of such comedies cannot but have had these woodcuts in mind. Terence's plays, as we have seen, were part of every gentleman's education, and they were studied doubtless in these illustrated editions, so that plays in a classical genre, such as the Pléiade's comedies, would inevitably call these woodcuts to the mind of the audience. The woodcuts would, then, take their place as one element within the close relationship of author and audience, in the small humanist and Court circles of the 1550s.

2. FARCES

It is remarkable how large a number of engravings, woodcuts, and paintings are inspired by Renaissance farces in France and the Low Countries: quite a large proportion of the whole iconographical evidence for French Renaissance stage design. This proportion, though, probably does not correspond to theatrical reality. Once again, we are dealing not with any kind of deliberate historical record of the theatre, but with the fine arts: a fashion of painting probably accounts for the large number of these pictures, just as at other times fashions for still-lifes or landscapes produced large numbers of paintings of those kinds. The simplicity and vigour of the farce stages may well have appealed and so begun this particular fashion, while other theatrical genres such as religious plays and formal tragedy and comedy attracted less attention from artists, even though we know from other sources that in terms of the actual theatre they were as important as farces.

But whereas the Terentian woodcuts gave us little reliable evidence about actual stages, these pictures of farces are probably rather nearer reality. The pictures all show a simple, even primitive platform stage.[1] The painting in the Cambrai set of part-books,[2] the 'Playerwater' detail,[3] and the pictures of Tabarin[4] all show trestles supporting the stage. Such stages were, then, portable; and indeed it was essential to the early professional troupes, before their establishment in Paris, that they and their equipment should be mobile. The earliest known travelling professional troupe, at Rouen in 1556, specifically performed farces as part of its repertory.[5] The equipment is rudimentary, generally including a curtain at the back. In the first two cases above, there is an area behind the curtain from which actors may appear. A table and chair, a few other small articles, and musical instruments in the case of Tabarin, are all the properties used,

---

[1] Such a stage is probably the descendant of a single element of the multiple décor of elaborate religious productions. In Fouquet's *Martyre de sainte Apolline*, the *maisons* are already independent, with their own stage and roof, and very like the farce stages of these later pictures. This origin is the more likely since farces were in fact acted as part of such religious productions. I am indebted for this suggestion to the unpublished thesis of A. Hindley, 'The Development and Diffusion of Farce in France towards the end of the Middle Ages' (University of Hull, 1965), p. 349.

[2] Cambrai, Bibliothèque municipale, MS. 126, f. 53. Cf. Plate IV.

[3] Amsterdam, Rijksmuseum. Detail of a painting attributed to Pieter Balten.

[4] Two engravings, reproduced respectively in L. Moussinac, *Le Théâtre* (Paris, 1957), p. 161, and in W. L. Wiley, *The Early Public Theatre in France* (Cambridge, Mass., 1960), pl. 10.

[5] Cf. Wiley, op. cit., pp. 37–9.

though others are referred to in the texts of farces. The beauty of the Cambrai painting is that it catches perfectly the atmosphere of one side of this kind of performance: sadness and desolation, dusk approaching, few spectators. The other pictures have mostly emphasized the other side: lively but cheap and brash fairground entertainment, paid for by collection and not by admission, often linked with commerce, as in the 'Orviétan' print.[1] The sadness is familiar to us today from Chaplin and from a whole tradition of music-hall; the brashness we still see set against that sadness, as in *Les Enfants du paradis*.

Can these farce pictures tell us anything about the stage for Renaissance comedies? Again, I think, primarily in the context of author–audience relationship. Farces were the only thriving comic form in the French theatre of the mid-sixteenth century, and their stages must therefore have been known to the audiences of the Pléiade comedies, plays which are themselves, as we have seen, so similar to the farces. Sébillet and Du Bellay certainly knew them and referred to them, the one to accept, the other to condemn. The authors of the comedies may well have had stages of this kind in mind. Jodelle's *L'Eugène*, the first French Renaissance comedy, really needs no more in the way of stage design than does a typical farce.

Indeed, in a sense it requires even less. Since the texts of many farces seem to suggest complex stages, but the pictures of farces show only simple ones, it seems that a good deal of miming on simple stages in fact took place in their performance.[2] *L'Eugène* and the other comedies do not even suggest such complex stages, so that in them there is no such *décalage* between text and practice. The demands that farce texts make may be seen, as an example, in the *Farce à trois personnages: Le savetier, le sergent et la laitière*[3] from the *Recueil Trepperel*, which the editors

---

[1] Reproduced, for example, in Allardyce Nicoll's *Masks, Mimes and Miracles* [1931] (New York, 1963), p. 225.

[2] A. Hindley, in *The Development and Diffusion of Farce*, pp. 328–44, comes to the same conclusion on the same grounds.

[3] *Le Recueil Trepperel: Les Farces*, ed. E. Droz and H. Lewicka (Geneva, 1961), pp. 25–40.

date in the 1480s or 1490s: this play seems to demand two distinct compartments and a neutral 'street' space, for example at ll. 14 and 81 'estes vous leans (ceans)', l. 88 'en ma maison', and l. 195 'hors de mon repaire'. The *Farce du porteur d'eau*, probably dating from the 1530s,[1] seems to need more still: each of the three secondary characters (the *entremetteur*, the *amoureuse*, and her mother) seems to have his or her own compartment, and all seem to move every few lines from compartment to compartment. At one point they even go to church to be married: 'Ils s'en vont à l'eglise et estant revenus le porteur d'eau commence à dire . . .' Miming is easier, though, at such high speed; and since the progress of time is certainly treated with scantier respect than in any play I know ('Car c'est demain, vous le sçavez, / Qu'il nous faut aller à l'église. / Soyons, d'une façon exquize, / Tous deux fort bien accommodez. / Voilà le dimanche venu . . .'), there is little reason to assume any very great respect for staging either. So also for *Le savetier, le sergent et la laitière*.

Another pictorial genre that awaits proper comment is the woodcut illustrations to early editions of farces. So few of these have been published that it is difficult to draw solid conclusions; but from the title-pages of the *Recueil Trepperel*,[2] and from the illustrations to *Pathelin* and others in the British Museum, it does seem that in general the pictures are drawn as though the scenes were happening in life and not in a theatre. The woodcut in *Le savetier, le sergent et la laitière*, for example, shows grass and a flower, and a horse in the background, and so tells us little about the stage.[3] Like the Terentian illustrations, these woodcuts were doubtless *primarily* intended as part of the design of a printed page, and scarcely at all as illustrations of stages. Sometimes they were possibly not even originally designed for these books, but for non-theatrical ones.[4]

[1] Text in E. Fournier, *Le Théâtre français avant la Renaissance* (Paris, 1872) [reprinted New York, 1966 (?)], pp. 456–60. Dating from Maxwell, *French Farce and John Heywood*, p. 131.

[2] Ed. cit.   [3] *Recueil Trepperel*, ed. cit., p. 29.

[4] The migratory nature of woodcuts in this period is well established. Thus, the illustrations to early editions of *Pathelin* were re-used for Verard's *Therence en Françoys* (Paris, n.d. [*c.* 1500]).

Neither the text of the farces, then, nor the woodcuts accompanying the early editions can tell us much about sixteenth-century stages. But the drawings and paintings can, precisely because they are scattered in time and in style and yet have common features: a small and simple stage, with a curtain or backcloth behind and few properties. Although by 1552 farces were in the hands of professionals and the new humanist comedy was to be amateur, nevertheless because the farces were the only living comic genre, and because their influence on the texts of the humanist comedies is plain to see, the farce stages should be kept in mind when we consider the stages for Pléiade comedy.

3. ITALIAN COMEDY

With the arrival of the Italian troupes in France from 1571, a new kind of theatrical illustration appears: engravings, woodcuts, and paintings of the Italian comedy. This pictorial genre is to some extent less clear-cut than either the Terentian woodcuts or the farce pictures; but as it is (at this early date at least) less formulated as an artistic genre than either of them, we may perhaps rely on these pictures rather more to find out about actual stage sets.

They are of two kinds: first, the engravings and woodcuts found in the *Recueil Fossard*, in the *Compositions de Rhétorique* (Lyons, 1601), and in isolated sources of a similar kind; and second, paintings of groups of actors on stage. The first clearly represents the *commedia dell'arte* in France; and as we move into the seventeenth century, the integration of Italian *commedia dell'arte* actors and French farce actors, begun already in the 1570s with Agnan Sarat and his troupe, becomes more apparent in them. The second kind is less farcical, more dignified. But the division is not sharp: some paintings of this second kind are certainly derived from Fossard engravings, and it is even possible that all of them are, as Charles Sterling has suggested.[1] However, it

[1] 'Early Paintings of the Commedia dell'arte in France', *Bulletin of the Metropolitan Museum of Art, New York* (1943), pp. 11–32.

may also be that some at least of these paintings represent not the *commedia dell'arte*, but performances of a *commedia erudita* or of some other genre—not necessarily other actors, but the same actors in different roles. I have not seen this suggestion made, but it seems probable: the first Italian troupes in France, we know, performed in both styles of acting. In that case, for instance, the pictures often referred to as the earliest representations of the *commedia dell'arte*—one in private possession in Paris,[1] the other in the Musée Carnavalet, Paris[2]—could equally well be pictures of learned comedy. The very essence of *commedia dell'arte* improvisation has meant that we know very little of its precise characteristics; but from the ease with which Fornaris, for example, could insert his character of Coccodrillo into a learned comedy, the two kinds of acting do not seem to have been so very far distant from each other, and were certainly practised by the same actors.

Most of the surviving paintings have been closely discussed by Charles Sterling, whose conclusion is that as a group they are derived from engravings such as those in the *Recueil Fossard*. This is demonstrable for paintings in the New York Metropolitan Museum, at Rennes, and at Béziers, which all show groups of actors in Italian comedy scenes. The paintings have stylistic affinities and generally show Flemish characteristics, so once again we have to some extent a defined artistic genre. The engravings are not discussed by Sterling, and would need a separate study.

One painting in the Musée Municipal at Bayeux particularly concerns us here. Dated by Sterling from the costumes at 1570–4, it shows a group of eleven actors in the foreground, one of whom wears the costume of Pantalone. Behind them is a second group of nine people difficult to identify. They are

---

[1] Reproduced in Sterling, p. 22, and in Nicoll, *Masks, Mimes and Miracles*, fig. 224; a group of seven actors, including a Pantalone figure with cuckold's horns, without stage setting.

[2] Reproduced in Sterling, p. 20, and in Wiley, *The Early Public Theater*, fig. 1; a group of five actors, with two other figures in the wings, with a plain curtain as background.

possibly further actors, or, as Sterling suggests, a courtly audience. No engraving like it is known, only a water-colour in the Hennin collection in the Bibliothèque Nationale, Cabinet des Estampes,[1] showing only the front group and possibly deriving from an identical source. The most interesting feature is the background: a façade with an arch in the centre showing a view in perspective—precisely as in the Teatro Olimpico stage at Vicenza. It is the only surviving Renaissance picture in France of such a stage set in the straight theatre.[2]

The other paintings, the Fossard prints, and the *Compositions de Rhétorique* all have either no background, or a simple curtain, or mere rudiments of the Serlian design such as the houses indicated on right and left in some of the engravings.

The Italian companies, then, who came to France from the 1570s onwards would seem from the pictures to have used surprisingly simple sets. One picture only (the painting at Bayeux) has a façade-type set with a scene behind it in perspective, as in the Teatro Olimpico; some only of the engravings in the *Recueil Fossard* and *Compositions de Rhétorique* have variants, and those primitive indeed, of Serlio's design. Otherwise, only back curtains are shown. Yet the plots of the learned comedies that existed by the hundred in Italy and some of which the actors brought with them demand more complex sets than these: Bibbiena's *La Calandria*, for instance, played at Lyons in 1548. In Italy, and doubtless in France too, more than a back curtain must have been provided. Serlio himself, whose comic scene is perhaps related to the sets actually used for such comedies, was in France from 1550 to 1554; if that was so, surely performances such as that of Alamanni's *Flora* at Fontainebleau in 1555 must have used more than a simple back curtain or the primitive structures seen in the *Compositions de Rhétorique*.

[1] Vol. xii, f. 34; cf. Sterling, p. 29.

[2] Sets with façades are, of course, found (cf. Lawrenson, *The French Stage*, passim), but only in genres such as entries and ballets, never in the straight theatre. Sterling (p. 19) considers it a normal *commedia dell'arte* set, but he does not refer to, and appears to ignore, the view in perspective through the central arch.

It may well be that a troupe with fair financial backing, such as the Confidenti playing for the Duc de Joyeuse, would have used some form of Serlio's design, but that no pictures of such performances have survived. As we have seen, the iconographical evidence forms a part of the world of the fine arts, and it may easily be that such performances did not find their artists. We should at any rate not rule out the possibility on methodological grounds, since there is internal evidence in the plays themselves to support the idea of developed stage design and not simply a back curtain. I shall return to discuss the type of set involved after examining the plays and their requirements in detail.[1]

4. MEDIEVAL STAGE SETS, SERLIO, AND THE *MÉMOIRE DE MAHELOT*

The question arises: how far are Serlio's designs, and the drawings in the *Mémoire de Mahelot*, survivals from medieval stage design? Jean Jacquot sees a continuity in Mahelot, and emphasizes the Italianate nature of his drawings—'Il a parfaitement assimilé les principes du décor "à l'italienne" '—while mentioning medieval elements such as ' "mansions" à claire-voie révélant un intérieur d'un caractère encore très médiéval'.[2] Professor Lawrenson, while not denying possible medieval elements in Mahelot, categorically denies the Serlio–Mahelot link: 'There is not one set which could even remotely be conjectured to be a direct imitation of Serlio.'[3] The balance between medieval and neo-classical designs is in fact a delicate one, both in France and in Italy. We have seen how a humanists' edition of Terence could give illustrations recalling the sets for mystery

---

[1] As far as I know, there exists no study of the stage requirements of Italian learned comedies, using internal evidence. The one over-all study of the genre, M. T. Herrick's *Italian Comedy in the Renaissance* (Urbana, 1960), discusses the plays only as literature, with very little reference to staging. Such a study would be valuable for the history of the Renaissance theatre, and would be particularly solid in that a very large number of texts survive.

[2] *La Vie théâtrale au temps de la Renaissance* (Paris, 1963), p. 160.

[3] *The French Stage*, p. 87.

PLATE V

Sebastiano Serlio's comic scene, from *Il primo libro d'architettura*, Paris, 1545

plays and farces. We have seen, too, how in France the farce still flourished in the 1550s, though by then a static genre, and influenced the Pléiade; while outside the comic theatre, as late as 1547 a wholly typical medieval set could still be used for the Valenciennes passion play. All the medieval genres—and hence presumably the stage designs associated with them—continued throughout the century, at the same time as the Renaissance genres gained their footing. Neo-classical designs flourished overwhelmingly in what Professor Lawrenson calls 'para-theatricals': entries, mascarades, ballets, and the like; is not the reason for this that the 'para-theatricals' were less formal genres, growing away from their medieval predecessors, and open to new ideas of design, whereas the 'straight' theatre, however new some genres such as tragedy might appear to be, still remained in a medieval tradition?

Two kinds of neo-classical design, derived from Italy, are especially applicable to the straight theatre. First, the façade with a number of doors in it (five according to theory) with parts of a set built in perspective behind the doors and visible through them. This, above all, is still visible in the Teatro Olimpico at Vicenza. For the French theatre (not 'para-theatricals'), as we saw, there exists only one picture of this kind of set: that at Bayeux.

The other kind is in the three theatre designs associated with the name of Serlio. These first appeared in France in the two-language first edition of two books of his works published in Paris in 1545.[1] Serlio himself came to France in 1541 and stayed until his death in 1554—that is, he was in France at the time of the first performance of Jodelle's comedies *L'Eugène* and *La Rencontre*. Serlio discusses the three types of décor specified by Vitruvius (tragic, comic, and satyric) and gives illustrations of his own model designs for each type, with emphasis on the

---

[1] *Il primo libro d'architettura* [*Il secondo libro di perspettiva*] *di Sebastiano Serlio . . . Le premier livre d'architecture* [*Le second livre de perspective*] *de Sebastiano Serlio . . . mis en langue françoyse par Jehan Martin* (Paris, 1545). Cf. Plate V. Some later editions have other woodcuts of these designs, differing in details; the comic scene is often reversed.

principles of perspective. The back of the stage, for example, should be higher by one-ninth than the front.[1]

But these designs, though they have the trappings of the Renaissance in their palaces, cities, north Italian Renaissance towers, and so on, seem in their essence to be derived from the medieval theatre. Nowhere in Vitruvius or other classical sources is there any reference to a central neutral space with buildings (or forests), supposedly realistic, on three sides;[2] whereas such an idea is perfectly reconcilable with medieval stage design. The Valenciennes stage, though more spread out, uses the principle. So does the set shown in Fouquet's picture of the martyrdom of Saint Apolline. Serlio's designs are not new, but are reworkings of an old principle.

In France in the late sixteenth century, Serlio's designs, even if consistently hailed as neo-classical, would have had an air of familiarity about them. For contemporary audiences, they would be a continuation of the medieval theatre, in a different guise. That some version of them was in fact used will appear from examination of the plays themselves.

The next major pictorial document for the French theatre is the *Mémoire de Mahelot*,[3] nearly one hundred years after Serlio's designs. Professor Lawrenson insists that Mahelot's sets are not directly related to Serlio, on the grounds that the essence of a Mahelot set is the independence of each separate compartment, whereas Serlio's sets are designed as unified wholes.[4] In view of

---

[1] Serlio, op. cit. (Paris, 1545), p. 65: 'communément il se faict une platte forme, eslevée de terre en sa partie de devant au nyveau de nostre veue, et la partie de derriere plus haulte seulement d'une neufiesme part.'

[2] Cf. Jean Jacquot, *La Vie théâtrale*, p. 109: 'Le souci [de la part de Serlio] de se conformer à Vitruve est d'autant plus curieux que la scène serlienne, avec sa grande ouverture centrale, n'a plus rien de commun avec la scène antique, avec sa façade ornée de colonnes et de statues et percée de trois ouvertures. Il n'est pas moins curieux de voir Jean Martin, dans son Vitruve, reproduire le plan du théâtre latin par Fra Giocondo, puis, sans explication, les trois types de décor de Serlio, qui résument la pratique des théâtres de la Renaissance. On n'aurait su admettre avec plus de désinvolture le divorce de la théorie et de la pratique.'

[3] Bibliothèque Nationale, MS. fr. 24330. Modern edition: *Le Mémoire de Mahelot, Laurent et d'autres décorateurs de l'Hôtel de Bourgogne*, ed. H. C. Lancaster (Paris, 1920).   [4] *The French Stage*, pp. 86–9.

the scanty evidence for the years preceding Mahelot, the question probably cannot be finally settled.[1] But the essence of a Mahelot set does not in fact lie in the independence of its compartments, but in something quite different: in the existence of a neutral central space surrounded on three sides by stage elements, which is precisely the essence of Serlio's sets also. In Mahelot, it is *always* the basic design, whereas he does not always have more than one or two compartments: for example, the specification for the anonymous *Les Trois Semblables* is simply 'Il faut que le theatre soit en pastoralle a la discretion du feinteur',[2] the corresponding drawing being of a single woodland scene; and Hardy's *La Folie d'Isabelle* has one compartment only whose placing on stage is a matter of indifference: 'Vous la pouves mettre au milieu du theatre si vous voulez',[3] an injunction which is in fact carried out in the drawing. In sets such as these, there is no juggling with a number of independent elements. It seems to me, therefore, that Mahelot and Serlio do share an essential concept of stage design.

A juggling of independent elements does take place in the sets for medieval religious plays, where the different *mansions* are in fact a series of different structures—even, in Fouquet's picture of the *Martyre de sainte Apolline*, a series of different theatres, each with its own stage and roof. We saw how one of these structures may have given rise to the common type of farce stage. In the mobile religious plays,[4] the different *mansions* were on separate carts and thus not fixed in any permanent spatial relationship at all. So that to the extent to which Mahelot's sets *do* involve combinations of pre-existent stage elements, they may be said to be in a medieval tradition.

---

[1] A new edition of the *Mémoire* is in preparation and may bring forward new evidence.

[2] *Mémoire*, ed. Lancaster, p. 79.   [3] Ibid., p. 74.

[4] Which were known to Grévin, writing in 1561: 'Et quant à moy je suis de ceste opinion que la Comédie a pris son nom ἀπὸ τῶν κωμῶν, c'est-à-dire des rues par lesquelles de ce premier temps elles estoyent jouées: et semble qu'encore ceste coustume soit demeurée en Flandres, et Pais bas, ou les joueurs de Comédies se font trainer par les carrefours sur des chariots et là jouent leurs histoires, Comédies, et farces' (*Brief discours: Théâtre complet*, ed. Pinvert, p. 8).

Each of Serlio's three sets shows this same basic design (of a neutral central space surrounded on three sides by stage elements), and moreover can *also* be regarded as consisting of a number of compartments, unified by the Italian into a more coherent whole than in some of Mahelot's designs. In all three sets, the idea of compartments as opposed to a less diversified set is neither emphasized nor excluded. His comic scene consists of seven buildings: a church at the back, two houses and an inn (or shop) on the left, and three houses on the right.[1] All seven have doors, and all five houses have windows or balconies (or both) above. The shape of the inn reminds us of the shop in, for instance, the drawing for Durval's *Agarite* in the *Mémoire*.[2] The plays for which he was designing—and we know that he had practical experience in Italy—did demand compartments, and such compartments are perfectly compatible with his sets. So would be the demands made by French comedies of the late sixteenth century.

It is difficult to escape the conclusion that there is a continuity of stage design in France *without* a break at 1500 or at 1550: the medieval designs being modified especially by Serlian ones, themselves medieval but in neo-classical dress, and enriched especially in the early seventeenth century until we see them again in Mahelot's drawings; iconographical evidence being lacking in between, but some support being found in the plays themselves. The continuity is of course relative. There are so many unknowns, and so many different kinds of staging in existence at this period, that it would be foolish to overrate the importance of this continuity, but it should be kept in mind.

5. PERFORMANCES

There is no need to recapitulate here the controversy, well over half a century old now, as to whether French Renaissance

---

[1] Serlio's text states that the houses are those of bourgeois citizens; that one of them is that of a *macquerelle*; and that there is a *temple* and a *hostellerie* (Serlio, op. cit.; cf. S. W. Holsboer, *L'Histoire de la mise en scène dans le théâtre français de 1600 à 1657* (Paris, 1933), pp. 280–1).

[2] *Le Mémoire de Mahelot*, ed. cit., pp. 80–1 and drawing.

tragedies and comedies were intended for the stage or the arm-chair. Lanson's investigations proved finally that the tragedies were in fact performed, while M. Lebègue's 'Tableau' gives us many details about performances of comedies.[1]

The evidence that we have for our particular plays relates mainly to the early ones (up to 1570) and to the late ones (1624–30).

The question of Jodelle's two comedies and their representation is a thorny one in its details. But those details need not concern us here. It is established, on the testimony of Étienne Pasquier, that *La Rencontre* was acted:

> Ceste Comedie [*La Rencontre*], et la Cleopatre furent representées devant le Roy Henry à Paris en l'hostel de Reims, avecqu'un grand applaudissement de toute la compaignie. Et depuis encores au College de Boncour, où toutes les fenestres estoient tapissees d'une infinité de personnages d'honneur, et la cour si plaine d'Escoliers que les portes du College en regorgeoient. Je le dy comme celuy qui estois present avecq'le grand Turnebus en une mesme Chambre. Et les entre parleurs estoient tous hommes de nom: Car mesme Remy Belleau, et Jean de la Peruse, joüoient les principaux roulets.[2]

Once, then, at the Hôtel de Reims, once at the Collège de Boncourt; both times, presumably, on a stage prepared or impro-vised for the occasion. The precise date is uncertain: M. Balmas, in his edition of *L'Eugène*, suggests early in 1553; he suggests also that *L'Eugène*, which he dates very precisely in the last fortnight of September 1552, was probably also performed in a college.[3]

Jodelle's example of an integrated performance of a tragedy and a comedy together, in a royal and academic milieu, was followed by Jacques Grévin a few years later. Problems of dating arise here also. Grévin himself tells us that *La Trésorière*, though

[1] Cf. esp. G. Lanson, 'Études sur les origines de la tragédie classique en France', *Revue d'histoire littéraire de la France*, x (1903), pp. 177–231 and 413–36; and M. Lebègue's 'Tableau'.
[2] *Les Recherches de la France* (Paris, 1617), p. 741.
[3] Étienne Jodelle, *L'Eugène*, ed. Balmas, pp. 5–12.

put off (for reasons which are not now clear) in 1557, was performed on 5 February 1558 (N.S. 1559) and *Les Ébahis* on 17
February 1560 (N.S. 1561):

> Ceste comedie [*La Trésoriere*] fut faicte par le commandement
> du roi Henry II pour servir aux nopces de madame Claude,
> duchesse de Lorraine, mais pour quelques empeschemens différée:
> et depuis mise en jeu à Paris au collège de Beauvais, après la
> satyre qu'on appelle communéement les Veaux, le v. de février
> M.D.LVIII.[1]

> Ceste comedie [*Les Ébahis*] fut mise en jeu au collège de Beauvais,
> à Paris, le XVIIIᵉ jour de février M.D.LX après la tragédie de J.
> César et les Jeux satyriques, appelez communéement les Veaux.[2]

No evidence survives about the staging of *La Maubertine*, if that
was indeed a third comedy by Grévin (see Appendix B).

Jean-Antoine de Baïf included details of the performance
of his *Brave* on the title-page of the first edition: 'Le Brave,
comedie de Jan Antoine de Baïf, jouee devant le Roy en
l'hostel de Guise, à Paris, le XXVIII de janvier M.D.LXVII.'[3]
The occasion was an important one, and again in a royal and
academic setting; again in a building with, presumably, an
improvised stage. The first edition in 1567 gives the 'chantz
recitez entre les actes de la comedie' by Ronsard, Baïf himself,
Desportes, Philieul, and Belleau; but they have already vanished
by the 1572 edition.

No performance of *L'Eunuque* is known to us, only a note
about its translation: the original manuscript, now in the
Bibliothèque Nationale, bears the note in a sixteenth-century
hand: 'Achevée Lendemain de Noel devant jour 1565.' Perhaps
it was intended for a Christmas entertainment, or for a performance in the early part of 1566.

External evidence about Pléiade plays, then, gives us a
picture of a specifically university milieu, sometimes with
university jokes or references (the Protenotaire in Grévin's *La*

---

[1] Quoted from Jacques Grévin, *Théâtre complet*, ed. Pinvert, pp. 353–4.
[2] Ibid., p. 355.
[3] J.-A. de Baïf, *Le Brave* (Paris, 1567).

Trésorière), and with royal patronage. Jean de la Taille tells us that he and his brother Jacques wrote plays in their youth, while students: that is, again, in the milieu of the University of Paris. The stages were presumably prepared for the occasions. There is no reason why they should not have been elaborate: after all, we have all seen present-day school and university productions whose sets are by no means simple or improvised. External evidence tells us no more.

To these royal and academic performances we should add the performances of Italian plays in royal and aristocratic circles: Bibbiena's *La Calandria* in 1548 at Lyons, Alamanni's *Flora* in 1555 at Fontainebleau, Fornaris's *Angelica* in 1584 or 1585 at the house of the Duc de Joyeuse in Paris. The first took place in the 'grande salle de Saint-Jean', a high vaulted room in which the set was built by the Italian Nannoccio, of Serlian type, specifically using perspective.[1]

Between La Taille and the 1620s, we never know when or where any given comedy—other than *Angelica*—was performed. Gérard de Vivre tells us that acting in schools is pedagogically effective, even giving stage directions in some detail for performance, and we may perhaps conclude from the many editions of de Vivre's plays (in which stage directions always appeared) that they were found useful for their purpose and so were in fact acted in schools. François d'Amboise tells us that his comedies were 'veuës et receuës avec un plaisir indicible', but does not say when or where. Gabriel Chappuis makes his Poëte say: 'La chose representée au vif ainsi qu'elle ha esté faite, ha plus d'energie et d'efficace, que ce qui se declare par parolles',[2] but this is not, of course, conclusive evidence for performance. M. Lebègue's 'Tableau' includes references to many performances of 'comédies', but the term is notoriously general and can refer to moralities or farces or other genres as well as to strict comedies.

[1] S. W. [Deierkauf-] Holsboer, *Histoire de la mise en scène dans le théâtre français de 1600 à 1657* (Paris, 1933), p. 53; Lawrenson, *The French Stage*, p. 126.
[2] Gabriel Chappuis, *Les mondes celestes . . . de Doni* (Lyons, 1583), p. 666.

In the British Museum copy of Larivey's comedies of 1579,[1] the page of *Dramatis personae* to *Le Morfondu* bears a list of actors in a late sixteenth- or early seventeenth-century hand, which appears to show that the play was indeed acted The actors prove difficult to identify. In the 1630s, a young François de La Motte could act Philippes (but he is otherwise not heard of until 1641); Fleury might be Fleury Jacob, by this time certainly apt for a *vieillard*'s part; Michel could be Michel de La Chappe (d. 1642), whose daughter La Motte later married; La Fonteine could be Étienne Ruffin, called La Fonteine, who was acting up to 1638; Bretone could be Noël Le Breton, called Hauteroche, who was born about 1616. On this assumption, Mostier and Lancelot cannot be identified at all.[2] One other performance of a play by Larivey or d'Amboise may have been that of the Château de Pougy which we discussed above. But in general, the references are very scattered. Perhaps more evidence once existed, and the notoriously ephemeral nature of records of this kind is to blame.

The performance of comedies in Hardy's time has been ably discussed by Mme Deierkauf-Holsboer in her 'Vie d'Alexandre Hardy' and by Professor Gill in his edition of *Les Ramoneurs*. Their conclusions were, as we saw, that Hardy certainly wrote comedies: and that in fact the very question of 'copyright' in connection with stage performance was probably responsible for the failure of these plays to reach print. It was the troupes of Valleran le Conte and later of Pierre le Messier (Bellerose) and Villiers, with Hardy as *poète à gages*, that acted such comedies. Supporting this evidence, we know on the testimony of Thomas Platter that Valleran's troupe, in 1599, specifically performed comedies:

A l'hôtel de Bourgogne il y a un comédien nommé Valeran, engagé par le Roi. Il joue tous les jours, après le repas, une comédie en vers français, et débite ensuite une farce sur ce qui peut être

[1] Shelf-mark 163. b. 24–6, 28, 62.
[2] Cf. G. Mongrédien, *Dictionnaire biographique des comédiens français du XVIIe siècle* (Paris, 1961), *passim*.

arrivé de drôle à Paris, en fait d'amourettes ou d'autres anecdotes du même genre.[1]

Platter's distinction between 'comédie en vers français' and 'farce' is quite clear.

Les Ramoneurs itself is connected with the Hôtel de Bourgogne: that is, probably with the 'Comédiens du Roi', a company including not only actors of Valleran's kind, but also the three farce actors Gros-Guillaume, Gaultier Garguille, and Turlupin. The author of the play makes the valet Martin say: 'Voila vrayement un bel exemple à vos disciples qui verront representer l'histoire de ces belles amours dans un hotel de Bourgogne',[2] a line which could have its full effect only in a performance in the Hôtel de Bourgogne itself. With this play, indeed, we are returning from conjecture to fact; and it was *Mélite*, played only some five years later (1629–30), that established (as Corneille tells us in his 'Examen') the troupe of Montdory in Paris, to begin a period in which the public theatre in France was to come once more to an acknowledged significance.

6. THE EVIDENCE OF THE PLAYS: 1552–1570

The internal evidence of the plays themselves has not, as far as I know, been used before to yield information about stage sets, perhaps because their evidence, as derived from possibly non-dramatic works, has been mistrusted. Let us put this objection aside for the moment, and examine what information the plays have to offer; we may then decide upon its value.

For *L'Eugène*, two compartments only are needed: the houses of Guillaume and of Eugène. I. iii is set *inside* Guillaume's house ('Mais comment? qui entre ceans? / Avez-vous laissé l'huis ouvert?'); it must have been a door through which Messire Jean enters, and it has an upper storey (III. iii) and a garden (I. iii), both of which may or may not be represented on stage. Eugène's house needs a door (v. v: 'Voylà l'Abbé et mon

[1] Translated from the original; cited by Lebègue, 'Tableau', p. 316.
[2] IV. x: ed. Gill, pp. 133–4.

Helene / Devant la porte'; 'Sus, entrons'), but no action takes place in the interior. Florimond's house is referred to (v. ii and iv) but need not be on stage. So, short of improvisation, there must be at least one compartment with an interior; one with only a door; and a neutral space for the street (II. i).

Jodelle's other comedy, *La Rencontre*, is lost, but we do know something about its staging. Étienne Pasquier says of it: 'La Rencontre ainsi appellée parce qu'au gros de la meslange, tous les personnages s'estoient trouvez pesle mesle casuellement dedans une maison, fuseau qui fut fort bien par luy demeslé par la closture du jeu.'[1] The scene where this confusion takes place, with all the characters within a single house, is presumably shown on stage, like the scene inside Guillaume's house in *L'Eugène*. It would be difficult to do without an interior. Staging clearly is of some importance when the very title and basis of the plot are derived from it.

In *La Trésorière*, the Trésorier's house is the only essential compartment: it has a door which is knocked at and used (III. v; IV. iii; etc.), and an upper storey is referred to. The whole play appears to take place outside this house: all action within it is reported. One might suppose from III. iii ('Il est chez le sire Sulpice') that II. iii took place at Sulpice's house; but Constance's appearance in that scene suggests otherwise, that it was rather at the Trésorier's house.

Les Ébahis is similarly undemanding. Only one compartment, Gérard's house, is needed. It has a door through which L'Advocat enters and emerges (III. iv; IV. i) and an upper storey (III. v: 'Je montray jusqu'en la chambrette') which is probably shown on stage, since Panthaleone appears to deliver his serenades to a window above in II. iii and v. i. II. iii definitely takes place in the street, 'devant l'huys du sire Gérard'. Otherwise references to places are often imprecise. No action necessarily takes place within Gérard's house. Compartments for Josse and Claude would be possible, but the neutral space could also be used for them. Although, as we saw, there is no *a priori* reason why a

---

[1] *Les Recherches de la France* (Paris, 1617), VI. vii. 741.

college production should not have an elaborate set, it does appear that Grévin has chosen to make only modest demands on his stage-builders. Unlike Jodelle in both his plays, Grévin does not set any of his action inside a compartment. A single 'flat' with a door and window in it, or even a back curtain with an aperture, would be adequate for either play.

In *La Reconnue*, action once more takes place inside a compartment. In I. ii, Madame refers to kitchen equipment ('ce chaudron', etc.), so that we are quite definitely inside the kitchen. The kitchen has a door communicating with the rest of the house, since Janne asks for it to be closed in IV. v. There is also a door from the street into the house, which Janne opens; it may lead into the kitchen, but this is not absolutely clear and would in any case be odd on social grounds. There is a room or rooms above (I. ii: 'Antoinette, descendez') and a window (V. i). One other compartment is essential, the Voisine's house (I. iv–v; IV. iii). There is definitely a neutral street area (Act V). An extra compartment for L'Amoureux (IV. vi) would be possible but is not essential. So—again, short of improvisation—the requirements are the same as for *L'Eugène*: a 'street' area, with two compartments, action taking place within one of them.

The set for *Les Corrivaux* also requires only two compartments, with a street in front. The compartments are Jacqueline's house and Fremin's house, in a residential part of Paris (II. iii: 'Je m'en vais à la ville'). In IV. iii Benard is outside Jacqueline's ('le logis où se tient mon fils') and in IV. v, without mention of his having moved, he is outside Fremin's ('Je ne demande autre chose, entron dedans'), so that the houses may be supposed to be near each other in terms of the play itself. Both of them have doors; Fremin's has a back door as well (I. iii; II. ii; etc.), but it is evidently supposed to be off stage (III. iii, etc.). Much of the action takes place specifically in the street, and none within the houses. *Le Négromant* is of course a translation; but in any case it follows the pattern in requiring two compartments, with a street in front. The two compartments are supposed to be near each other in terms of the play (I. ii); and there is a reference (IV. vi) to 'ces maisons prochaines', which may be mere 'flats'.

Baïf's two plays follow the staging requirements of their originals. *Le Brave* in particular requires two compartments, the houses of Taillebras and Bontams (corresponding to those of Pyrgopolynices and Periplectomenus in the *Miles gloriosus*), but all the action takes place outside them.

The stage requirements of these first comedies, then, are quite consistent. There are five original plays, three translations, and the missing *La Rencontre*. The most that is needed is a neutral space with two compartments, with action inside one of them and a door in the other (*L'Eugène*, *La Reconnue*). The least is a neutral space with one compartment with a door (Grévin's two plays). La Taille's two plays need two compartments, but no action takes place within them; Jodelle's other play, *La Rencontre*, has action within a compartment, but it is possibly the only compartment—we cannot know.

This is not the staging required for Terence's plays at any period, for there no action is ever seen happening inside a house. It could correspond to the décor of the illustrations to Renaissance editions of Terence; in those illustrations curtains are used and sometimes the drawn curtain reveals a character inside,[1] a procedure that could be followed for *L'Eugène* and *La Reconnue*. But the décors of the Terentian illustrations are essentially rows or groups of numbers of compartments, whereas here there are only one or at most two.

Nor has it any Italian character;[2] nor is it the staging of the farces. In reading farce, one becomes used to the vertiginous changes of scene depending doubtless on improvisation, whereas here the atmosphere is different, calmer, rather suggesting that an actual set is being used than implying improvisation.

It does seem that a kind of set is implied, especially in *L'Eugène*

---

[1] For example, in an illustration to *Phormio* in the 1518 Venice edition, reproduced in Lawrenson and Purkis, 'Les éditions illustrées de Térence', fig. 13.

[2] The farce-like character of *L'Eugène* is quite at variance with Serlio's elaborate comic scene, which Balmas nevertheless reproduces in his edition of Jodelle's play.

and *La Reconnue*, and also in *Les Corrivaux* and *La Rencontre*, which is different from anything known to us from pictorial evidence. A reasonable solution could be that the model for these writers in conceiving the setting for their plays was the Terentian illustrations, but that since their plays were less complex structurally than Terence's, so were their sets. A very simple design for *L'Eugène* might be:

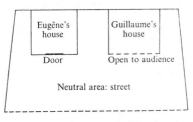

FIG. I. Possible set for Jodelle's *L'Eugène*.

7. THE EVIDENCE OF THE PLAYS: 1571–1630

De Vivre's *La Fidélité nuptiale*, as we saw, is the first comedy in French to imitate the Italian players newly established in France in the 1570s. Already its staging is different from that of the earlier generation. It is not elaborate, but it does make full use of the possibilities of the décor. There is a window above— from which a servant, Pardalisca, throws down water as it were into the street, shouting as she does so: 'Garde l'eaue. Garde l'eaue.' There are pillars supporting the 'fenestrages' or balcony —and a masked figure who stands hidden as though he were one of the pillars:

Cependant qu'il chantera, sortira un autre accoustré legiere-ment ayant un masque devant la face, lequel se mectra devant la porte tout debout en un coin, là ou l'autre ira chanter, et se tiendra là coy, comme si c'estoit une colomne à soustenir les fenestrages.

This active use of stage elements seems different from the more passive use seen in the comedies of the earlier generation.

There is something of it in Larivey's *Les Esprits*. Two com-partments are needed: Severin's house and Hilaire's house.

They are near each other in terms of the play (III. iii). Severin's needs a door and a window above, and both of these are actively used, the first in III. iii, where the door can be heard opening, and the second in II. iii, where tiles are thrown down from it. Hilaire's needs only a door, through which Frontin enters and emerges (I. v); it also has a 'Huys de derrière' (III. ii), but this is not necessarily on stage. The stage must represent, or at least give the illusion of, two or more streets (I. ii: 'Je le veux appeler devant qu'il change de rue'). Near Severin's house there is a 'trou' in which he hides his purse (II. iii, etc.). Gérard's relation's house, and Ruffin's house, are referred to and said to be in the same street as each other, but are not necessarily on stage.

Turnèbe's *Les Contents* requires three compartments: the houses of Girard, Louise, and Monsieur Bartole the lawyer.[1] The first needs a door, and in IV. v a window above is implied ('Qui est là-bas?'). The second needs a door which can be locked with a key (it is so locked at V. iii) and a window above which opens and closes (V. iii). None of the action other than reported action needs to go on inside Louise's house,[2] but we know some things about its interior: it has a 'petit oratoire' (III. vii), a 'salle' below (III. vii, etc.), and a room or rooms above (I. i: 'Qu'on se despesche de descendre'). The 'salle' has windows opening into the *cour* (Act IV). The house also has a 'huys de derriere' (V. ii). Monsieur Bartole's house needs only a door (IV. iv–v). These three compartments are supposed to be near each other in terms of the play itself (in III. iv Basile, who is outside Girard's house, speaks of the door of Louise's house as 'ceste prochaine porte', while from IV. v we gather that M.

---

[1] Dr. Spector, in his edition of the play, p. xxxvi, only counts two, omitting Monsieur Bartole's house. Although it is true that in production this house could be set off stage, there seems no reason to suppose that it is not a third compartment on stage: cf. IV. iv: 'Mon frere, allons trouver ce fameux advocat Monsieur Bartole, qui demeure tout icy-contre', and IV. v: 'Tenez, la voyla qui sort de chez Monsieur Bartole.'

[2] Part of I. i could well be set inside, but M. Lebègue is wrong in assuming this to be essential ('Unité et pluralité de lieu dans le théâtre français 1450–1600', *Le Lieu théâtral à la Renaissance* (Paris, 1964), p. 352).

Bartole's house is near Girard's). Girard's house appears to be a mere 'flat', because in IV. v Girard and Eustache speak in the street, rather than in the house, for no dramatic reason at all; the only reason that suggests itself is that the set does not allow them to enter.[1] As well as the main neutral space, there are at least two 'ruelles' (I. i). In I. iii Rodomont hides under an 'auvent', but v. iv referring to this same scene says that he hid behind a 'charrète', a cart; this is an inconsistency, but one or other, or both, is necessary.

Les Néapolitaines similarly needs three compartments: Angélique's house, the Collège des Lombards, and the inn, the Escu de France. The first is supposed to be in the Faubourg Saint-Germain (I. i); it has a door, through which exit Camille, running (III. vi); it has a window (II. iii); and it probably has an 'haute gallerie', otherwise Gaster's lie (III. iii) would have no point. It has an upper storey where Angélique and Virginie live (II. viii). No action takes place within it; in III. viii Virginie delivers her monologue outside the house when it would be more normally spoken inside, the reason for which may well be that the house is not intended to have an interior. The Collège des Lombards has a window: in v. iv the innkeeper calls Camille: 'Je le vay appeler par la fenestre', and Camille appears there. The Escu de France has a door through which the innkeeper enters and emerges (v. iii). The street is used (v. x, etc.) as neutral territory. Other compartments are possible, but not essential; one likely one is Augustin's house, for in I. i he is calling out to Loys, who, precisely, is staying at home, and another possible one is the house where Dieghos is staying (I. iii; III. vi). Other places are named, which the characters visit within the time of the play's action, but they are not on stage: the pâtisserie (II. ii), Isabeau's house (IV. iv), etc.

The evidence of Fornaris's *Angelica* and Bruno's *Il Candelaio*, both published in France, merely supports our data so far:

[1] Dr. Spector suggests in his edition, p. xxxvii, that the reason is to preserve the unity of place. This theoretical reason may well be correct; the conclusion regarding the staging is nevertheless also valid.

neither presupposes a stage in any way different from that of
Les Contents or *Les Néapolitaines*. 'L. C.' 's *Angélique* is a close
translation of *Angelica*. As we saw, it is doubtful whether
Lasphrise's *Nouvelle Tragicomique* was ever acted; but if it were
acted, it would be an exception to the practice so far; it would
need five compartments: Dominicque's castle outside Paris,
with a gate that opens; the magician's cave; a city gate of Paris,
again which opens; an inn with a window, a door that opens, and
a scene inside the inn; and a prison.

Perrin's *Les Écoliers* is far simpler than any of the plays we
have been discussing. As we have seen, it stands outside the
Italianate tradition, and the stage of the *commedia erudita* is
foreign to it. In this as in other ways, the play is a return to other,
simpler forms. There is only one compartment, Marin's house;
this has a door which can be heard opening (II. ii). If Friquet in
I. v is not speaking in general terms, it seems that from the
outside of the house one can see a staircase, a door, and a window. Some of the action is definitely in the street (IV. v).

Les Déguisés, although an adaptation from the Italian, is also
simple. Only one compartment is essential: Grégoire's house in
a residential part of Toulouse (v. i; III. v: 'Mon père doit
retourner . . . bientost de la ville'). It has a door through which
Louise enters and emerges (II. ii; IV. iii). III. v–vi could take place
within the house, but need not. Other possible compartments
are Prouventard's house (III. iv) and Passetrouvant's house
(IV. viii); any of these could be on stage, but need not. Some
action definitely takes place in the street (III. i and iv), and the
stage seems to have two streets or at least their appearance
(III. iv: 'il a jà gagné l'autre rue').

Troterel's two plays, like *Les Écoliers*, look back to farce in
many ways, and not least in their staging. The awareness of
stage décor which we saw in *La Fidélité nuptiale* and *Les Esprits* is
absent here, and we have only occasional references to basic
stage elements such as a door (*Les Corrivaux*, II. iv). One of the
rare references to a curtain in French Renaissance comedy is in
Les Corrivaux, III. iii.

The set for *Les Ramoneurs*, on the other hand, is relatively complex. It consists of four compartments, every one of them this time with doors. The play opens outside the Captain's house, 'ce malotru de logis' (ed. Gill, p. 24), 'ce misérable Toict à pourceaux' (p. 4); it has a door out of which Galaffre chases the Crocheteur (p. 6; cf. *Les Néapolitaines*, III. vi) and which the Captain slams (p. 56), and a window above (pp. 13, 32). Part at least of III. iv takes place within the house, when the chimney is swept; this is a room separate from but communicating with Diane's room, the one which has the window (p. 91). Separated from the Captain's house by a drain or 'ruisseau' (p. 21) is Dame Bonne's fruit shop, which has a window 'opposite' (p. 43) and commanding a view of the Captain's house. People go in and out of her door (pp. 70, 72). Claude's house has a bedroom inside (pp. 120–34) in which, as in the Captain's house, action takes place; the door of the bedroom is even broken in (p. 127). Besides this, there are references to a 'Chambre de nantissement' above (p. 137), a 'salle' (p. 150) which is possibly the same as the 'chambre' (p. 97) but which is specifically not used (p. 150), and a 'porte de derriére' (p. 127). Finally, there is the house of Dame Louise, the Lingère, which has a window (p. 153) and a room above (p. 145). This is certainly the most complicated set of any of our plays; unless a very great deal of improvisation were employed, the bare stage of the Hôtel de Bourgogne as we see it in Bosse's print (reproduced, for example, in Gill's edition, frontispiece) would be wholly insufficient. If the play was acted at the Hôtel de Bourgogne, as it would appear (p. 134; and introduction, pp. xxxv ff.), then we surely must assume a more elaborate set, similar to those in the Mahelot drawings. As for the arrangement of the compartments, we know that the Captain's and Bonne's houses are very near each other, that Philippes turns *left* out of the Captain's house to go to Claude's (p. 87), so that Claude's must be on stage left of the Captain's; and that the Lingère's house is probably not meant to be very far from Claude's, as Galaffre easily follows Martin from one to the other. Finally, the number of references to streets, particularly small ones (pp. 71, 73, 87, 92, 119, 143), suggests gaps between the compartments, perhaps alleys as in the Vicenza set. One arrangement of the whole might be:

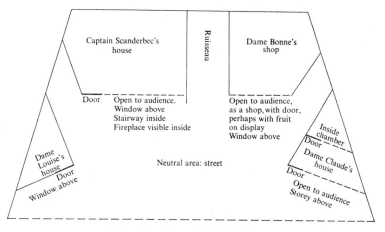

FIG. 2. Possible set for *Les Ramoneurs*.

Corneille's *Mélite*, written in the same decade as *Les Ramoneurs*, stands firmly in the tradition of multiple décor, even though in the 'Examen' which he published in 1660, he wrote:

Ce sens commun qui estoit toute ma Regle . . . m'avoit donné assez d'aversion de cet horrible déreglement qui mettoit Paris, Rome, et Constantinople sur le mesme Theatre, pour reduire le mien dans une seule Ville.[1]

The three necessary compartments—the houses of Mélite, of Cliton, and of Tirsis and Cloris—are indeed supposed to be in the same town, but nevertheless in different quarters and far enough away for Tirsis never to have seen Mélite before ('Examen': 'ces quartiers doivent estre si esloignez l'un de l'autre, que les Acteurs ayent lieu de ne pas s'entreconnoistre'[2]). We saw that Turnèbe in his play has minimized the artificiality of the convention; but Corneille, forty years later, here still accepts it.

[1] *Mélite*, ed. cit., p. 135.   [2] Ibid., p. 138.

Later, in the 'Examen', he was to consider it a fault that characters were allowed only a short time to move from one quarter to another; but, of course, in terms of the convention, there is no objection to this.[1] Mélite's house, like so many others, has a window at first-floor level at which she appears (II. viii: 'Elle paroist au travers d'une jalousie . . . Melite se retire de la jalousie et descend'); Cloris's has a door (III. vii: 'Elle luy ferme la porte au nez').

What are the constant features of this convention? First, it is quite clear that a form of *décor simultané* is involved, a single set with a number of houses.[2] And the stages in the illustrated editions of Terence will no longer do, because they do not have windows, doors which can be heard opening, and so on; while the elaborate set of Serlio's comic scene, with its church and tower, inn, and five houses, is never necessary.

It is clear that a change has taken place with the coming of the Italian troupes. From Jodelle to La Taille, the maximum number of compartments needed was two, with action taking place in one of them (*L'Eugène, La Reconnue*). From Larivey to *Les Ramoneurs*, two to four or even five compartments are needed, with action inside them in *Les Ramoneurs*, and the compartments need to be more complex. But the staging seems to have altered only in degree and not in essence. The example of La Taille should warn us against assuming that a sharp break occurred overnight. La Taille's models were Italian (though admittedly he wrote before the Italian troupes came), but still, as an admirer of the Pléiade he demands no more complex sets than they do. The Italians may have scored a great success in France in the 1570s, but the stage demands of French comedy do not seem to have altered essentially as a result: with Perrin and even

[1] Thus Tirsis in Act I between scenes iii and v, 82 lines; Tirsis in Act II between scenes v and viii, 84 lines; Cloris in Act v between scenes iii and v, 54 lines.

[2] Is it necessary to refute the idea of successive changes of scene? In the nineteenth century, Thomas Love Peacock, translating *Gl'Ingannati*, wrote: 'I have . . . marked three changes of scene: A street, with two hotels and the house of Gherardo. A street, with the house of Flaminio. A street, with the house of Virginio', an error which has found its way, without comment, into a modern reprint: *The Genius of the Italian Theater* (New York, 1964), p. 100.

Godard, adaptor from the Italian as he was, it was still possible to return to a set demanding only a single compartment. This continuity supports the particular ideas about continuity of stage design which I suggested in part four of this chapter.

Separate compartments, then, with a neutral street area are used throughout our period. The town is always Paris (except Orléans for *Le Brave*, Toulouse for *Les Déguisés*, and Saumur for *L'Avare cornu*), although references to the provinces are more frequent than they will be, for example, in post-Richelieu plays. The two old men in *La Néphélococugie* come from Toulouse. Some of the action takes place in the street, and sometimes it is specifically made clear that the characters are in neutral territory and not outside a specific character's house (*Les Néapolitaines*, III. xi, etc.). In *Les Esprits*, *Les Contents*, *Les Déguisés*, and *Les Ramoneurs* it appears that there is more than one street, or at least the illusion of more than one street, on stage. To this extent, the convention corresponds to Serlio's 'comic scene', where small alleys open off the main central space.

The number of essential compartments, even in the later period, varies from one to four. In Perrin's *Les Écoliers*, Marin's house is the only one, and there is no reference whatsoever to any other compartment. At the other extreme, *Les Ramoneurs* needs four compartments; and *Les Néapolitaines* needs at least three, probably four or even five, while in addition four other places visited by the characters off stage in the course of the play are precisely named.

The compartments in the comedies, then, are always town houses with a street or streets in front of them. It is perhaps noteworthy that no comedy has any compartment representing anything other than a town house. The *Mémoire de Mahelot*, from a later period in the history of the theatre, has compartments of many other kinds (caves, castles, cemeteries, prisons, gardens, oceans, etc.), not merely in tragedies, tragi-comedies, and pastorals, but also in comedies such as Du Ryer's *Les Vendanges de Suresnes*.[1]

---

[1] *Le Mémoire de Mahelot*, ed. Lancaster, p. 94.

The town houses regularly have certain features in common. Every one has a door opening directly on to the street, in view of the audience; in every case without exception a character (or characters) goes through these doors, and in *Les Esprits* and *Les Écoliers* one can be heard opening. In *Les Contents* Louise locks one with a key. Sometimes the door is all that the compartment requires; sometimes it needs considerably more. Thus, in *Les Contents* Louise's house has an upper storey with a visible window that opens and closes; and several others also have upper storeys and windows. Angélique's house in *Les Néapolitaines* appears to have an 'haute gallerie', but there is never a balcony of the *Romeo and Juliet* kind. Any serenading (*Les Ébahis*, *La Fidélité nuptiale*, *Les Ramoneurs*) is done to an open window. A print in the *Recueil Fossard* shows a serenade being given to the upper window of a structure on stage (cf. Plate VI).[1]

It is clear, however, that some compartments, although they may have a door, could perfectly well be mere 'flats' or curtains, without an interior which can be acted in. Such are Girard's house in *Les Contents* (IV. iv) and Angélique's house in *Les Néapolitaines* where, as I have said, there is some dramatic awkwardness in both cases when characters are forced to remain outside a house. In other plays, there is no such awkwardness, but nevertheless there is often no evidence whether a particular scene is taking place inside a house or in the street outside. Many compartments thus have no need to be anything other than 'flats' or curtains.

Others certainly have interiors within which action takes place. Such are Guillaume's house, *L'Eugène*, I. iii; presumably the house in Jodelle's lost play *La Rencontre*; Monsieur's house, *La Reconnue*, I. ii; Claude's and the Captain's houses in *Les Ramoneurs*; and perhaps Grégoire's house, *Les Déguisés*, III. v and vi (the action inside Louise's house in *Les Contents*, though considerable, is merely reported). All six houses have a door, communicating with the street, through which characters pass

---

[1] A painting related to this print is in the Drottningholm Theatre Museum, and is reproduced in Allardyce Nicoll's *The World of Harlequin*, p. 21.

in the course of the play, action taking place in both house and street. It is necessary, therefore, that both the inside of the house *and* the street should be in view of the audience. There are two solutions. First, for the earlier plays I suggested the use of a curtain, as in the Terentian illustrations; this could be used for the later ones too, for such a curtain was certainly used a few years later in the Mahelot drawings.[1] Or it might be done by deliberately omitting the wall of a house, that is on the audience's side, so that the interior is visible to the audience; Serlio illustrates this in his *tragic* scene, but not in the comic scene. In *Les Ramoneurs*, IV. x (and in Lasphrise's *Nouvelle Tragicomique*), an *interior* door is broken down, suggesting something of the kind. There would have to be at least a *loggia*.

Some of the Mahelot sets are close to the sets required for these plays. For one thing, they are pictures of sets built on the Hôtel de Bourgogne stage, where *Les Ramoneurs* for one was performed, the set for *Les Ramoneurs* not being essentially different from that required for the earlier plays. In general, Mahelot's sets are more complex; but where it happens that a play makes demands similar to those of our comedies, the set is similar. The closest is probably that for Rotrou's *Les Ménechmes*, with four town houses, each having a door and a window above, and with a neutral street area and alleys between the houses.[2] None of the houses of this set, though, has an interior for acting in.

It is, of course, an artificial convention that places which might be supposed to be some distance apart are set close to each other on stage. Potiron in *La Reconnue*, arriving at Monsieur's house from off stage, is 'hors d'haleine' (IV. vi). But at least in the comedies the various houses are all supposed to be within the same town, thus fulfilling any theoretical requirement for the unity of place; whereas in the tragedies and tragi-comedies of the turn of the century (such as Chrétien de

---

[1] Cf. *Le Mémoire de Mahelot*, ed. cit., pp. 73–4 (Hardy's *La Folie de Clidamant* and *La Folie d'Isabelle*), and *Les Ramoneurs*, ed. Gill, p. xxix.

[2] *Le Mémoire de Mahelot*, ed. cit., p. 89 and drawing. Cf. Plate VII.

PLATE VI

A serenade from the *Recueil Fossard*, showing a structure with window on stage

PLATE VII

The set for Rotrou's *Les Ménechmes* (acted 1631) from the *Mémoire de Mahelot*, showing four houses disposed round a central space, each house with a door and window

Croix's *Les Portugais infortunés*) distances of many miles can be involved. In one play, *Les Contents*, the three compartments are supposed to be very near each other *in terms of the play itself* (III. iv and IV. v), a touch of realism peculiar to this play and strictly unnecessary in terms of the convention of *décor simultané*.[1]

A problem presents itself in the cases of *L'Eugène* and *Les Néapolitaines* which may be solved according to the degree of artificiality which is assumed. In *L'Eugène*, it is reported that in the interval between II. ii and III. i Arnault goes to Guillaume's house, enters, confronts the company present, and departs. In *Les Néapolitaines* it is similarly reported that between III. xiii and IV. i Camille enters Angélique's house and sends Cornélie off to do the shopping, Cornélie returns, is delayed by some students, Camille leaves, Cornélie enters and then emerges. We learn these things by report; but in both cases the house concerned is a compartment on stage and in full view of the audience. Are we to assume that the audience 'forgets' that it has not seen the action? Or that in both cases there is a break in the performance, an interval, perhaps even with a curtain drawn? The elaborate dumbshows that would otherwise be necessary can hardly be considered.

All this suggests a remarkably stable scenic convention, in which the same features recur continually. Three considerations lead me to think that they represent an actual stage convention throughout the period and not at any time a literary and hypothetical one. One is their very stability: the basic décor requirements, like the time-sequence, hardly change through seventy-five years, whereas freedom from the limitations of the stage might have suggested variants which we do not in fact find. Second, the details have had to be gleaned from texts where they are scattered haphazardly and often ambiguously; if a literary convention were involved and not a practical one, they might surely be expected to be more systematic. They occur incidentally in the plays, usually having a dramatic

---

[1] The two compartments of *Les Corrivaux* are similarly supposed to be near each other; but the fact has to be deduced and is less obvious than in *Les Contents*.

function as well as giving mere scenic information: thus in *Les Néapolitaines*, v. iv, Marc-Aurel admiring all the colleges is not merely indicating 'scenery' to a reader, he is expressing the astonishment and naïvety supposed to be proper to a stranger visiting Paris for the first time. Often it is not clear whether a scene is supposed to be at one house or another, inside or outside, and the very lack of system, when one considers it together with the consistency of the detail that *can* be gleaned, seems to be a good indication that the convention we are dealing with is a practical and not merely a literary one. And finally and more convincingly, actual production seems to be suggested by the two passages where characters, at the cost of some dramatic awkwardness, choose to remain *outside* a compartment rather than to enter it. The only reason that presents itself is scenic necessity, in that the compartments in question are mere 'flats' or curtains, and that action cannot take place within them. Had the plays not been written with production in mind, the characters could quite simply have 'entered' their compartments and continued their conversation.

The question of miming was mentioned in connection with the farces. Miming by a good actor would, of course, at once remove the necessity for many of the pieces of stage set which we have been discussing, and for properties as well. The Jean-Louis Barrault of *Les Enfants du paradis* did not need an actual pocket watch to convey to us the idea of one, and the Italian actors so closely connected with the French comedy of this time had a reputation for miming and improvisation as great as any in theatre history. A 'realist' school of acting at this time is most unlikely, and it would be naïve to take literally each single reference to staging in these plays. But there is hardly any other evidence; and if a play refers to a serenade sung to a window above, it is at least difficult to do without the window. And above all, the continuity of the references to windows and the like, and to the nature of the total set, does suggest that throughout our period actual stage sets were used, of the kind which I have described.

7. ACTION ON STAGE; STYLES OF ACTING; COSTUMES; PROPERTIES; MASKS; STAGE DIRECTIONS

The point about miming leads on to the whole question of acting and action on stage.[1] Most violent action, we find, is set off stage, a standard theoretical principle of course for tragedies up to the end of the sixteenth century, and following in the comedies too. The riot in *Les Corrivaux*, the escape through the window in *Les Contents*, and all the seductions happen off stage, just as all the deaths and murders in the tragedies of the sixteenth century do. The texts of French Renaissance farces show that a good deal of physical action went on in them; but little physical action is apparent from the texts of the comedies, where the most violent actions that can be cited are Camille's hasty exit from a house in *Les Néapolitaines* (III. vi), the tile-throwing in *Les Esprits* (II. iii), Rodomont's arrest in *Les Contents* (III. ii), and the breaking down of a door in *La Trésorière* (IV. iii) and in *Les Ramoneurs* (IV. x). One consequence of setting certain kinds of action off stage is that the women's parts can be made very small.

Other stage business can be deduced from the text. We have already seen how characters continually go in and out of doors. Other action involves the use of properties, for example, Panthaleone singing to his lute in *Les Ébahis*, or the use of disguise. In *Les Contents*, characters hide their faces with their cloaks (III. v; IV. i and iii), not to overhear, but simply in order not to be recognized. Many other characters overhear without being seen, such as Potiron in *La Reconnue* (III. iv) or Désiré in *Les Esprits* (II. iii). The pictures of Fabrizio de Fornaris show him 'overhearing' on stage, listening to a dialogue but not attempting to conceal himself otherwise than with his cloak (cf. Plates VIII and IX). Turnèbe, on the other hand, has his braggart Rodomont hide behind a cart or an 'auvent', thus mitigating once again in his play the artificiality of a convention. There are

---

[1] More details about acting will be found in Chapter III, where asides and soliloquies, and the speech proper to certain characters, are discussed.

particularly lively actions in de Vivre's *La Fidélité nuptiale*, which were described by La Vallière in 1768 as *lazzi*: 'Ascanio, valet de Charès, est aussi sorti avec un luth, et va chanter dans les rues. Tout cet acte se passe en lazzis [*sic*] entre ce valet et une figure masquée qui lui fait plusieurs niches.'[1] To judge from this knockabout scene, from the bright costumes, from the masks, and from the Italian names in the play, it does look very much as though, already in the 1570s, de Vivre has been more influenced by the *commedia dell'arte* than has either d'Amboise or Turnèbe.

There are three serenades. Panthaleone in *Les Ébahis* (II. iii and v. i) sings lines from *Orlando furioso* to the lute. Charès in *La Fidélité nuptiale*, 'jeune gentilhomme, avecques la cappe et l'espée', sings parts of no less than five of the most popular *chansons* of the day: *Toutes les nuits, Susanne un jour, Bon jour mon cœur, Douce mémoire*, and *Mon cœur se recommande à vous*; his 'garson' Ascanio ('car vous savez Messieurs Tel Maistre, tel valet') sings parts of *D'Amours me va tout au rebours, En entrant en un jardinet, Changeons propos*, and *Qui veut entrer en grace*. In *Les Ramoneurs*, Philippes even hires a consort of voices, lutes, and guitars to serenade Diane: 'Bon Dieu, quelle ravissante melodie, quel agréable meslange de voix, de luts, et de guittarres; Escoute unair où ton nom est inseré . . .' (I. viii).[1]

References to facial and bodily expression occur, but are not common. We may gather from the text that the delivery is pompous (Maudolé in *Les Déguisés*, III. iv: 'Je pompe, je morgue, je brave'), or lyrical, or violent, but there is not much other evidence about the kind of delivery intended or expected by the author. In *L'Eugène*, II. ii, Florimond says to Arnault 'Tu t'en venois trepignant / Pour me trouver' and 'Je te voyois mouvoir le doy, / Et marmonner en tes deux levres', and in *Les Déguisés*, II. iv, Grégoire says of Prouventard 'Il s'en va furieusement'. Details of stage delivery, as in the succeeding century, do not

---

[1] La Vallière, *Bibliothèque du théâtre françois depuis son origine*, vol. i (Dresden, 1768), p. 217.

[2] Ed. Gill, p. 34. Cf. Plate VI.

PLATE VIII

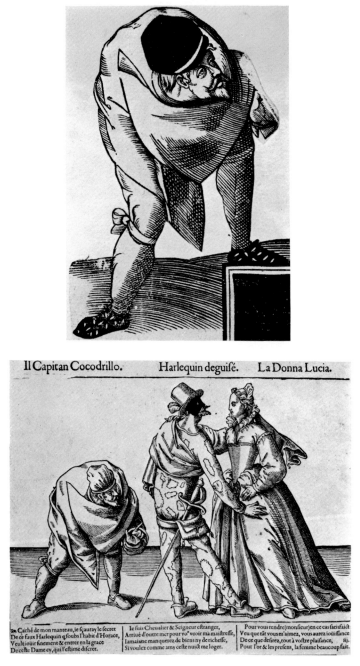

Il Capitan Cocodrillo.   Harlequin deguisé.   La Donna Lucia.

Caché de mon manteau, ie sçauray le secret
De ce faux Harlequin q̃ soubs l'habit d'Horace,
Veult iouïr finement & entrer en la grace
De ceste Dame cy, qui l'estime discret.

Ie suis Cheualier & Seigneur estranger,
Arriué d'outre mer pour vo' vooir ma maistresse,
Iamaisne manquerez de biens ny de richesse,
Si voulez comme amy ceste nuict me loger.

Pour vous rendre(monsieur)en ce cas satisfaict
Veu que tãt vous m'aimez, vous aurez iouïssance   iij.
De ce que desirez, tout à vostre plaisance,
Pour l'or & les presens, la femme beaucoup fait.

Two prints from the *Recueil Fossard* showing Fabrizio de Fornaris as
Il Capitan Cocodrillo eavesdropping

PLATE IX

A painting in Drottningholms Teatermuseum, related to the prints in Plate VIII, also showing Cocodrillo eavesdropping

appear to have been part of the author's province; we may perhaps compare Renaissance music, where the notes before the performance could certainly be played in many different ways and on many different instruments, to be decided by the performers, not specified by the composer.

Mr. Joseph devotes much of his book, *Elizabethan Acting*, to discussing the hand positions and gestures in John Bulwer's *Chirologia* and *Chironomia*, published together in 1644. We find that many of these same hand gestures are demonstrated in the pictures of the *Recueil Fossard*, and by their precision and detail they are an important part of the acting styles seen in that collection, showing that they were in active use in France and Italy as well as in England. The gestures often seem natural enough, so that agreement between Bulwer and the *Recueil Fossard* is not surprising, but some of the gestures found in both sources are more unusual. Two of these more unusual ones found in both sources are the flicking of the thumb as a sign of contempt, and surrender by extending one's hands to the front (instead of above one's head). In the first of the two pictures of Coccodrillo in the *Recueil Fossard*, the captain's left hand is in a position similar to Bulwer's *Exprobrabit*, the index and little fingers extended, the other two half closed, and the whole hand raised for the audience's attention. A variant of it is used by Zani in a print of 1594 or earlier, and Mr. Joseph shows us Ellen Terry using it in 1885.[1]

Costumes are often varied and colourful, such as Josse's fur coat in *Les Ébahis*, the sweeps' clothes in *Les Ramoneurs*, or Dom Dieghos's cloak in *Les Néapolitaines*. Disguise is commonly part of the plays' comic structure: in *Les Ramoneurs* sweeps' clothes

[1] B. L. Joseph, *Elizabethan Acting*, second edition (Oxford, 1964) (the first edition, of 1951, differs a good deal). The flicking of the thumb is Bulwer's *Floccifacit*; cf. Joseph, p. 53 and fig. 5, I, and the *Recueil Fossard*, plate xv. The surrender is seen in Bulwer's *Libertatem resigno*; cf. Joseph, p. 17 and fig. 2, N, and the *Recueil Fossard*, plate xii. *Exprobrabit* is seen in Joseph's fig. 6, V, in the plate facing his p. 17, and in Plate viii of the present volume. The picture of Zani is in Alain Dufour's 'Le catéchisme du docteur Pantalon et de Zani, son disciple (1594)', *Aspects de la propagande religieuse*, *Travaux d'Humanisme et Renaissance*, xxviii (1957), 361–72.

with a little soot are used to disguise a woman as a man, in *Les Contents* Alix is disguised also as a man, and in *Les Déguisés* the device is of course fundamental to the play. Costume is more important still in *Les Contents*, where Turnèbe has made of a scarlet cloak something more than a stock disguise. It and a second cloak exactly like it are integrated into the plot, and are essential to no less than six different scenes of the play, worn by four different characters. The scarlet colour, as Dr. Spector points out, is an ironic comment on the supposed virtue of Geneviefve to which the cloaks are always related.[1] Gérard de Vivre, too, though he says in the preface 'Aux lecteurs' to his collection of plays that comedies deal with 'matiere vulgaire' and therefore do not require elaborate costumes, nevertheless uses several costumes to some meaning in *La Fidélité nuptiale*, such as a black dress signifying melancholy and mourning, or the white sleeves of Palestra signifying wifely virtue.

References to other 'scenery' or to 'properties' other than clothing are not frequent. In *Les Ébahis, La Fidélité nuptiale*, and *Les Ramoneurs* we have the lutes and guitars needed for the serenades. In *La Reconnue* there is kitchen equipment, in *Les Esprits* tiles and a purse and a 'trou' to hide the purse in, in *Les Contents* an 'auvent' and/or a cart, in *Les Déguisés* a purse. A piece of 'scenery' or more compartments or 'flats' are implied in *Les Néapolitaines*, v. iv: 'Toutes ces grandes maisons, sont-ce colléges?' *Les Ramoneurs* is unique in needing quite a collection of small 'props'. A good use of them is found in *Les Corrivaux*, III. iii, where the two servants Alizon and Claude find themselves in the street embarrassed by the distaff and torch which they are respectively carrying and which each intends to wave as a secret signal to the lover who has bribed him for the purpose.

The Italian actors, as we see them in the pictures of Italian comedy in France, wear masks for some characters but not for others: that is, for some plays at least we are to assume the

---

[1] *Les Contents*, ed. Spector, introduction, pp. xlvi–xlvii, lxvi–lxix.

PLATE X

La signification des signes, desquels i'vse-
ray en toutes mes Comedies.

Ce signe signifie vne pause.

Cestuy deux.

Cestuy trois, chascune pause vaut vne
reprise d'haleine.

Vn pourmenemēt par tout le Theatre

Ceci signifie parler bas.

Ceci signifie, de parler plus viste que
le reste.

Cecy de parler plus lentement que le
reste.

ACTE

The list of signs used by Gérard de Vivre as stage directions throughout his plays. This list is from his *Comédie de la Fidélité Nuptiale*, Antwerp, 1577

rather odd theatrical technique whereby some actors wear them while others do not. This may well apply to the *commedia dell' arte*, but probably not to the *commedie erudite* performed by the same actors. The French farce actors certainly used them, as we see from the *Testament de feu Gaultier Garguille* which refers to 'Mon habit noir, mon masque, ma chevelure blanche',[1] and their use survives into the character of Mascarille in Molière's *Les Précieuses ridicules*. Masks were among the equipment of Valleran le Conte in 1598.[2] In our plays, although actors may possibly have used them, only one play specifies a mask, and that only for one character: de Vivre's *La Fidélité nuptiale* (cf. p. 77 above). In addition, in the last scene of *Les Néapolitaines*, Gaster the parasite turns to the audience for the final speech of the play which includes the words: 'Mon nez, tel que vous le voyez, sçait bien à quoy s'en tenir: qui bien fera bien trouvera', which may possibly refer to a mask. But in general, in these learned comedies, masks were probably rarely used.

As for stage directions, they are found in quantity only in one source, once again the plays of Gérard de Vivre, which have much to tell us about the Renaissance stage. Every edition of de Vivre's plays includes a table of signs which are liberally used in the plays themselves (cf. Plate X). In addition to the table of signs, de Vivre's plays also contain stage directions given in full, such as the one quoted above for its mention of a mask. Occasional stage directions are found in the other plays, but they are rare and isolated, like this from *Les Esprits*: 'Il crache, et ceux de dedans jettent des tuiles' (II. iii). The words 'Tich tach toch' are curiously put into the mouth of characters in Larivey's, Turnèbe's, and d'Amboise's plays to indicate that they are knocking at a door. They may therefore be classed as a stage direction.[3]

[1] Cf. D. Roy, 'Conditions and Conventions of the early Seventeenth-century Theatre in France' (unpublished dissertation for the degree of M.A., University of Wales, 1954), p. 304. [2] Ibid.

[3] Orazio Vecchi's *L'Amfiparnaso* (Venice, 1597), which, if not quite the first opera, is a play sung in madrigal form, most extraordinarily sets the words 'Tich tach toch' to music, as though they were indeed spoken by the character concerned and not merely representing the sound of his knocking.

But details of acting technique and of stage conditions at this time are unlikely to be peculiar to the genre of comedy; so that these details, gleaned from the text of French Renaissance comedies, can be seen to be relevant to the French Renaissance stage as a whole, about which we have such scanty evidence today.

CHAPTER THREE

The Conventions

I. COMIC THEORY IN THE FRENCH RENAISSANCE

DRAMATIC criticism in Renaissance France is at first sight small in quantity. There is no parallel to Corneille's 'Discours', for example, nor to the ample prologues and epistles which Ben Jonson added to his plays. We have today three sources for French Renaissance dramatic theories: the treatises on poetry in general, the liminary material to actual comedies, and (for comedy) the commentaries on Terence. The first of these gives drama a small place indeed; the second is fragmentary; and the third is primarily pedagogic, even pedantic. At first sight, this is perhaps surprising, to us for whom the dramatic production of the Renaissance is one of its principal legacies. But in France, for various social, political, and economic reasons, drama never achieved the flowering that it did, for example, in England: in the last decade of the sixteenth century, when aristocratic patronage and popular support combined in England to encourage a rapidly increasing dramatic activity, France was in the grip of a far sadder political situation, and the English fusion of classical influences with the experiences of the Italian actors and with the native drama was never achieved there.

But all the same, the dearth of theoretical material is partly an illusion. The extracts from treatises, and the liminary material to plays, may seem fragmentary indeed, but the appearance is deceptive, for two reasons. Firstly, drama in general was not, in the sixteenth century, considered as anything other than a species of poetry, along with the ode, the hymn, the epic, and other forms. Scaliger, praising the comic form, praises it specifically in its context as such a species: comedy is the first and true form of poetry in general, because of the special role of invention in it: 'Tantum enim abest, ut Comoedia Poema non sit: ut pene omnium et primum, et verum existimem. In eo enim ficta omnia, et materia quaesita tota.'[1] Specifically dramatic criticism as such was less possible then than it is today, when theories of the drama—as of the novel or of lyric poetry—are often readily discussed in isolation. It follows that many ideas which are certainly relevant to Renaissance views on drama are to be found expressed as relevant to poetry in general. It is essential to keep this broader view in mind. Where the author of a treatise writes a section on tragedy or comedy (or on the epic, the hymn, or the ode), he will put in it only such ideas as are supplementary to ideas which he has expressed as relevant to poetry in general: ideas on imitation, invention, decorum, and the like. We must therefore take full notice of those more widely applicable ideas. And secondly, one form of comic theory was inescapably part of every cultivated man's education during the Renaissance: Terence's plays and the commentaries on them, both those ascribed to Donatus and those by more recent critics. Marvin T. Herrick has discussed the influence of the commentaries in a European context, while H. W. Lawton has shown particularly how great was the number of editions of Terence published in France at this time.

All the sources of comic theory in France are normally descriptive, usually of Terentian or of contemporary French practice. They are less often prescriptive, even though they may ostensibly appear so, or historical in any diachronistic sense. When Jean Vauquelin de la Fresnaye in 1605 prescribes rules for the observance of decorum of speech in comedy:

> Grand' différence y a faire un maistre parler,
> Ou Davus qui ne doit au maistre s'égaller,
> Ou le bon Pantelon, ou Zany dont Ganasse
> Nous a representé la façon et la grace[2]

---

[1] *Poetices libri septem*, 5th ed. (Heidelberg, 1617), I. ii. 11.
[2] Jean Vauquelin de la Fresnaye, *L'Art poétique* (1605), i, ll. 857–60; ed. Pellissier, pp. 50–1.

he is certainly referring to the *Andria* of Terence and to plays performed in France by the Italian troupe of Ganassa.[1] His prescriptive or didactic form is, as so often with Renaissance instruction books, in fact a cloak for description, in this case of Terence and the *commedia dell'arte*. When a genuinely prescriptive approach is in fact adopted, it is usually in general terms, not in terms of detailed dramatic practice; thus Du Bellay:

Quand aux comedies et tragedies, si les roys et les republiques les vouloint restituer en leur ancienne dignité, qu'ont usurpée les farces et moralitez, je seroy' bien d'opinion que tu t'y employasses, et si tu le veux faire pour l'ornement de ta Langue, tu scais ou tu en doibs trouver les archetypes.[2]

The dramatic theory that is to be found in Renaissance treatises on poetry—those of Sébillet, Du Bellay, Peletier du Mans, Scaliger, Laudun d'Aigaliers, Vauquelin de la Fresnaye—and most of the relevant liminary material have been valuably gathered together by H. W. Lawton in his *Handbook of French Renaissance Dramatic Theory* (Manchester, 1949). The material is necessarily isolated; in the case of the theory, from the rest of the treatise, and in the case of the liminary material, from the plays that accompany it. W. F. Patterson's *Three Centuries of French Poetic Theory*, 2 vols. (Ann Arbor, 1935), amplifies the context in the first case, while the examination of the plays themselves in the present work should give the context of the second. A brief survey of the sources that survive, their statements on comedy, and the context of those statements is as follows.

We may begin with the period just before the Pléiade. Earlier than that, comic theory was certainly discussed, but primarily in connection with the plays of Terence and the commentaries on them, and the ideas were broadly identical

---

[1] On Ganassa, cf. A. Baschet, *Les Comédiens italiens à la cour de France* (Paris, 1882), chapter I.

[2] *La Deffence et illustration de la langue françoyse* (Paris, 1549), II. iv; ed. H. Chamard (Paris, 1961), pp. 125–6.

with those of Donatus and his successors. And as far as comic practice is concerned, our material begins at the mid century; the literal translations of the earlier period, and the other genres such as the plays of Marguerite de Navarre, do not concern us here. With these theoretical ideas in mind, it should be possible in the succeeding chapters to approach the dramatic practice of the time and in particular the use that is made of dramatic conventions directed towards audiences with certain known tastes and literary training.

The first full-length treatise relevant to comedy is Thomas Sébillet's *Art poétique françois* (Paris, 1548). Its author's interest in drama is shown by his translation into French of Euripides' *Iphigenia at Aulis*. It precedes Jodelle's *L'Eugène* by some four years, and by its date already has a particular interest, because of the somewhat embarrassed position in which the Pléiade as a group found themselves towards its author's ideas. Henri Chamard has shown how doctrines which the Pléiade would have liked to proclaim resoundingly as new and their own had already been expressed, awkwardly for them, by Sébillet.[1] As far as comedy is concerned, it turns out that the situation is complex. Sébillet's section on the theatre is primarily descriptive, accepting the medieval genres as they still actively survived in his own day. He is concerned with questions of terminology: Farces, Sotties, Comedies Latines, Comedies Grecques et Latines, Moralités, Tragedies, Mimes ou Priapées are the terms whose relationships and differences he discusses in two short paragraphs. Earlier, he has discussed moralities and farces, accepting them (despite his disapproval of the indecency of the farces) as part of the state of the theatre in his time, and indeed giving certain maxims and instructions for writing them. His commentary on them is, then, descriptive ('nous ne faisons aujourd'-huy ne pures Moralités, ne simples farces'), also didactic: 'A quoy exprimer [farces] tu ne doutes point que les vers de huit syllabes ne soient plus plaisans, et la ryme platte plus coulante.' It is strange, to say the least, that he does not discuss Terentian

---

[1] Chamard, *Histoire de la Pléiade*, i. 160–3 and 192–221.

comedy despite the several commentaries on, translations of, and discussions of Terence which had appeared before his time, nor Italian comedy despite the famous Court performance of the *Calandria* at Lyons in 1548 and despite Estienne's translation of *Gl'Ingannati* into French in 1543; he is concerned with the contemporary medieval survivals only. From the more forward-looking ideas found in the rest of the *Art poétique françois*, one might have expected, if not an awareness of Italian theatre, at least more interest in Terence.

Du Bellay, as one might expect, rejects Sébillet's tolerant attitude. For him, the classical theatre is alone worthy of imitation. But the short paragraph in which he expresses this view (quoted above) is a meagre statement indeed in a treatise supposed to prepare the way for a new national literature. Not only are the Italian comedies not mentioned in the *Deffence et illustration* (which in the field of lyric poetry strongly and of course successfully advocates among other things the imitation of Italian models), but even the name of Terence, the obvious model, does not appear.

The questions of imitating ancient comedies, and of abandoning or preserving medieval forms, which have so far been answered only with lack of perception on Sébillet's part and lack of attention on Du Bellay's, take a more interesting turn with the theory and practice of Étienne Jodelle. These are, as one would expect, totally opposed to Sébillet's. Jodelle does not accept the *status quo*; for him, moralities and farces are part of the medievalism which is to be rejected in favour of antiquity. They are impatiently dismissed:

> Sans que, brouillant avecques nos farceurs
> Le sainct ruisseau de nos plus sainctes Sœurs,
> On moralise un conseil, un escrit,
> Un temps, un tout, une chair, un esprit,
> Et tels fatras . . .[1]

But a discrepancy clearly exists between Jodelle's theory and his practice. In theory, farces cause an unwelcome muddying of 'Le

[1] *L'Eugène*, ed. Balmas, prologue, ll. 37–41.

sainct ruisseau de nos plus sainctes Sœurs'; in practice, *L'Eugène*
owes much to farce technique and conventions. So that whereas
in the field of serious drama Jodelle's claims to have broken with
the medieval genres in favour of a classical one (Senecan tragedy)
were fully justified, in the field of comedy his similar claims were
not substantiated.

The next treatise is Jacques Peletier du Mans's *Art poëtique*
(Lyons, 1555). Here again, as one would expect of a member of
the Pléiade writing a theoretical work, medieval genres are dismissed: 'Nous espérons que les Farces qu'on nous a si longtemps
jouées se convertiront au genre de la Comédie: les Jeux des
Martyrs, en la forme de Tragédie.'[1] What is perhaps more surprising is that creation of comedy in France is expressed as a
pious hope and not as something which has already been begun;
according to Peletier, the French comic theatre still consists of
worthless medieval genres: 'Nous n'avons point encore vu en
notre Français aucuns Écrits, qui eussent la vraie forme Comique:
mais bien force Moralités, et telles sortes de jeux. Auxquels le
nom de Comédie n'est pas dû.'[2] In fact, Jodelle's *L'Eugène* dates
from some three years before this treatise; did Peletier simply
not know of it? It may well be so, for he admits that he knows
the *Cléopâtre* only at second hand ('une [tragédie] par Étienne
Jodelle Parisien, de laquelle j'ai ouï seulement le bruit').[3] Or
could it be that the farcical elements in the play made it un-
worthy, for Peletier, of the name of comedy? In any case, with
the exclusion of medieval genres and the omission of Jodelle, it
is clear that what Peletier has to say about comedy will describe
classical practice, and not practice in France in his own time.

Peletier's discussion of comedy is the longest that had as yet
been written in France. He discusses in succession comedy as
a mirror of life which shows us certain types of people; plot-
structure; the merits and demerits of Terence, Plautus, and
others; the desirability of comedy in France; the differences be-

---

[1] *Art poëtique*, II. v; ed. A. Boulanger (Paris, 1930), p. 172. For practical
reasons, the spelling has been modernized.
[2] Ibid., II. vii, p. 189.   [3] Ibid., pp. 192–3.

tween comedy and tragedy (rank of characters, ending, elements of the plot, diction). His starting-point is Cicero's description of comedy as 'imitationem vitae, speculum consuetudinis, imaginem veritatis'; his analysis is from Donatus; and his model is Terence. It may be worth discussing these points.

The Ciceronian description was known only through Donatus's *De tragoedia et comoedia*. But it was widely known and continually quoted; we shall find it again, for example, in Larivey's dedication of his 1579 collection: 'La Comedie, vray miroüer de noz œuvres.' For these men, it is of course only a statement in particular terms of the Renaissance principle of *imitatio*: art is not something created anew, something 'original', but an imitation, either of nature, directly, or of nature through other (generally classical) writers. The idea is Platonic, and may have been familiar to Donatus, as well as to his Renaissance successors. Thus comedy, like all other forms of art, is a re-creation, a mirror to life. For Peletier, the things it reflects are:

l'avarice ou la prudence des vieillards: les amours et ardeurs des jeunes enfants de maison: les astuces et ruses de leurs Amies: la vilenie et déshonnêteté des Maquereaux: la façon des Pères tantôt sévères, tantôt faciles: l'assention et vileté des Parasites: la vanterie et braveté d'un Soldat retiré de la guerre: la diligence des Nourrices: l'indulgence des Mères[1]

that is, the characteristics of middle-class people and their servants and hangers-on, selected according to Terentian models, as opposed to the kings and nobles of tragedy.

Donatus, and not 'les Grecs', provides the terminology for Peletier's discussion of plot-structure: prologue, protasis, epitasis, catastrophe. They are the standard terms used in that familiar commentary, and I shall discuss them further in the section on plot-structure below.

About speech or diction, he says that 'La Comédie parle facilement et . . . populairement', and refers to Caecilius, called 'mauvais auteur de Latinité'.[2] His discussion of comedy and of the difference between tragedy and comedy is in terms of plot,

---

[1] Ibid., pp. 186–7.   [2] Ibid., pp. 190, 189.

character, and speech. Although the discussion is Donatan, these three divisions are *ultimately* derived from the first three of Aristotle's six divisions of a play: Plot, Character, Diction, Thought, Spectacle, and Melody (*Poetics*, VI). The three are readily though tacitly accepted here, as in most of the subsequent theoretical writings on comedy. Their innings is not yet over: the three next chapters in this book are based on the same division.

Peletier proclaims the excellence of Terence. Theorist after theorist will later do the same thing; and the popularity of that author has been clearly shown by Professor Lawton in his *Térence en France au XVIe siècle*. It should only be remembered here, first, that this popularity was not exclusively based on dramatic merit in Terence; and second, that Terence is not the only model for the actual comedies (as opposed to theories of comedy) that were written in France before Corneille. As for the reasons for the popularity, Professor Herrick has suggested that the main one may have been quite simply the existence of Donatus's excellent commentary.[1] Also, Aristophanes may have been better in many ways, but he was too immoral for schools; Plautus too may have been better, but his Latin is not as admirable as Terence's and therefore, again, not so suitable for teaching in schools. Scaliger says that he prefers Plautus as a comic writer, Terence as a stylist.[2] These pedant's reasons may not be the whole story, for Terence's plays still hold the stage today; but they are important.

Most of Peletier's ideas reappear, treated at greater length, in J. C. Scaliger's *Poetices libri septem*, first published at Lyons in 1561. The subjects treated are: the definition of comedy; peril in comedy; the differences between tragedy and comedy in terms of plot-elements, character, and diction; plot-structure, at some length; the merits and demerits of Terence. We have the Ciceronian statement, slightly changed ('Caeterum, vel

---

[1] Herrick, *Comic Theory*, p. 5.
[2] 'Nam equidem Plautum ut Comicum, Terentium ut loquutorem admirabor' (*Poetices libri septem*, 5th ed. (Heidelberg, 1617), VI. ii, p. 707).

ex authoribus, vel ipsius vitae nostrae exemplis sibi quisque quantum volet sumet'), the Donatan analysis of structure, with changes by Scaliger, while Terence is the model for the whole of the analysis, with occasional reference to Plautus. The discussion is a very full one, and based on firm knowledge of his models. His most individual contribution is the addition of a fourth division, catastasis, to Donatus's three which are protasis, epitasis, and catastrophe: this I shall re-examine in the next chapter.

From Scaliger onwards, the same ideas reappear. Jacques Grévin quotes his Cicero on comedy: 'Cicéron l'appelle imitation de vie, mirouer des coustumes, et image de vérité', before entering into a history of the genre from earliest times.[1] It is quite clear that there was a solid body of critical statements which was well known to all and could be assumed as basic knowledge in any audience. In a sense, then, this body of knowledge forms a convention, a framework upon which variations can be built. In 1577 Gérard de Vivre wrote: 'Amis Lecteurs, chascun sçait desja bien que c'est que la Comedie, pourtant ne m'amuseray à la vous deschiffrer en ce lieu ci, à cause, qu'il y en a tant d'autres qui en ont faict mention.'[2]

Pierre de Laudun d'Aigaliers's *Art poëtique françois* (Paris, 1579) contains similar ideas, grouped under subject-matter, types of character, plot-structure, and diction. He says, interestingly, that comedy and farce are not really very different from each other by their content: it is only that farces are shorter and do not have acts, and may not introduce gods or goddesses or characters from moralities (comedies of course may not introduce them either—but de Laudun has now turned to the most general definition of 'comedie').[3] Jean Vauquelin de la Fresnaye, in his full but diffuse *Art poétique* (Paris, 1605), uses similar ideas: he adds to them some evident knowledge of the Italian actors in France, as we saw, and of both Grévin's and Belleau's work. It is interesting to find this literary theorist insisting that rules

[1] *Brief discours pour l'intelligence de ce théatre*, in *Théâtre complet*, ed. Pinvert, p. 7.
[2] *Comédie de la Fidélité nuptiale* (Antwerp, 1577), preface 'Aux Lecteurs'.
[3] Lawton, *Handbook*, p. 92.

are not important compared with following the model of nature. Even a farce, if it does that, is better than a comedy:

> Quelquefois une farce au vray Patelinee,
> Où par art on ne voit nulle rime ordonnee . . .
> Pour ce qu'au vray les mœurs y sont representees,
> Les personnes rendra beaucoup plus contentees,
> Et les amusera plustost cent mile fois
> Que des vers sans plaisir rangez dessous les lois,
> N'ayant sauce ni suc, ni rendant exprimee
> La Nature en ses mœurs de chacun bien aimee.
> Nature est le Patron sur qui se doit former
> Ce qu'on veut pour long temps en ce monde animer.[1]

To these treatises must be added the scattered liminary material: Larivey's dedication to François d'Amboise, where he defends his use of prose on the grounds that ordinary people do not speak in verse; or François d'Amboise's prologue in which he claims that his play is, by exception, not based on an invented action but on a true story; or Godard's moralizing on his pairing a tragedy with a comedy to illustrate something about life.[2] D'Amboise even applies the theory to his own play, telling us precisely which part is the protasis, which the epitasis, and which the catastrophe.[3]

We have not yet considered the ethical view of comedy. Sir Philip Sidney, in his *Defence of Poesie*, expresses such a view:

The *Comedy* is an imitation of the common errors of our life, which he [the comic writer] representeth in the most ridiculous

[1] Ed. Pellissier, pp. 153–4.
[2] *Ancien Théâtre français*, v. 2–3; ibid., vii. 241–2; Lawton, *Handbook*, p. 90.
[3] *Les Néapolitaines* (Paris, 1584), ff. 4–13: 'Sommaire de ceste histoire Comique.' The 'Sommaire' is not reprinted in *Ancien théâtre français*, vii, nor in Fournier's *Le Théâtre français*. Throughout the period, the editions of Terence, with commentaries, continued to appear. In the year that *L'Eugène* was written, 1552, for instance, appeared the monster edition at Paris, containing, besides Terence's plays, writings and commentaries by eighteen critics. It would certainly be of value to examine in detail the commentaries that may have been known to, and used by, the French Renaissance writers of comedy. This I have not done in full detail, aiming rather at an examination of the plays themselves, within the context of Donatus's commentaries (certainly the best known of them) and of French Renaissance theorists.

and scornful sort that may be: so as it is impossible that any beholder can be content to be such a one. Now as in *Geometrie*, the oblique must be knowne as well as the right, and in *Arithmetick*, the odde as well as the even, so in the actions of our life, who seeth not the filthinesse of evill, wanteth a great foile to perceive the bewtie of vertue.[1]

In France, as throughout Europe in the Renaissance, this ethical point was discussed as well as the aesthetic one. De Vivre writes at some length about the moral function of his plays, which are intended to show the 'variables accidents de Fortune'. Larivey too develops the Ciceronian image of the mirror to show his plays' moral function:

Toutes fois, considerant que la Comedie, vrai miroüer de noz œuvres, n'est qu'une morale filosofie, donnant lumière à toute honneste discipline, et par consequent à toute vertu, ainsi que le tesmoigne Andronique, qui premier l'a faict veoir aux Latins, j'en ay voulu jetter ces premiers fondemens, où j'ay mis, comme en bloc, divers enseignemens fort profitables, blasmant les vitieuses actions et louant les honnestes, affin de faire cognoistre combien le mal est à eviter, et avec quel courage et affection la vertu doibt estre embrassée, pour meriter louange, acquerir honneur en ceste vie et esperer non seulement une gloire entre les hommes, mais une celeste recompense après le trespas.[2]

How far did this view turn out to be an excuse for immorality, and how far was it real?

Morality is not important in the Pléiade comedies. Though those plays were born in a university milieu, they were not intended to have pedagogic value. The difference is important, for at the Collège de Boncourt, comedies were written only by students, whereas when teachers such as Muret and Buchanan wrote drama, they wrote edifying tragedies. Jodelle's aims were to make his own reputation, and to achieve an aesthetically

[1] Sir Philip Sidney, *The Complete Works*, ed. A. Feuillerat, vol. iii (Cambridge, 1923), p. 23.
[2] *Épistre* to François d'Amboise in his 1579 collection, *Ancien Théâtre français*, v. 1–2.

successful example of the new classical genre in French, but not to teach anything. In fact, *L'Eugène* is immoral both in its action and in its outcome: Alix at the end of the play promises fidelity not to her husband but to her lover, the churchman Eugène. Grévin's *La Trésorière* is about attempted adultery, once successful and once unsuccessful, and about unscrupulous financial dealings: no word of condemnation of these things is uttered. Later, Turnèbe's *Les Contents* plays ironically with the gap between real morality and the bourgeois concern for appearances: the irony is aesthetically successful, but has no reforming intent. Most of the other plays end with a marriage after a successful, and often forcible, seduction. 'They say the comedies rather teach than reprehend amorous conceits', wrote Sidney—and so indeed it appears.[1] The anonymous *Les Ramoneurs* in the early 1620s, with its two prostitutes and two procuresses, is thoroughly in the same tradition. Corneille's *Mélite*, some five years later, is much more decent, and in it infidelity is specifically condemned; but nevertheless impropriety continues in the comedy of the seventeenth century, from Mairet's *Galanteries du duc d'Ossone* onwards.

In practice, then, Renaissance comedy seems to have aimed at delight rather than moral reform. Perhaps the Englishman Lyly had the most honest attitude when he wrote that his plays were made for pleasure, were 'mere pastime or plays of the imagination'. He writes, too, that they were made 'to move inward delight . . . to breed soft smiling, not loud laughing'.[2] Laughter is not an important aim of the French playwrights either, whether in theory or in practice: we laugh at the predicaments in *L'Eugène* or La Taille's *Les Corrivaux*, at the puns,

[1] Cf. Des Autelz's similar statement about comedy (though not about native French comedy, which did not exist when he wrote): 'Or que la Moralité . . . soit plus profitable que ny la Comedie, ny la Tragedie, il en appert, pource que ces deux tendent plus à la corruption, que à la bonne information des mœurs: l'une proposant tout exemple de lascivité, l'autre de cruauté et tyrannie' (*Replique . . . aux furieuses defenses de Louis Meigret* (Lyons, 1551): quoted from Margaret L. M. Young, *Guillaume Des Autelz* (Geneva, 1961), p. 46).

[2] Prologues to *The Woman in the Moon* (1597), *Endimion* (1579), and *Sapho and Phao* (1582?). Quoted from J. W. H. Atkins, *English Literary Criticism: The Renascence* (London, 1947), p. 240.

at the braggarts, but these are all elements incidental to the principal aim, which is delight.

To sum up: the comic theory follows a constant pattern throughout our period. Also, it appears in many different sources, pedagogic, theoretical, and theatrical; so that a majority of any cultivated audience must have been aware of it. Variations on it must have been recognized, such as, for plot, Belleau's unusual delaying of his action to a sudden quickening in Act V; for character, the variety of servants and masters; and for speech, the interplay of kinds of language proper to captains, valets, heroines, and the rest. The rest of this book is about those variations.

2. PLOT

Comedy as one part of a performance

The Greek ideal of an over-all dramatic performance on a single occasion could hardly fail to appeal to the Pléiade, anxious as they were to revive the practice of the ancients in every way possible. They revived Greek practice, for example, in the famous ceremony of the 'bouc' which they connected with the supposed etymology of 'tragoedia' as 'goat-song'. But despite their lip-service to Athens, it was Rome that gave them their principal models (Seneca for tragedy and Terence for comedy), and in Rome, as far as the surviving evidence shows, such over-all dramatic performances were not the general practice.[1] On these grounds alone, then, it is hardly surprising that the Pléiade and their successors only rarely achieved such performances.

Jodelle and Grévin are the first to have done so. The famous productions at the Hôtel de Reims and the Collège de Boncourt consisted of *Cléopâtre* and *La Rencontre* together, and their author was regularly praised for his introduction of both the tragic and the comic genres into France.[2] Grévin went a step further than

[1] The first known Latin dramatist, Livius Andronicus, produced a tragedy *and* a comedy at the Ludi Romani of 239 B.C., according to Cassiodorus (W. Beare, *The Roman Stage*, 3rd ed. (London, 1964), p. 27). But Beare and other sources otherwise have little to say about such combinations.

[2] For example, in the letter of Denys Lambin cited by M. Balmas, in his

Jodelle in including what he considered a third dramatic genre of the ancients:

> Ceste comédie [*La Trésorière*] fut . . . mise en jeu à Paris au collège de Beauvais, après la satyre qu'on appelle communéement les Veaux, le v. de février M.D.LVIII.[1]

> Ceste comédie [*Les Ébahis*] fut mise en jeu au collège de Beauvais, à Paris, le XVIIe jour de février M.D.LX. après la tragédie de J. César et les Jeux satyriques, appelez communéement les Veaux.[2]

He calls *Les Veaux* a 'satyre' and 'Jeux satyriques'. The word 'satyre' to describe plays and other works of literature has recently been studied in two articles by C. A. Mayer and J. W. Jolliffe.[3] Grévin's use of the term is complicated by uncertainty about *Les Veaux*. It could be the entirely unexceptional farce or *sotie*, *Les Veaux*, whose text survives to us in the La Vallière collection; but internal evidence shows that that was definitely performed by the Connards of Rouen for a royal entry, probably in 1550[4]—why should Grévin choose such a piece to precede his own plays? Or it could be a variant spelling of *Les Vaux*, i.e. *vaux-de-vire*; but it is likewise difficult to understand why Grévin should have chosen such a genre for his 'Jeux satyriques'. In favour of the first solution is the fact that Grévin certainly identified, in his own mind, the French farce with an ancient genre, the 'Mimus ou Bastelerie':

> Les anciens avoyent encores une autre sorte de Comédie qu'ils appeloyent Mimus ou Bastelerie, pour autant qu'elle estoit faicte

---

edition of *L'Eugène*, p. 10: 'Delectavit me in primis epistolae tuae locus de comoediis et tragoediis Gallicis. Libenter enim audio linguam nostram, quam ceterae nationes barbaram et inopem esse dicunt, antiquarum poetarum veneres et ornamenta capere, interpretari et exprimere posse.'

[1] Quoted from J. Grévin, *Théâtre complet*, ed. Pinvert, pp. 353–4.

[2] Ibid., p. 355.

[3] 'Satyre as a Dramatic Genre', *Bibliothèque d'Humanisme et Renaissance*, xiii (1951), 327–33. 'Satyre: satura: *ΣΑΤΥΡΟΣ*, a Study in Confusion', ibid. xviii (1956), 86–95.

[4] Cf. L. Petit de Julleville, *Répertoire du théâtre comique en France au moyen âge* (Paris, 1886), pp. 252–4. M. de Julleville mentions Grévin's *Les Veaux*, but without comment. Text in A. J. V. Leroux de Lincy and F. Michel, *Recueil de farces, moralités, et sermons joyeux* (Paris, 1837), vol. ii.

de parolles ordes et villaines, et de matières assez deshonnestes . . .
De là sont venues les farces des François, comme nous pouvons
facilement voir.[1]

But why in the same volume should he equate the farce once with
'Mimus ou Bastelerie' and once with 'satyre' and 'Jeux satyriques'?
At least it is clear, however, that the tragedy *César* and the
comedy *Les Ébahis* were united in a single performance with a
second comic form, which on another occasion was combined
with the comedy *La Trésorière*. Such an emulation of classical
practice may have been all the more important for Grévin, since
he claimed that his plays were the first French plays on classical
models (perhaps because he published his plays, which Jodelle
had not done).

Even with this early generation of enthusiasts for antiquity,
however, other influences may have come to bear. A 'farce', we
know, was originally something used to stuff ('farcir') a performance of another kind of play, and still in the sixteenth century was used in this way in the mystery plays.[2] Grévin himself
writes that he knows two other kinds of theatre where this sort
of programme-building took place: the perambulating theatre
of the Low Countries, and the stages of the University of Paris
itself:

Et semble qu'encore ceste coustume [of acting in the street]
soit demeurée en Flandres, et Pais bas, où les joueurs de Comédies
se font trainer par les carrefours sur des chariots et là jouent leurs
histoires, Comédies et farces.[3]

ils font à la manière des basteleurs un massacre sur un eschaffaut,
ou un discours de deux ou trois mois . . . et autres telles badineries,
que je laisse pour estre plus bref.[4]

This is an obvious kind of programme-building in all ages,
perfectly normal to Boswell, for example ('At night I was with

---

[1] *Théâtre complet*, ed. Pinvert, p. 8: from the *Brief discours pour l'intelligence de ce théâtre*.
[2] Cf. Grace Frank, *The Medieval French Drama* (Oxford, 1954), pp. 245–6.
[3] J. Grévin, *Théâtre complet*, ed. cit., p. 8.   [4] Ibid., p. 10.

Lady Crawford at *The Beggar's Opera* . . . The farce was *The Vintner Tricked*'; 'The play was *False Delicacy*, and the farce, *A Peep behind the Curtain*'),[1] though in the professional theatre of our own day it is perhaps less frequent. Furthermore, as Grévin says, the question of the personal specialization of the dramatist, according to his temperament, must be considered:

car comme ainsi soit que des hommes, les uns soyent graves et sévères, les autres gaillards et joyeux, il est advenu que les premiers se sont mis à escrire des Tragédies graves et sévères, les seconds se sont exercez en Comédies gaillardes et joyeuses.[2]

Belleau's *La Reconnue* and Jean-Antoine de Baïf's *Le Brave* and *L'Eunuque* are in comparison quite isolated. The title-page of *Le Brave*, as we saw, tells us that it was performed on 28 January 1567 (N.S. 1568), but there is no record of a play of any other genre accompanying it. The 'chantz recitez entre les actes de la comedie' are the only extraneous element; in view of Baïf's known interest in music,[3] 'recitez' may well mean 'sung'. It is only surprising that Baïf, who even founded the Académie de Musique et de Poésie precisely in order to re-create the practice of the ancients in uniting poetry and music, was not also interested (as far as we know) in uniting forms of drama.

After the Pléiade, no such ideals of the union of the forms of drama seem to have existed. Writers certainly wrote both tragedies and comedies—both the La Taille brothers, d'Amboise, Perrin—but not usually, apparently, for performance together. In the prologue to Godard's *Les Déguisés*, there is a reference to the performance together of Godard's tragedy *La Franciade* and his comedy:

> Car on a bien voulu, pour mieux vous contenter,
> Dessus cette eschaffaut ici representer
> Ces deux poèmes-là, qui vous feront entendre
> Que la fortune peut ses longues mains estendre
> Aussi bien sur les grands comme sur les petits[4]

---

[1] *Boswell in Search of a Wife*, ed. F. Brady and F. A. Pottle (London, 1957), pp. 141, 146.   [2] Grévin, *Théâtre complet*, ed. cit., p. 9.
[3] Cf. Frances Yates, *The French Academies of the Sixteenth Century* (London, 1947), chapter III.   [4] *Ancien Théâtre français*, vii. 340.

and although this is not reliable evidence of an actual performance, it does show that Godard is attempting some meaningful
relation between the two plays. He also claimed that he was the
first in France to write both kinds of play, but this is the claim
either of ignorance or of impudence. Finally, with the classical
generation—Mairet, Corneille, Rotrou—we have plays of both
kinds, in considerable numbers, but written rather as part of
their authors' varied dramatic production, not for performance
together on a single occasion.

Comic structure in theory and practice

Comic theory in the Renaissance, as we saw, was based above
all on the commentaries of Donatus on Terentian practice. Beare
quotes Michaut as saying that 'the remarks of . . . Donatus involve absurdities which would do honour to a professional
humorist',[1] but at least in the Renaissance the remarks were
taken perfectly seriously. On the question of the over-all structure of a comedy, the central point at issue is that according to
Horatian precept and the versions of Greek and Roman plays
which the Renaissance knew, plays should have, and did have,
five acts; yet the Aristotelian division involves only three parts
a beginning, a middle, and an end, or as Donatus puts it (apart
from the prologue which is a mere introduction), protasis, epitasis, and catastrophe. Donatus's statement is as follows:

Comoedia per quatuor partes dividitur: Prologum, Protasin,
Epitasin, Catastrophen. Prologus est velut praefatio quaedam
Fabulae, in quo solo licet praeter argumentum aliquid ad popu-
lum, vel ex Poetae vel ex ipsius fabulae vel ex actoris commodo,
loqui. Protasis primus est actus, initium drammatis. Epitasis
incrementum, processusque turbarum, ac totus, ut ita dixerim,
nodus erroris. Catastrophe conversio rerum est ad iucundos exitus,
patefacta cunctis cognitione gestorum.[2]

---

[1] Beare, *The Roman Stage* (1964), p. 217.
[2] *De Tragoedia et Comoedia*; quoted from Lawton, *Handbook*, p. 12.

Jacques Peletier du Mans takes over these ideas:

La Comédie a trois parties principales, sans le Prologue. La première, est la proposition du fait, au premier Acte: laquelle est appelée des Grecs Protasie. Et en elle s'explique une partie de tout l'Argument, pour tenir le Peuple en attente de connaître le surplus. La seconde, est l'avancement ou progrès, que les Grecs disent Épitasie. C'est quand les affaires tombent en difficulté, et entre peur et espérance. La tierce, est la Catastrophe, soudaine conversion des choses au mieux.[1]

And the same ideas were taken over by most Renaissance theorists. Beare put it as follows: 'The scholars of the Renaissance did their best to reconcile the two theories, five-act and three-part, but I agree with Leo . . . that the two are mutually exclusive.'[2] The difficulty was certainly present. But in fact, as we shall see below, the act-division of Renaissance comedies was relatively unimportant, the action sometimes appearing to be perfectly continuous from the end of one act to the beginning of the next. And theoretical discussion of the parts of a comedy and their disposition was much more often concerned with Donatus's three parts than with act-division. Scaliger, for instance, apparently analysing the structure of actual plays more closely than many other critics,[3] concluded that a fourth division was necessary, which he called catastasis:

Protasis est, in qua proponitur et narratur summa rei sine declaratione exitus . . . Epitasis, in qua turbae aut excitantur, aut intenduntur. Catastasis, est vigor, ac status Fabulae, in quae res miscetur in ea fortunae tempestate, in quam subducat est. Hanc partem multi non animadvertere, necessaria tamen est. Catastrophe, conversio negotii exagitati in tranquillitatem non expectatam. His partibus additus, uti dicebamus, Prologus . . .[4]

I propose to examine the plays themselves, which after all are the important texts, to see what kind of structure was used in

---

[1] *Art poëtique*, ed. cit., II. vii, p. 187.
[2] Beare, *The Roman Stage* (1964), p. 217.
[3] 'Scio a nonnullis tres tantum enumeratas, nos autem ad subtiliora semper animum appulimus' (*Poetices libri septem* (Heidelberg, 1617), I. ix. 32).
[4] Ibid., p. 33.

practice. In fact, all the surviving Renaissance comedies could be analysed according to Donatus's and Scaliger's principles, and it will be convenient to follow to some extent their divisions in discussing first the prologue (and epilogue) and then the other parts of the plays—which may or may not correspond to their divisions. The emphasis will be, however, rather on discovering the function of such parts in the total dramatic effect than on establishing them on any theoretical grounds.

Prologues and epilogues

These two sections of the play lie outside the formal act- and scene-division. Both of them are normally found: *La Reconnue* and *Les Ramoneurs* are the only ones of the regular comedies before *Mélite* without a prologue, and *Les Déguisés* the only one without an epilogue. *Mélite* includes an epilogue.

The prologue has a long ancestry, both classical and medieval. Every play of Terence has a prologue, the *Hecyra* even two, in which the author addresses his audience more or less in polemical fashion. Jean Bodel's *Jeu de saint Nicolas* has a prologue calling, quite traditionally by that time, for silence.[1] Giordano Bruno's *Il Candelaio* has an Antiprologo, a Proprologo, and a conventional Prologo; Troterel in his *Les Corrivaux*, as we saw, plays with the tradition too, by having his prologue interrupted by someone behind the curtain. Throughout this long period, the prologue's main function in terms of the theatre was to ease the transition from the audience's world to the players' world. This function is never essential, but it can be used for comic or other effect. It is only one of a number of devices used to establish a relationship with the audience (others are the soliloquy, the aside, the chorus in tragedy), but by virtue of its position its uses are different from any of these.

First, although the prologue is a less integral part of the play than, say, a chorus, it has the advantage of addressing the audience directly. In every one of the prologues we are considering, the audience is addressed as 'vous'. The speaker usually

[1] Ed. F. J. Warne (Oxford, 1951), p. 4.

specifically states that he is not the author. But neither does he say he is an 'actor', in cold reality; he usually leads the audience from the knowledge of where they are, over the boundary of illusion, until they and he are within the action of the play. For example:

> Ce nonobstant, j'ai sceu de luy [le poète],
> Comme une chose bien secrette,
> Que ceste Comédie est faicte
> Sur le discours de quelque amour,
> Qui s'est conduit au carefour
> De Sainct Sevrin; mais je vous prie,
> D'autant que vous avez envie
> D'estre secrets, de tenir coy,
> Car je voy cy derrière moy
> Le sire Josse.
>
> (*Les Ébahis*, prologue, ll. 62–71)[1]

Although the speaker is specifically never the author, it is never said who he is. One may perhaps compare the epilogues, which perform the corresponding function of leading the audience back over the boundary of illusion; they are all spoken by one of the dramatis personae, who turns to the audience and addresses them directly. In production, any of the nine prologues could similarly be spoken by one of the dramatis personae, and may well have been so intended.[2]

But if this were all, the prologue would be superfluous; it would be naïve to suppose that an audience is really in need of help over the boundary of illusion. In these plays, it has another function: to prepare the audience for the play by discussing comic practice and theory and how the particular play fits into these.[3]

---

[1] Grévin, *Théâtre complet*, ed. Pinvert, p. 117.

[2] Orazio Vecchi's *L'Amfiparnaso* (Venice, 1597) is perhaps not strictly comparable. But the prologue of this musical setting of a *commedia erudita* is definitely put into the mouth of one of the characters, Lelio (cf. Plate XI). So is the prologue (the third, normal one) to *Il Candelaio*, which is spoken by a beadle. And it is fairly clear (though not conclusively so) that the speaker of the prologue in Troterel's *Les Corrivaux*, and Le Caché, are the two characters who open the play proper: Bragard and Gaullard.

[3] The prologue to the *Jeu de saint Nicolas* does this too; cf. F. J. Warne's edition (Oxford, 1951), pp. xvii–xviii.

PLATE XI

PROLOGO. LELIO.

Benche fiat'ufi ò Spettatori Illuftri, Solo di rimirar Tragici afpetti, O Comici apparati In varie gúife ornati, Voi però non fdegnate Quefta Comedia noftra, Se non di ricca, e vaga Scena adorna, Almen di dopia nouità compofta. E la città doue fi rappresenta	Queft'opra, è'l gran Theatro Del mondo, perch'ognun defia d'udirla: Ma voi fappiat'in tanto, Che quefto di cui parlo Spettacolo, fi mira con la mente, Dou'entra per l'orecchie, e non per gl'occhi Però filentio fate, E'n vece di vedere hora afcoltase.

A print from Orazio Vecchi's *L'Amfiparnaso*, Venice, 1597, in which the prologue is being spoken by a member of the cast

The prologue to *L'Eugène*, for example, claims that it is the first French comedy. The prologue to *Les Néapolitaines* explains that it is an exception to the usual rule that comedies are invented to please the 'simple populace', and why. Godard's *Les Déguisés* was printed together with his tragedy, *La Franciade*, and the prologue is at pains to point out that this juxtaposition is intended to show how fortune strikes down the great but merely plays with the humble and leaves them happy in the end. These ideas can be pedantic, as those of *Les Déguisés* certainly are, but they appear to show at least that the audiences of these plays, as well as the authors, were interested in the theory behind them. For us, the examination of the prologues, besides other purely theoretical writings about comedy, has some points of interest to offer. First, in the later plays, the references to variety as a merit:

Or, j'espère qu'elle [cette comédie] vous plaira, pour estre toute plaine de *variables* humeurs, affections, plaisirs et passions[1]

. . . la gentillesse de l'invention, le bel ordre, la *diversité* du subject . . .[2]

Second, the emphasis on verbal style: the above extract from *Les Néapolitaines* continues: 'Les sages discours, les bons enseignements, sentences, exemples et proverbes, les faceties et sornettes dont elle est semée de toutes parts', while in the prologue to *L'Eugène* the list of qualities desirable in a comedy reads: 'Quels vers, quels ris, quel honneur, et quels *mots*.'[3]

The prologues usually say that their aim is to entertain the audience. Only two, those to *Les Déguisés* and to Perrin's *Les Écoliers*, overtly state a moral aim; the other seven have no reference at all to any didactic purpose (cf. *Les Néapolitaines*, 'plaisante et facetieuse'; *Les Esprits*, p. 201: 'J'espère qu'elle vous plaira'). The supposed aim of the prologues, as we have seen,

---

[1] *Les Esprits* (*Ancien Théâtre français*, v. 201). My italics (also in the quotation below). The fact that this prologue is translated from the Italian need not affect its validity as an expression of Larivey's ideas.

[2] *Les Néapolitaines* (*Ancien Théâtre français*, vii. 239).

[3] *L'Eugène*, ed. Balmas, p. 32.

is to ease the audience gently into the play, and it appears to have been concluded that edification was not a recommendation; for of these seven prologues, four belong to plays whose authors, we know, expressed elsewhere their didactic intentions:

> Or je reviens à la Comédie, qui est un discours fabuleux . . . par lequel on peult apprendre ce qui est utile pour la vie, et au contraire cognoistre ce que l'on doit fuir, enseignez par le bonheur ou malheur d'autruy.[1]

> Toutesfois, considerant que la Comedie, vray miroüer de noz œuvres, n'est qu'une morale filosofie, donnant lumière à toute honneste discipline, et par consequent à toute vertu . . .[2]

> aux autres qui la liront elle apportera aussi un grand *proffict* et contentement.[3]

None of the prologues includes the full 'Argument',[4] but four of them (to *L'Eugène*, *Les Ébahis*, *Les Esprits*, and *Les Contents*) state specifically that they are *not* going to give details of the plot because the play in itself will do that well enough. One play, *La Reconnue*, which has no prologue, has a printed 'Argument'.

For us, the knowledge of theory of comedy that we can gain from these prologues has its interest. But their chief function, as we saw, lay in establishing a relationship with the audience; and it is here that their main interest, and such dramatic qualities as they have, are to be found. We shall return to them, and to the epilogues, in this context.

The epilogues perform the reverse function to the prologues, in bringing the audience back to their own world. They are always spoken by one of the actors, who turns to the audience and speaks to them. They are generally shorter than the prologues (*L'Eugène* has only one line). As the prologues contained

---

[1] J. Grévin, *Brief discours* (*Théâtre complet*, ed. Pinvert, p. 7).

[2] Pierre de Larivey, *Épistre* to François d'Amboise in the 1579 collection, *Ancien Théâtre français*, v. 1–2.

[3] François d'Amboise, *Les Néapolitaines*, preface, *Ancien Théâtre français*, vii. 239.

[4] The prologue to La Taille's *Les Corrivaux* gives a good deal of the plot, but still leaves the outcome for the play itself to show.

the *Silete*, so the epilogues contain the *Plaudite*. Thus Rodomont in Turnèbe's *Les Contents*:

Mesdames, qui avez pris patience de nous ouïr ceste après-disnée, s'il vous plaist revenir en ce lieu le jour des noces de Basile et Geneviefve, vous aurez le plaisir de voir courir la bague. . . . Cependant, vous ferez bien de vous retirer chez vous. Car voicy l'heure que l'on commence à souper aux bonnes maisons. Et si nostre comedie vous a esté agreable, je vous prie de nous le faire cognoistre à quelque signe d'allegresse. (v. vi)[1]

Exposition

The first part of a comedy in contemporary theory was the protasis. According to Donatus, the protasis is the first act of the play: 'Protasis primus est actus, initium drammatis'; and again: 'Protasis est primus actus fabulae, quo pars argumenti explicatur, pars reticetur ad populi expectationem tenendam.'[2] To some extent, then, it is what we call the exposition. But clearly, the exposition and the first act are not necessarily synonymous: for instance, in Larivey's *Les Esprits* the exposition is still going on in Act II, by which time Urbain has obtained his Feliciane: the action has begun. Scaliger himself pointed out that the protasis (evidently for him meaning 'exposition') of the *Miles gloriosus* comes in Act II (though Baïf, in his adaptation *Le Brave*, moved it slightly backwards into Act I, scene ii). By 'actus', Donatus seems to have meant not necessarily an act in our sense (one of five formal sections of the play) but simply a part of the play; and the sixteenth century understood protasis in that sense, as the beginning, including the exposition, but if necessary also including some action. Professor Herrick quotes Dryden's Eugenius: 'First the *protasis*, or entrance, which gives light only to the characters of the persons, and proceeds very little into any part of the action.'[3] The important point seems to be how the exposition as such is handled, especially as act-division in

[1] Ed. Spector, pp. 141–2.
[2] *De Tragoedia et Comoedia*; Lawton, *Handbook*, pp. 12, 14, 16.
[3] *Essay of Dramatic Poetry*; Herrick, *Comic Theory in the Sixteenth Century*, p. 117.

our sense, and in this period, is not so very significant in practice.

It is handled with a varying degree of conventionality. At its stiffest, it consists of one character telling another details that that character cannot but know already, the technique satirized by Sheridan in *The Critic*: 'Mr. Puff, as he *knows* all this, why does Sir Walter go on telling him?'[1] This is found in only one play: surprisingly, Larivey's *Les Esprits*, which is otherwise not a stiff or excessively conventional play. Hilaire tells his wife Elizabet details that she certainly knows already, and she is so obviously a protatic character, a puppet figure provided for the purpose of the exposition, that she does not even appear at all in the rest of the play.

One degree less stiff—at least it is more honest—is the exposition by soliloquy. This is used in three plays: *Les Ébahis*, *La Reconnue*, and *Les Déguisés*. The first two share a peculiar feature: that the young lover (L'Advocat and L'Amoureux respectively) is not even mentioned in the opening soliloquy, and hardly at all until his arrival, in each case at II. i. Apart from this, in *Les Ébahis* one soliloquy suffices (I. i); in *La Reconnue* Janne's first soliloquy and Maistre Jehan's asides (I. i) tell us all except a minor detail or two; in *Les Déguisés* two successive soliloquies are necessary.

The other plays all open with dialogue that is to some extent motivated. *Les Contents* is the best motivated of all: at the opening of this play Louise has roused her daughter Geneviève at an unnaturally early hour, so that Geneviève has perfectly good reasons for wanting to know why—thus justifying the exposition. This seems to be another example of the deliberate disguise of the conventions in this play; similar 'realistic' preoccupations also blur the conventions of *décor simultané* and of time-sequence in it. *Les Néapolitaines* and *Les Écoliers* use dialogue in which some action is already taking place: Augustine is trying to get Beta on to his side, and Marin is trying to get some

[1] *The Critic*, II. ii, *Sheridan's Plays and Poems*, ed. R. C. Rhodes, vol. ii (Oxford, 1928), p. 219.

truth out of Finet. In the first case, some slightly stiff expository
details by Beta are necessary, and in the second, a supplementary
monologue by Finet. *L'Eugène* is perhaps the most pleasing of
all: Jodelle quite simply entertains us with the pleasures of the
churchman's life, and of Eugène's in particular, before ever
getting down to the exposition. When he does, he introduces it
frankly with:

> d'un cas nouveau . . .
> M'est à ceste heure souvenu
> Pour lequel appellé t'avois.
> (*L'Eugène*, I. i)[1]

and the rest of the exposition is made in the same dialogue and
in a supplementary monologue by Messire Jean (Florimond's
late arrival in II. i is perhaps surprising; compare the late
appearance of the lovers in *Les Ébahis* and *La Reconnue*). The
technical ease of the exposition in this play is paralleled only
in *Les Contents*.

The division between exposition and action varies in sharp-
ness. Sometimes an attempt is made to avoid an excessively
conventional beginning by interlinking the two: thus in
L'Eugène, I. iii, Messire Jean appears at Guillaume's house,
obeying orders received in I. i, before Florimond appears to
complete the exposition in II. i. The plot of *Les Esprits* is so complex that the exposition is not complete until II. ii, well after
Urbain has bargained with Ruffin and got his Feliciane (even
the denouement of this play takes more than the usual fifth act
and overflows backwards into the fourth). An opening *in medias
res*, with explanations following, is never used in these plays.[2]

As well as being integrated with the action, it is necessary
that the exposition should be integrated with character. It is
so in *L'Eugène*, where Eugène's sensuality is dwelt on in the
first part of the play before ever the exposition begins. It is so

---

[1] Ed. Balmas, p. 37.

[2] In three plays, the exposition is strictly speaking not complete until the
end, when facts unknown to characters and audience alike, and necessary to the
plot, are revealed: *La Reconnue*, *Les Corrivaux*, and *Les Néapolitaines*.

also in *Les Néapolitaines*, where the dialogue of Augustin and Beta shows both their characters clearly (Augustin the devoted and determined lover, Beta the ready-witted and bribable servant). In fact, all these plays, even *Les Écoliers*, do considerably more than merely expound at the beginning: the individual character of the speakers is always made quite clear (even Elizabet in *Les Esprits*, who only appears in I. i), and the exposition of the plays generally shows, very competently, the atmosphere that is going to dominate (the hedonism of *Les Néapolitaines*, the sour misanthropy of *La Reconnue*). In plays as dependent on convention as these, one might perhaps have expected the expositions to be stiffer than they are.

Catastrophe or denouement

It is convenient to take the last part of the structure next. Here practice bears out theory. The catastrophe in Donatus's words is the 'conversio rerum . . . ad iucundos exitus, patefacta cunctis, cognitione gestorum', and again, the 'explicatio fabulae' —that is, a change in the action leading to a happy ending (the opposite of Aristotle's μετάβασις in tragedy) and the revelation to everyone of the true state of things (e.g. that Pamphila is after all free-born, in the *Eunuchus*). Scaliger adds that the happy ending must be 'non expectatam'. All this is very similar to the extremely conventional ending of the modern detective story: a happy ending and the unexpected revelation of the true state of things.

Like the expositions, the catastrophes or denouements are treated in practice with a varying degree of conventionality. *Dei ex machina* are not uncommon. Seven of the plays employ new characters who arrive more or less out of the blue to reveal new facts, or to influence the situation in a new way, so that the 'happy ending' may be achieved. *Les Néapolitaines* introduces the new character of Marc-Aurel, a jeweller from Naples who has not been mentioned in the four preceding acts. He reveals new facts which resolve the situation. Nor is he the only one: the sub-plot (Dieghos and Gaster) is given another completely new character, the messenger Louppes, who reveals facts that persuade Dieghos to leave and thus remove his presence from the 'happy ending'. The arrival of these two new characters is certainly artificial; but the mystery surrounding Angélique's past and the constant references to it are bound to warn the reader that something of the kind will happen.

In *La Reconnue, Les Corrivaux, Les Esprits, Les Déguisés,* and *Les Ramoneurs,* a parent (or parents) of one of the lovers involved arrives at the end of the play and makes the 'happy ending' possible. Since the 'happy ending' always involves marriage, and since in terms of the plays marriage always involves settlements and family details, the very absence of the parent concerned in a way prepares his arrival. In addition, there is generally other preparation. In *Les Déguisés* the plot at the end is already turning upon Olivier's father, and Passetrouvant is having to impersonate him, so that his arrival is prepared and effective. In *Les Corrivaux,* the prologue has already told us of the father's existence. In *Les Esprits,* the Urbain–Feliciane relationship has been prepared from as early as Act I, and moreover Gérard's arrival is prepared two scenes before he actually arrives (IV. v). In *La Reconnue,* some slight indication of Antoinette's father's arrival in Paris is given early in the play (I. v) when Maistre Jehan says:

> il y a trois nuits
> Que, sans me reposer, je suis
> A faire l'extrait d'un procès,
> En droit et matière d'excès,
> D'un gentilhomme de Poitou.[1]

But the main preparation lies in the obvious *lack* of parents of this girl whose marriage involves so many people. There is a second new character as well, in the denouement of this play: the *capitaine,* who has been so much discussed in the preceding acts.

Much more preparation is made for the arrival of Agnès at the end of *Les Ébahis,* whose function is to get Josse out of the

[1] *Ancien Théâtre français,* iv. 358.

way of the 'happy ending'. We gradually learn a lot about her past, and about her affair with the Gentilhomme, before she appears in Act v.

In all these cases, however, preparation must not be confused with motivation. In *Les Déguisés*, it fits the pattern of the plot very well that Pierre Galand should arrive when he does, but that is not to say that his arrival is motivated in terms of the play. He has simply arrived in Toulouse, looking for his son, by chance at this particular time. The same applies to all the other examples: Agnès's arrival may be prepared, but it is mere coincidence that she, the Gentilhomme's whore, should turn out to be the same person as Josse's wife. Jodelle, in *L'Eugène*, achieves a better-motivated plot by making the arrival of a new character, Florimond, the source of his plot and not a mere accidental impingement upon it. But in the later plays, it is clear that the arrival of new characters has become a convention that does not need to be motivated.

The acceptance of this convention is shown by comparing Grévin's *Les Ébahis* with his *La Trésorière*. *La Trésorière* is the earlier play, and it is completely motivated by character, not by *dei ex machina*. Loys's anger at his rival's success precipitates the climax, all the reactions to which are in character. Despite this early production, however, in the later play Grévin introduces new characters at the end, showing that the internally motivated denouement was not, for him, something that need necessarily be aimed at.

The other plays have a denouement that does not depend on new characters or facts: *Les Contents* and *Les Écoliers*. The technique of *Les Écoliers* is primitive when compared with *Les Contents*, but nevertheless it is true of both that the denouement derives from character and not from chance. In *Les Écoliers*, the inquisitive and meddlesome neighbour Friquet is credibly bullied into persuading his neighbour Maclou to allow the marriage of Sobrin and Grassette; and the fathers Maclou and Marin, seeing that it is after all a perfectly suitable marriage, credibly decide to allow it after scolding their children. In *Les*

Contents similarly, after a good deal of quarrelling, the parents of Basile and Geneviève, seeing that it is also a perfectly suitable marriage, decide to allow it. This is not, of course, to condemn the convention of *dei ex machina* merely on grounds of artificiality; nevertheless, it is of interest that the convention is not universal and that *La Trésorière*, *Les Contents*, and *Les Écoliers*, at least, successfully avoid it. The denouement of *Mélite*, too, is internally motivated.

Loose ends are seldom left over. The captains often have a marriage provided for them as a consolation prize (*La Reconnue*, *Les Néapolitaines*, *Les Déguisés*). Belleau in *La Reconnue* is so concerned with rounding off his play that practically all the characters, and what they will receive, are passed in review in order: L'Amoureux and Antoinette, Potiron, Monsieur, Madame, Maistre Jehan, the captain, Janne. The plot of *Les Esprits* is complex enough with its three pairs of eventually united lovers not to involve additional loose ends in any case. *Les Écoliers* and *Les Corrivaux* also have no loose ends. In *L'Eugène*, Matthieu the creditor is introduced so late into the play that he is hardly an integral part of the plot; nevertheless, he is not merely a loose end to be dealt with, for the way Eugène satisfies him is an effective demonstration of their respective characters. *Les Ébahis* alone does not end so tidily. At the end of the play, L'Advocat's disguise is still unknown to Gérard, the guilt being attributed to Panthaleone. The revelation of the facts, and the marriage of L'Advocat and Madalène, are merely promised to the audience in the epilogue and not actually arranged within the play. But this is a solitary and not particularly significant example. There are no cases in these comedies where the play significantly ends with a question mark, like *Le Misanthrope* or *Twelfth Night*.

Epitasis and catastasis

The part of the play between exposition and denouement is less clear-cut than either of them. One significant question is whether or not a climax occurs at any point to divide it up.

La Reconnue, *Les Esprits*, and *Les Déguisés* have no such obvious climax. In the first, the unusual lack of a climax serves to build up the suspense: Monsieur's machinations come nearer and nearer success until, only in the last act, he is finally foiled and the atmosphere cleared. In the second, the plot's complexity is sufficient entertainment in itself to sustain a single level of action throughout, and the three pairs of lovers simply continue to manage or mismanage their affairs until the denouement. The success of *Les Déguisés* depends on the gradual complication of the intrigue through four acts, one disguise and deception involving another, until the disguises are broken down, in strictly reverse order, in the last act.

In six other plays, the course of the action is changed about the half-way point. The change is precipitated by a seduction in *Les Contents*, Act III, and in *Les Ébahis* and *Les Néapolitaines* between Acts III and IV; by Richard's discovery of his master's rival's success in Act III of *La Trésorière*; by Florimond's violent removal of his furniture in Act III of *L'Eugène*; and by an attempted rape in Act III of *Les Corrivaux*. In each case a reaction is provoked. Act IV of *Les Contents* is occupied by Basile's attempted prevention of that reaction; Act IV and part of Act V of *Les Ébahis* by Gérard's chaffing of Josse about the seduction, and Josse's violent reaction; Act IV of *Les Néapolitaines* by discussion until the *dei ex machina* of Act V provide the solution; Acts IV and V of *Les Corrivaux* by gradual reaction and solution; so that in each case the climax changes the course of the action. In *L'Eugène* there is a difference, in that the removal of the furniture is not an unexpected disaster, but in a similar way reactions and eventually a solution are provoked.

Les Écoliers represents a variation on this technique. The climax occurs, not half-way through the plot, but in Act IV. After three acts of discussion and plotting, suddenly in Act IV the pace quickens, a plot is laid, carried out, and discovered all in the course of the act. It is quick, and effective; but the execution of this play as a whole is not good enough to carry it off.

The theoretical discussion of this part of a comedy, in the

sixteenth century, concerns the meaning of Donatus's third part, epitasis, and of Scaliger's added fourth part, catastasis. Donatus calls the epitasis 'incrementum, processusque turbarum, ac totus, ut ita dixerim, nodus erroris',[1] but as the term by elimination has to cover everything between the protasis and the catastrophe, this seems a little vague. It seems to me that Scaliger's two terms, between them, are much more closely related to actual dramatic practice both in Terence and in our comedies: 'Epitasis, in qua turbae aut excitantur, aut intenduntur. Catastasis, est vigor, ac status Fabulae, in qua res miscetur in ea fortunae tempestate, in quam subducta est.' For example, in *Les Néapolitaines* the epitasis would cover everything that happens up to Camille's seduction of Virginie; that seduction and its immediate sequels would be the catastasis; and the solution of the problem, the catastrophe. It will be seen that the 'climax' I have been discussing, and which I see as an important part of the dramatic structure, is in fact very close to Scaliger's catastasis.

Perils and obstacles

One of the main principles of plot-structure in these plays is the gradual removal of obstacles or perils in the way of the principal characters' ends. Those ends may be either moral or immoral. Eugène's aim is to enjoy Alix at his leisure; Loys's and the Protenotaire's aim in *La Trésorière* is to enjoy Constante; Basile's aim in *Les Contents* is to marry Geneviève (even though his methods may be the reverse of moral); Olivier's aim in *Les Déguisés* is to marry Louise. The morality is irrelevant. In terms of plot-structure, the action is built on the removal of the perils or obstacles: Florimond's anger in *L'Eugène*, Louise's obstinacy in *Les Contents*, and so on. The most frequent pattern is a double one: the young lover first has to win the girl, and then has to obtain the approval of society for marrying her (*Les Ébahis*, *La Reconnue*, *Les Corrivaux*, *Les Esprits*, *Les Contents*, *Les Néapolitaines*,

[1] Lawton, *Handbook*, p. 12.

Les Déguisés, Les Écoliers, Les Ramoneurs). In terms of the structures we have been discussing, the overcoming of the first obstacle is Scaliger's catastasis; the overcoming of the second, the catastrophe. Although this applies to most of our comedies, some like *L'Eugène* have only one obstacle and so are outside this definition.

Mélite is a variant on this pattern. The obstacles to Tirsis and Mélite are Eraste's jealousy and machinations: we see how they begin, succeed, are discovered and overcome, and almost the whole action is built on them. The second obstacle, obtaining social approbation, is still there in the shape of Mélite's mother's approval, but it is so played down that we are hardly aware of it. The perils and obstacles are still the basis of the plot, but they come from the characters themselves, not from society outside; from other members of the same generation, not from an older generation.

The multiplication and removal of obstacles, then, form a principal feature of the plot-structure of these comedies. We have the testimony of De Rayssiguier on the audience's reaction to it:

> La plus grande part de ceux qui portent le teston à l'Hostel de Bourgongne veulent que l'on contente leurs yeux par la diversité et changement de la face du Theatre et que le grand nombre des accidens et adventures extraordinaires leur ostent la cognoissance du sujet.[1]

Though De Rayssiguier was doubtless referring mainly to tragicomedy, behind his exaggeration there is some truth for comedy too. The truth is that there *are* often a number of 'accidens et adventures extraordinaires'; the exaggeration, that an audience, if it is attentive, is never forced to lose the thread of the plot. Characters on stage may be deceived, but we, the audience, are always aware of the deception. Thus, in *Les Ébahis*, IV. ii, Gérard believes that L'Advocat is Josse, but it has been made quite clear to us that in fact L'Advocat is disguised. In the same

---

[1] De Rayssiguier, preface to *L'Aminte du Tasse, Tragi-comedie pastoralle accommodée au Theatre François* (Paris, 1632), quoted from H. C. Lancaster, 'De Rayssiguier', *Revue d'histoire littéraire de la France*, xxix (1922), 263.

play, the woman discussed by Claude and Le Gentilhomme in Act III is in fact Agnès, Josse's wife; as soon as it becomes necessary for us to know this, we are told.

Disguises and plot-structure

One might have supposed, from the reputation that Renaissance comedies have as plays of complex intrigue, that disguise and deceit played a fundamental part in them. But in fact, only one of them uses disguise and deceit as the main structural principle of the plot; and it is indeed called *Les Déguisés*. In this play Olivier, the hero, disguises himself as a valet, but then, needing to introduce himself in person, is obliged to use his valet disguised as himself; when his valet promises to produce his father, and this is not possible, a further impersonation becomes necessary. At one point in the play, we are confronted with a true Olivier and Pierre Galand, and a false pair of the same. The plot is built up upon the multiplication of disguises and upon their removal in reverse order.[1]

In all the others, disguise and deceit are only a means of complicating the plot. The *climax* of the play is sometimes the discovery of the disguise or deceit; but this is not to say that the theme is the fundamental basis of the plot. In *Les Écoliers*, three and a half acts pass before the disguise is adopted to enable the hero to attain his ends, and then it is put on and discovered in the course of a single act. In *Les Néapolitaines*, the only deceit is Camille's method of getting Cornélie out of the way, a very minor part of the plot. In *L'Eugène*, only Guillaume is deceived; but the action does not turn upon Guillaume, but upon Florimond, who is perfectly aware of the situation. In *Les Ébahis* and *Les Contents* the climax results from the disguise, but nevertheless it is only one element in the plot among others. *La Reconnue*, admittedly, uses the theme rather more: Monsieur's attempt to

[1] The sequence of disguises is taken from the play's model, Ariosto's *I Suppositi*. Nevertheless, some important ways in which it is used and developed are Godard's: Maudolé's bragging in his master's clothes, and his confrontation with Prouventard.

deceive his wife runs through all the play, while one pretence gets out of hand: the captain is announced to be dead, L'Amoureux plans to pretend he is alive, and in fact he turns out to have been alive all the time. Although the theme occurs in all these plays to some extent, it is never fundamental to the plot in the way in which it is in, say, Du Ryer's *Les Vendanges de Suresnes* or Molière's *Tartuffe*. Nor do we yet have a pretence leading to a reality (as in Rotrou's *Saint-Genest*, where the actor playing a Christian *becomes* a Christian). Perhaps its most significant use is in the irony of *Les Contents*, where real and pretended piety are continually played off against each other.

Nevertheless, the theme has its importance in the relationship which it makes possible with the audience. As we have seen, the audience is not deceived in these plays, but always knows perfectly well who is disguised as whom, and precisely what deceits are being attempted. The interest lies in watching the characters' reactions, and how the deceits are made and exposed.

Linked with this, and with the same kind of function, is the discrepancy between what is and what is not. The braggart soldiers claim to be brave but are regularly shown to be, in fact, the opposite. Josse in *Les Ébahis* claims to be strong and capable of making love; in fact he has a cold and has to wear a fur coat. The audience knew the facts very well in each case, not only from the plays themselves, but from the tradition which told them that a braggart soldier or an old man in love were not to be taken seriously.

Act- and scene-division

In twentieth-century plays, it is normal for an author to specify the divisions and subdivisions which he requires and which a producer will generally respect. He may use the division as a means of variety and contrast; after a scene of gaiety and movement the lights may be dimmed, or the scenery changed, for a more subdued scene. In the plays we are considering, the divisions are much less clear. Since the stage set was bound to to remain the same, or almost the same, throughout the performance, changes of scene could not be used in this way for contrast. Speech and the entry and exit of characters were the main means of contrast available; and the formal scene-division in these plays is in fact based entirely on the entrance and exit of characters. A character may leave the stage entirely; or he may simply draw aside to another part of it, whence he may return a scene or two later (thus, perhaps, *Les Déguisés*, IV. ii–v). Often it is not clear which is intended, nor does it need to be made clear, the question being left in the hands of the actors. The result is that the indicated scene-division is less formalized than in twentieth-century (or even seventeenth-century) plays, and that there are considerable inconsistencies from play to play, and even within a single play.[1]

The theoretical basis is simple. Charles Estienne is typical:

Quand deux personnaiges ou trois avoient devisé et tenu propos ensemble, et que l'ung se retiroit, ou qu'il en venoit ung aultre en nouveau propos, ilz appelloient cela une scene, c'est adire commutation ou variation de propos.[2]

Donatus also linked acts and scenes with entrances and exits, but took the principle to absurdity: 'No character who has left the stage five times can exit any more'—which Scaliger saw was, to start with, literally untrue.[3]

The idea that a play should have acts and scenes at all was derived by Renaissance authors from Donatus. Donatus states that act-division of Terence's plays went back to the time of Varro; so that by 1550 the idea had a tradition of some 1600 years behind it. But the actual comedies of Terence and Plautus date from before that time, and as Professor Duckworth says: 'We may conclude that neither Plautus nor Terence applied any rule of act-division to their comedies, and that the plays

---

[1] The scene-division is not necessarily entirely the work of the author; and it may be that the printer, or a copyist or other intermediary, had a hand in any inconsistencies.

[2] 'Epistre du traducteur au lecteur', *Andrie* (1542) (Lawton, *Handbook*, p. 38).

[3] Donatus quoted from Herrick, *Comic Theory*, p. 109. Scaliger: 'Personam eandem negat Donatus plus quinquies exire in proscenium, falso. Vel statim ipsa in Andria Davus ostendit haud ita esse, tum alibi saepe' (I. ix; ed. cit., p. 35).

were usually produced on the stage with complete continuity of action.'[1]

The principles according to which French Renaissance comedies were divided vary a great deal. *La Trésorière*, *Les Ébahis*, and *Les Contents* are, in fact, the only plays which are consistent within themselves. *La Trésorière* and *Les Ébahis* adopt one simple principle: the entry of a new character entails the declaration of a new scene. Thus, in *Les Ébahis*, v. i, Panthaleone has a soliloquy overheard by Julien; dialogue between the two follows. Then new characters enter and v. ii is declared; but Panthaleone and Julien remain on stage and a page or two later, within the same scene, return into the conversation. *Les Contents* adds to this the principle that when a character is left alone on stage for a soliloquy, a new scene is declared (I. vi, etc.).

Not one of the other plays is so consistent. The two basic principles remain the same: that the entry of a new character or his isolation on stage for a soliloquy entails the declaration of a new scene. But in every case there are exceptions. In *La Reconnue*, IV. ii, Madame enters in the middle of a scene, and a new scene is declared, whereas when she entered after III. i the normal procedure was followed. In *Les Esprits*, v. i, Ruffin knocks at the door, Severin appears, and a new scene is declared (v. ii) as one would expect; but in III. i, Frontin had knocked at the door, Urbain had appeared in exactly the same way, and a new scene was not declared. After *Les Déguisés*, III. vii, Olivier has a soliloquy entailing a new scene; but in II. iii, Grégoire's soliloquy does not entail one. Similar examples are found in all the other plays, including *Mélite*.

It might be thought that these inconsistencies are in fact intended, that they represent something to do with stage production. This does not appear to be so: in the examples I have cited (and others could be given) the inconsistencies occur in passages as nearly parallel as could be. We must conclude that although the basic principles remain constant, the details of the scene-division cannot have been regarded as greatly significant. And

[1] Duckworth, *The Nature of Roman Comedy*, pp. 98–101.

in fact, of course, they are not of the greatest significance. If
the entry of a character (possibly a very minor one) should
justify a new scene, why should not his exit? Important divisions
in the plays must be based on more fundamental criteria (e.g.
an empty stage, a turning-point in the plot, or an obviously
important entry) which the producer and actors then as now
must decide upon.

In one isolated case things are different: Perrin's *Les Écoliers*.
The division here is based upon other principles, and neither the
entry nor the exit of a character entails a new scene. Thus, in
the middle of IV. i, Corbon enters and no new scene is declared;
and a typical plan for a scene in this play precisely involves an
entry in the middle: soliloquy by A, entry of B, soliloquy by
B, dialogue between A and B (thus I. v; II. i; II. ii; II. iv; III. ii;
III. v; IV. ii; IV. vi; IV. viii; V. iii). The principle that is adopted
appears to be that of a break of a tableau in performance, as is
perfectly possible with *décor simultané*. The acts are much more
split up than usual; whereas, for example, in *Les Esprits* the first
act, like the others, continues without a break, here the first act
consists of four separate tableaux: scenes i and ii show Maclou
and Finet, scene iii shows Grassette and Babille, scene iv Sobrin,
and scene v Friquet and Marin. The principles of construction
and consequently of scene-division are quite different.

Act-division is less important here than it is in post-Renaissance
plays. The structure of the plot does correspond to some extent
with the act-division, but the correspondence is not at all strict.[1]
As far as either narrative or stage production is concerned, the
division between two acts often has little more significance than
a division between scenes. In *Les Néapolitaines*, II. i simply carries
on the action of the last scene of Act I (iv), the same two characters being on stage without any apparent break in time. In *Les*

[1] Far less strict, either in classical or in Renaissance practice, than Badius's
analysis of Terence would suggest: 'In primo horum actuum ut plurimum
explicatur argumentum. In secundo fabula agi incipit et ad finem tendere cupit.
In tertio inseritur perturbatio et impedimentum et desperatio rei concupitae.
In quarto remedium alicuius interventus affertur. In quinto autem omnia ad
optatum finem ut iam saepe dixi perducuntur' (*Praenotamenta* (Lyons, 1502),
xix; Lawton, *Handbook*, p. 30).

Déguisés, moving to the other extreme, a day or more seems to elapse at some point within Act III. If the division were normally more important, one might say that in both these cases (and in others) the dramatists concerned were deliberately departing from a convention in order to obtain a particular effect; but this does not appear to be the case. Sometimes it would be difficult, without the written indications, to arrive at the same division into five acts as the author has established. That division may well be a concession to the contemporary theory of comedy, not an obstacle but at the same time not a thoroughly integral part of the structure of the play. It is clear that we should not give too great significance to it. The principles of construction are not dependent on formal scene-division, nor are they 'realistic'. Chamard criticized the scene-division in *L'Eugène* and *La Reconnue*: 'Les scènes ses uivent et ne se lient pas.'[1] 'Les scènes s'y succèdent à peu près au hasard, sans préparation, sans enchaînement.'[2] But these plays gain their effect in other ways, and the criticism, though possibly valid for the twentieth-century armchair reader, is anachronistic.

Time-sequence

In every play except *Les Déguisés*, *Les Ramoneurs*, and *Mélite*, the unity of time is observed, the action taking place within at most one day. Sometimes the time of day is explicitly and carefully stated as the play goes on; sometimes it is very vague. Five plays begin in the morning and end just before 'souper' (about 6 p.m., according to *Les Contents*, v. vi);[3] four state no

---

[1] *Histoire de la Pléiade*, ii. 18.   [2] Ibid., iii. 291.

[3] The terms used for the two main meals of the day were 'disner' and 'souper', which I shall translate, for purposes of clarity, as 'lunch' and 'supper' respectively. The examples given by E. Huguet, *Dictionnaire de la langue française du seizième siècle*, vol. iii (Paris, 1946), pp. 208–9, show that 'disner', when it did not mean 'breakfast' (and it appears not to be used in this sense in the plays, where 'déjeuner' is used, as in *La Reconnue*, I. i), meant a meal at midday or shortly after. O. Block and W. von Wartburg, in their *Dictionnaire étymologique de la langue française*) (Paris, 1950), p. 176, state that 'le premier des deux principaux repas quotidiens . . . avait lieu ordinairement vers 10 heures au XVIᵉ siècle', but this is not confirmed by any text that I know. 'Souper' is regularly the evening meal, served about 6 p.m. Cf. Montaigne, 'De l'expérience', *Essais*, ed. A. Thibaudet,

precise time; *Les Déguisés* occupies two not necessarily consecutive days; *Les Ramoneurs* occupies only 24 hours, since it begins in the afternoon of one day and finishes two hours before supper at least two days later; while *Mélite*, surprisingly, is the most loosely constructed of all.

L'Eugène is one of the five. At some time before III. i, Messire Jean was 'banqueting' with Guillaume and Alix; we presume this was the midday meal. In V. iv, Florimond says 'desja la nuict s'approche', and in V. v, the greeting 'Bon soir' is used and supper is being prepared. Other indications of the passing of time, however, are few.

La Reconnue also occupies one day: it begins straight after the night (I. i) and ends just before supper on the same day (V. v). As in *L'Eugène*, other indications are few.

Les Esprits begins in the morning. In I. ii, Hilaire gives orders for the preparation of lunch. In I. v, Frontin goes off to prepare lunch for Fortuné, and one might assume that by his next appearance (II. i) he had lunched. But as late as III. vi, Frontin says to Severin 'Venez disner'; this may be simply inadvertence, or more likely may serve a dramatic purpose in emphasizing the fact that Severin is so harrassed that he has not eaten. In V. vii, Frontin goes off to prepare supper.

Les Contents contains more precisions about time than any of the above, but each one serves a dramatic purpose. Thus in I. i, it is so early that the sun is not even up, and the conversation bears very largely on why Louise and Geneviève are up at this unusually early hour. In II. v, it strikes 10 a.m. A little later, lunch is eaten. An assignation made for 1 p.m. is carried out in III. iv. In IV. iv, the greeting 'Bon vespre' is used. In IV. vi, Louise says it is an hour and a half since she locked 'Eustache' into her 'salle' (III. vii). In V. i, Anthoine says it is an hour since he went on his errand (VI. i). In the last scene of the play (V. vi) Basile says 'Bon soir' rather than 'Bon vespre'; Louise says it is nearly 6 p.m. and invites the company to supper.

Bibl. de la Pléiade, p. 1232: 'je ne disne ny avant onze, ny ne soupe qu'apres six heures.'

Les Néapolitaines is also precise. It occupies from 'early' in the morning (I. ii) until just before supper. In III. iii, Dieghos says 'Je croy qu'il s'approche de midi'. It is the hour for lunch; Augustin and Angélique have this meal between III. ii and III. v, and Dieghos and Gaster between III. iii and III. vi. As early as III. xiii, Camille is able to plan to send Cornélie to do the shopping for supper, and in v. ii, the host of the Escu de France gives orders for Marc-Aurel's supper. In v. x, Louppes says he has been looking for Dieghos for eight hours—presumably since the morning. At the end of the play, supper is about to be served; the 'Plaudite' takes the form: 'Demenez les mains, et moy les dents.'

The four plays that are not precise are *La Trésorière*, *Les Ébahis*, *Les Corrivaux*, and *Les Écoliers*. The total references to time in these plays are as follows: in *La Trésorière*, as early as II. iii, we hear 'Vous sçavez qu'il est desjà tard', and the epilogue refers to a banquet which is about to be prepared. In *Les Ébahis*, by II. iv the mass is over. In I. iii, Panthaleone is said to come in the evening; but this can hardly be true of both his serenading appearances. There are, I think, no other indications; but the play could well take place in a single day. *Les Corrivaux*, too, could occupy one day only. By I. ii, some of the day has certainly passed ('je n'ay fait que tracasser par toute la ville pour voir si je trouverois Claude . . .'). In IV. iii, Felix says 'nous n'avons point souppé', suggesting that supper-time is not far away. The traditional invitation to supper that one might have expected at the end does not occur. *Les Écoliers* is not merely imprecise, but clumsy. Already in II. i, Finet says 'Le jour commence à se baisser'; but still in v. iii, it is not yet sunset. Between IV. iv and vi Sobrin has entered Marin's house, seduced Grassette, and had a long conversation with her which is reported in scene vi; the shortness of the time is excessive even for the convention.

Les Déguisés, the last of the sixteenth-century comedies, is the only one of them that does not observe the unity of time. In III. ii, Olivier offers his services to Grégoire as valet, and in III. v he is well established in the household, having shown that he can play the spinet, read and write, and please Grégoire. The artificiality of this speed might perhaps be overlooked; but in fact even within the play's own terms two separate days must be concerned. In I. iii, lunch is served and Olivier and Maudolé go off to eat. In II. v, Maudolé has fresh news for Olivier, so that we must assume that time has passed; then Olivier offers his services, is accepted, and establishes himself; and then in III. v, Louise says 'despeschons nous, de grace, / D'aller aprester à disner'. This would be impossible if one day only were meant, but on the other hand there is no clear gap, so that whatever intention one assumes, the execution is clumsy. It is perhaps best to assume two days for the action. In v. v, a banquet, presumably supper, is about to be served, so that the first day occupies from before lunch to after it, and the second, not necessarily consecutive, from before lunch to just before supper.

All the plays up to 1600, then, except only the last one, *Les Déguisés*, seem to take place within one day. Four of them do not give details of the passing of time. All the others occupy from morning until just before supper: that is, a time longer than the play would take in actual production. In them, therefore, an artificial dramatic convention is regularly being observed, that the supposed time is longer than the acting time. This is normal and acceptable enough; but sometimes the artificiality is pressed to such a point that the convention demands more than passive acceptance. Thus, in *Les Néapolitaines*, III. xiii, Camille tells us what Angélique, Augustin, and he have done since scene xi; and in III. xii, Gaster tells us what Dieghos has done since scene vii; in each case the time needed would be obviously much more than the acting time. At two points in this same play, no time at all is allowed for an action: in II. viii, Augustin sends Loys on an errand and already in the next scene (III. i) is impatiently awaiting his return, while in III. xiii, Camille plans the seduction of Virginie and already in the next scene (IV. i) he has carried it out. Perhaps intervals or at least gaps in the performance are to be assumed (cf. also *L'Eugène*, III. i–ii;

III. iii–IV. i; IV. v–V. i; *La Reconnue*, V. i–ii; *Les Corrivaux*, III. ii–iv; III. vi–IV. i; *Les Esprits*, II. v–III. i).

Les Contents, as we saw, minimized the artificiality of the *décor simultané* convention by the assumption that the compartments were near each other in terms of the play itself. It also minimizes the artificiality of the time convention, in two ways. First, whereas *Les Néapolitaines* usually allows only a scene or two for a reported action to take place (see above), *Les Contents* usually allows plenty of time (e.g. Rodomont is led off to prison in III. ii, and returns free in IV. ii). And second, although the play is precise when need be (for example, in the hurry of the early morning in I. i, when the church bell is heard sounding the parts of the mass), when there is no dramatic need, it is vague. Most of Acts III and IV take place simply in the 'aprés-disnée', and we feel no lack of any indication of time, whereas in *Les Ébahis* such a lack was jarring (why does Panthaleone give two serenades in one day, etc.?).

In *La Reconnue*, a particular kind of atmosphere is created by the passing of time. Everyone is in a hurry. It is time for Janne to get supper, or for Potiron to report to his master, or Monsieur cannot wait until night falls. The play is unique in this, and gains by it in two ways. First, the play is obviously more lively if speeded along; second, this sense of hurry fits in well with the atmosphere that Belleau is creating. In fact, he has drawn for us a set of complaining and selfish people: Janne sick of her job, Madame tormenting Janne and her husband, the inquisitive Voisine, the adulterous Monsieur, Maistre Jean and the Gentil-homme de Poictou complaining of the law courts. Their inability to be content with the moment is part of their character, and part of the character of the play.

The two seventeenth-century plays *Les Ramoneurs* and *Mélite*, perhaps surprisingly, are the only French Renaissance comedies whose action frankly occupies more than one day. In *Les Ramoneurs*, I. vii, the Captain says 'Allons nous coucher', and in I. viii there is a serenade in the 'douce et favorable nuit', after which the Captain says 'Il sera demain jour'. A whole night, then, must be supposed between Acts I and II. Another elapses between Acts IV and V. It cannot be the same night that is in question, for in III. v it is day ('Repassez sur le soir, marauts'). On the other hand, the action ends, exceptionally, some hours before dinner: in the last scene of the play the Captain asks for 'une couple d'heures de loisir au preparatif du souper'. The entire action, then, involves at least two nights and must occupy at least forty-eight hours. *Mélite* is the loosest of the plays, since on Corneille's own admission in his 'Examen' a week or fortnight must be assumed between Acts I and II and again between Acts II and III (e.g. l. 542: 'Ce que depuis huict jours je bruslois de sçavoir'). This looseness, as well as that of *Les Ramoneurs*, is perhaps derived from the lack of precision in such matters in the whole of the French theatre of Hardy's generation. Certainly it is not derived from any earlier French or classical comic tradition.

As with the décor, the details of the time-sequence can be discovered only by combing through the plays. We generally find them there only when they are essential to the plot (indeed, sometimes they are omitted where they seem necessary) and where they serve some dramatic purpose (especially *L'Eugène* and *Les Néapolitaines*). They do not seem to be there as part of a purely literary and non-scenic convention.

3. CHARACTER

Sixteenth-century theories of character in drama are dominated by the principles of decorum found in Aristotle, Cicero, and Horace. Aristotle names six circumstances that differentiate individual men: emotions, habits, age, fortunes, sex, and nationality, and says that the writer should

endeavour always after the necessary or the probable; so that whenever such-and-such a personage says or does such-and-such a thing, it shall be the necessary or probable outcome of his character.[1]

[1] *Poetics*, 1454[a]35 (*The Works of Aristotle*, ed. W. D. Ross, vol. xi (Oxford, 1924)).

Cicero, writing in the *Orator*, says:

Moreover the orator must have an eye to propriety not only in thought but in language. For the same style and the same thoughts must not be used in portraying every condition in life, or every rank, position or age, and in fact a similar distinction must be made in respect of place, time and audience. The universal rule, in oratory as in life, is to consider propriety. This depends on the subject under discussion, and on the character of both the speaker and the audience.[1]

—a statement about rhetoric applicable to literature and therefore to comedy too. In life, Castiglione's *Courtier* applied the concept to social intercourse. Quintilian's discussion of the term with reference to oratory even compared comedy:

In the case of the declaimers indeed it is of the first importance that they should consider what best suits each character; for they rarely play the role of advocates in their declamations. As a rule they impersonate sons, parents, rich men, old men, gentle or harsh of temper, misers, superstitious persons, cowards, and mockers, so that hardly even comic actors have to assume more numerous roles in their performances on the stage than these in their declamations.[2]

The list sounds like any of the lists in French Renaissance theorists, clearly derived from Terentian practice, which we examined in the chapter on comic theory above.

Such ideas, of course, tell us how dramatists ought to handle characters once they have created them, but not what sort of characters they ought to create. In fact, in French Renaissance comedy the characters are those of French bourgeois society, systematized into a number of types at first based on native farces and on Terence, and later set into a whole comic tradition.[3] Sometimes they have generalized names like 'Monsieur' or 'L'Advocat' or 'Le Protenotaire', a technique which reminds us

[1] Quoted from Herrick, *Comic Theory in the Sixteenth Century*, p. 136.
[2] Ibid., p. 133.
[3] Cf. H. W. Lawton, 'La survivance des personnages térentiens', *Bulletin de l'Association Guillaume Budé* (1964), pp. 85–94.

of characters in farces such as 'Le Sergent' or 'Le Porteur d'eau'. They are figures of their own time: for example, the relationship of the valet to his master is the sixteenth-century relationship, not the Roman one, and the relationship of the younger and older generations to each other is entirely that of Renaissance society. Since comedy in France was born in a university milieu, university characters are often found in the plays: the young lover, especially, is often a student (*La Reconnue*, *Les Néapolitaines*, *Les Ramoneurs*, etc.). Sometimes he is specifically a law student like L'Amoureux in *La Reconnue*—and indeed, at a later date, like Corneille's hero Dorante in *Le Menteur*.

It was concluded that these characters were fictional, and therefore might have whatever names the dramatist chose to give them, and might behave as the dramatist wished. However, the very fact that people established lists of characters found in Terentian comedy, considered as standard for comedy in general, meant that comic characters were looked upon not in the first place as individuals, but as a series of figures representative of defined human types. The question of how far a character in a comedy should represent a human type, and how far he might be independent according to the demands of the comedy, was much discussed: that is, how far he should observe *social* decorum and how far *dramatic* decorum. Thus, the impertinence of the slave Davus in *Andria*, III. ii, was condemned as indecorous by Willichius,[1] because a slave should never mock his master. Dramatically, however, it is clear that Davus's impertinence is effective. Donatus applies the different kinds of decorum: thus, on *Andria*, V. ii, he remarks that Simo's anger is reflected in his speech in that he says nothing but calls repeatedly for his slave— an example of decorum of emotions.[2] It is a question that comes to the fore in any discussion of characterization not only in Terence but in any of the kinds of sixteenth-century comedy that ultimately derive from him.

And if we turn to actual comic practice in France in the Renaissance, we find a breadth of possibilities parallel to the theoretical

---

[1] Herrick, *Comic Theory*, p. 140. [2] Robbins, *Dramatic Characterization*, p. 43.

ones. In theory, a valet should respect his master: in fact, in Godard's *Les Déguisés*, Maudolé almost fights his master for a suit of clothes. In theory, a soldier brags; in fact, in *L'Eugène*, Florimond does not behave particularly as a soldier at all. Our twentieth-century ideas about 'des personnages fixes, stéréotypés' should be modified. The set types resemble the masks which in any case Renaissance actors often wore: and it is clear, for instance from Professor Nicoll's work, that the mask of the *commedia dell'arte* players were no hindrance to variety— indeed, in the hands of these particular highly experienced and technically accomplished actors, they were rather an aid. Similarly, in Renaissance comedy, when the audience saw an old man, a young lover, a soldier, they expected certain things. But these things were only a basis, a foundation upon which first the author and then the actor were free to make their own variations: the relationship between stage and auditorium was helped rather than hindered by the convention. Eugène Rigal's older study, 'Les personnages conventionnels de la comédie au XVIe siècle',[1] did not recognize this but assumed that masks of all kinds were hindrances to good theatre.

In the mixed genres, decorum of character is important. Plautus called his *Amphitruo* a 'tragicomoedia' almost as a joke, in that the play had both gods and ordinary mortals in it. Gods belong properly to tragedy, where they have certain norms of behaviour. If, as here, they are found in comedy, behaving and speaking like the normal middle-class figures of comedy, then a reason of decorum is invoked for calling the play a tragicomedy.

So, too, in Garnier's *Bradamante*. According to the principles of decorum, a paladin of Charlemagne's court and his wife ought to behave and speak with proper dignity. Instead, Aymon and Beatrix are in a tragi-comedy with a plot which is structurally very like that of a Renaissance comedy, and they behave like normal middle-class people in such a comedy. There results the curious spectacle of Charlemagne's court coming forcibly down

---

[1] *Revue d'histoire littéraire de la France*, iv (1897), 161–79.

to earth without the justification of the mockery of the gods which was Plautus' and later Lucian's.

The definition of 'stock' characters, then, is a delicate one. Characters like the braggart or the young lover are recognizable from play to play; their social groupings are generally the same; yet in a number of ways it would be wrong to regard them only as a series of types.[1] Plautus, in the prologue to the *Captivi* (ll. 57 ff.), boasts that his play is unusual in *not* containing characters such as the perjured slave dealer, the evil courtesan, or the braggart warrior, which are common in his other plays. The Renaissance authors, however, do not avoid types; how, precisely, do they use them?

Nearly always, the stock characters are used as a basis for variation. The old man in love, the timid heroine, and so on, are all certainly found again and again, but it is rare to find any one of them unelaborated, that is without the addition of some feature or other which makes the character in question more than a mere example of the type. Nineteenth-century Molière critics thought it important—as did Molière's contemporaries—that characters should be universal, typical of the human race as a whole. But this cannot be done literally. Drama demands something more than a character so general, or than a simple type; and in these plays nearly always the stock characters are used as a basis for variation: recognition by the audience is assumed, so that upon a familiar type may be built up an individual character for use within the play in question. Thus, Josse in *Les Ébahis* is an 'old man in love'; but in Act v he is given certain 'braggart' characteristics which make him something more than the stock character. In *Le Catéchisme du docteur Pantalon et de Zani, son disciple*,

[1] On the braggart, cf. especially O. Fest, *Der Miles Gloriosus in der französischen Komödie von Beginn der Renaissance bis zu Molière* (Erlangen and Leipzig, 1897) (Münchener Beiträge zur romanischen und englischen Philologie, xiii); D. C. Boughner, *The Braggart in Renaissance Comedy* (Minneapolis, 1954); and M. R. Lida de Malkiel, 'El fanfarrón en el teatro del Renacimiento', *Romance Philology*, xi (1957–8), 268–91. There is literature on the other types of Renaissance comedy; cf. for example C. Dietschy, *Die 'Dame d'intrigue' in der französischen Originalkomödie des XVI. und XVII. Jahrhunderts* (Halle, 1916) (Beihefte zur Zeitschrift für romanische Philologie, 64).

the very title shows how Pantalon is not merely Pantalon but a 'Docteur' as well.[1]

On the other hand, the characters are never very profound. They are usually developed enough to hold the audience's attention, but not deeply enough ever to make character more important and significant than plot.[2] Seldom, too, does a character develop in the course of a play: the abbé Eugène in Jodelle's play is the only example I have found, who at the beginning of the play, according to Messire Jean, does not think enough of the future to guard against misfortune (I. ii), in the middle shows himself quite unable to think of a solution (II. iv; III. ii; IV. ii; IV. iv), and at the end shows himself practical both in thinking of a solution (V. i) and in carrying it out (V. ii–v). Development was not expected of characters in comedy. Quintilian had said that comedy resembled *ethos*, or the set definition of a fixed personality, as distinct from tragedy which resembled *pathos*, a mood or phase of feeling.[3]

It would be wrong to suggest too many qualities for these plays; and it may be a fault in them, considered as a group, that their characters are in fact not profound. We admire *Twelfth*

---

[1] Cf. Alain Dufour, 'Le Catéchisme du docteur Pantalon et de Zani, son disciple (1594)', *Aspects de la propagande religieuse* (*Travaux d'Humanisme et Renaissance*, xxviii (1957), 361–72).

[2] If the evaluation of a play is in question, factors must be considered other than the mere relative importance in it of 'comédie d'intrigue' and 'comédie de caractère'. The two must be integrated. Chasles gave excessive importance to the latter when he wrote: 'La comédie d'intrigue, qui se plaît à exciter la curiosité et à satisfaire l'imagination, recherche les aventures, les surprises du hasard; elle peint l'imbroglio des événements, l'imprévu de la vie extérieure, tout ce qui ne dépend pas de l'homme, tout ce qui, par l'illusion ou l'équivoque, trouble l'intelligence. . . . La comédie de caractère offre un autre spectacle aux hommes, qu'elle suppose nés libres et raisonnables. . . . Son objet, qui est l'étude, la connaissance et la peinture de l'humanité, l'élèveelle-même au degré le plus haut de la littérature' (*La Comédie*, pp. 213–14). The tendency to make comedy of character the basis for evaluative judgements of comedies has been strong in the history of French criticism. In France, where the acknowledged master is Molière and where comedy of character has been acknowledged as the forte of that master, the tendency has hindered until recently the proper study of either foreign or French comedy.

[3] Cf. M. C. Bradbrook, *Elizabethan Comedy*, p. 43.

Night for the depth of Malvolio's character as well as for the suppleness of the plot or the beauty of the language; we admire the *Eunuchus* in the same way. Even in the best of these plays— *L'Eugène*, *Les Contents*, *Les Ramoneurs*—though the characterization may be skilful, it very seldom shows us any character in depth, a fault that Professor Lawton blames on the excessively bookish quality of the imitation in them.[1] The most profound is probably Severin in *Les Esprits*. This miser goes through deceits and misfortunes, his beloved treasure has been stolen: and then (IV. iii) he is able to realize that his miserliness has in fact been an offence to himself:

> En un mesme jour j'ay perdu deux mille escuz, j'ay esté desnyaisé d'un ruby, trompé par Frontin et deshonoré par Urbain, de façon que je n'atten plus que la mort. O fortune, que tu es cruelle quand tu delibères faire mal à quelcun! je n'ay jamais offencé que moy-mesme.[2]

But however this may be, it is certainly apparent that in the hands of a skilful author, the stock characters provide not a mere Punch and Judy show with unvarying characters, but an entertainment in which variation upon the familiar figures serves to ring the changes upon the many relationships possible. The variation of each character is done with the ensemble of all the rest in mind.

A good example is Josse in Grévin's *Les Ébahis*. We saw that he is the 'old man in love' who in Act V is given some 'braggart' characteristics. But there is already a braggart in love in the play, Panthaleone; and he for his part, compared with the braggarts in later plays, is greatly toned down.[3] Much of the

---

[1] 'La survivance des personnages térentiens', pp. 93–4.
[2] *Ancien Théâtre français*, v. 266.
[3] Pantalone in the Italian plays is of course not usually a braggart; he is properly a *magnifico*, an elderly citizen (cf. Allardyce Nicoll, *The World of Harlequin*, esp. pp. 44–55). When he becomes a serenading lover, as he often does in Italian comedy, this is only as a variation on his normal character, not as a replacement for it. It appears that Grévin did not know, or deliberately ignored, the characteristics of Pantalone in Italy. Cf. R. C. D. Perman, 'The Influence

last act is built upon these two characters and the interrelation-
ship of their two different kinds of braggadocio. 'Braggarts' are
also used in this way in *Les Déguisés*, where the regular stock
character, Prouventard, is fairly standard, but where he is put
side by side with a valet given certain 'braggart' characteristics
(Maudolé). In *Les Néapolitaines*, a stock 'timid heroine' (Virginie)
is used side by side with a supposed widow and her mother,
Angélique, who is not a stock character. In *Les Contents*, the
entremetteuse Françoise is developed by supposed piety, played
off against the real piety of Geneviève's mother, Louise.

   In short, to use a stock character as such, without development,
is to treat him only as an individual, with very limited reference
to those around him, and is therefore suitable only for comparatively undeveloped drama. These plays, on the other hand, are
built up on the relationship between all the characters; and for
this, it is necessary that a stock character, if used at all, should
be modified to suit the dramatic situations envisaged. And in
fact, we find that a stock character pure and simple is a rarity
in these plays. Giordano Bruno has a comment which is to the
point on his own use of stock characters in *Il Candelaio*, and which
is entirely true for the French comedies:

   Son tré materie principali intessute insieme nela presante comedia L'amor di Bonifa[cio] l'alchimia di Bartholomeo et la pedan-
   taria di Mamphurio. Peró per la cognition distinta de suggetti,
   raggion dell'ordine, et evidenza dell'artificiosa testura: Rappor-
   tiamo prima da per lui l'insipido amante, secondo il sordido avaro.
   Terzo il goffo pedante, Dequali l'insipido non é senza goffaria,
   et sordidezza. Il sordido é parimente insipido et goffo, Et il goffo
   non é men sordido et insipido che goffo.[1]

None of the comedies spotlights one single character at the
expense of the others. It is seldom even possible to say that one
character is more important than the others: indeed, the very
titles of nearly all the comedies are in the plural: *Les Ébahis*, *Les*

---

of the commedia dell'arte on the French Theatre before 1640', *French Studies*, ix
(1955), 295.
   [1] Giordano Bruno, *Candelaio comedia del Bruno Nolano* (Paris, 1582), f. ã iii^v.

Esprits, *Les Ramoneurs*. The plot-structure is always constructed on a group, as with the *commedia dell'arte*, and as with Terence; whereas Molière, for instance, following Corneille, often focused his plots on a single character: *L'Avare*, *Le Médecin malgré lui*, *Le Malade imaginaire*. (It is true, though, that titles have only limited significance. Italian comedies, whose plots are usually constructed on a group, do often have titles in the singular: *La Mandragola*, *Il Candelaio*, *Olimpia*.)

As examples, I shall discuss four types: the old man in love, the servant, the braggart soldier, and the young heroine. The old man in love is one of the simplest. He appears in Josse in *Les Ébahis* and Monsieur in *La Reconnue*. Josse believes his wife is dead, and he wishes to marry Madalène; he has a cough and a cold, but otherwise believes himself vigorous. This might be the end of his character; but Grévin has widened the canvas by the comic contrast with another (similarly unconventional) braggart type. Monsieur has the more complex aim of marrying Antoinette off to his clerk to serve his own ends, and the interest of his character lies not only in his being an 'old man in love', but in the considerable amount of ingenuity he is forced to deploy towards those ends.

The servant is a new creation of Renaissance comedy, although certain features of the Roman slave and parasite survive in him.[1] He is part of the same process of sixteenth-century modernization of comedy which resulted in the substitution of European proper names for Graeco-Roman ones, and of Italian and French marriage customs and problems for Roman ones. The Roman slave was bound to obey his master, and might fear a beating if he did not. The Renaissance servant, however, is not bound in the same way, whether he is called *valet*, *serviteur*, or *laquais*. He is based upon something in sixteenth-century society which had no precise equivalent in the Roman.

Servants in these plays are never used except in conjunction with their masters: as one of a pair. There is no such thing as a

---

[1] Cf. Duckworth, *The Nature of Roman Comedy*, pp. 249–53 and 265–7 respectively.

'servant' type isolated in a play, looking for a job. Whether in the social context of carrying out orders for his master, or in other dramatic terms, the servant is never seen as anything other than a foil to a master. He may be a fool and the master self-possessed (Maudolé and Olivier in *Les Déguisés*); or the reverse (the parasite Gaster and Dom Dieghos in *Les Néapolitaines*). He may talk to the audience about his master (Antoine in *Les Ébahis*, Messire Jean in *L'Eugène*). Or he may express ideas that balance his master's (anti-heroism, or anti-Petrarchan love). No one detail (such as anti-heroism) is common to all these servants; their social standing and their balancing against their masters are the only constant features.

Once these principles of the novelty of the role and its function are grasped, the almost infinite variety of the servants in these plays makes sense. Some mock their masters (Gaster in *Le Néapolitaines*), some serve them faithfully (Antoine in *Les Contents*). Some are moral and serious-minded (Finet in *Les Écoliers*), most are cynical. And so on. The servant figure is in fact probably the role in which the technique of variation upon a stock character is best applied.

Among all the different creations, the two most successful are probably Gaster in *Les Néapolitaines* and Maudolé in *Les Déguisés*. Gaster is a development of the Gnatho of Terence's *Eunuchus*, and is therefore a parasite rather than a *valet* or *laquais*. In a fine soliloquy (I. iv), he proclaims his policy: to attach himself to a master and get as much out of him as possible. He is a *maquereau* with no compunctions about it; a lively cynic, drawn with much verve and verbal richness. Maudolé is the best thing about *Les Déguisés*, and an original creation by Godard.[1] He is a fool as well as a valet; timid, but swaggering when he is in his master's clothes ('Je pompe, je morgue, je brave')—until he is attacked. He cannot even wear his master's clothes properly (III. i), while he quite forgets himself in thinking about the coming banquet in v. v. His bragging and his folly, however,

---

[1] Neither he nor Prouventard, against whom he is set, appears in Ariosto's *I Suppositi*, which is the model for *Les Déguisés*.

make him a figure of fun himself, so that he cannot be so much an intermediary between the audience and the principal characters as some of the other servants are. That function is performed in this play by Vadupié, Prouventard's *laquais*. It is done mostly by means of asides: of Vadupié's thirty speeches exactly half are asides,[1] while in the other plays, such asides as there are are nearly always in the mouth of servants.

We have seen that one of the servant's functions is to serve as a counter-balance, in the audience's eyes, to his master's ideas. This applies in particular to two kinds of ideas: uplifted senti-ments in love, and valour in combat. The servant regularly expresses his more down-to-earth views on love, and his greater care for his own skin, respectively. Thus, in La Taille's *Les Corrivaux*, I. ii, Filadelfe expresses his love for Fleurdelys:

> Mais quoy? qui est celuy qui ne connoit les forces d'amour? Qui ne connoit qu'il est aveugle, jeune et volage, sans loy et sans raison? C'est par luy que je n'ay non plus de repos que si j'avois le vif argent soubs les pieds.

while in scene iv his valet Gillet is overheard:

> Vrayement je seroy bien un grand sot, pendant que mon maistre demeine une vie amoureuse, si de ma part je ne me jettois aussi sur l'amour: non point de la sorte qu'il fait, car il est de ces amoureux transis, qui ne s'amusent qu'à une, et sont deux ou trois ans à lanterner, sans qu'à la fin ils viennent au poinct.[2]

Boniface's cowardliness in *La Trésorière*, IV. v, is typical:

> Car, quand j'ai ouy ce beau mesnage,
> Ainsi qu'un homme de courage
> J'ai gaigné le grenier au foin.

Like the servants, the braggart soldiers differ considerably from each other, perhaps because of the widely differing sources used. Florimond and Arnault in *L'Eugène* are the first examples

---

[1] Fourteen are asides; fourteen are direct speech; two contain both asides and direct speech.
[2] Ed. de Maulde, pp. xxii and xxvii–xxviii.

in date, owing more to Terence and Plautus than to Italian models. But they are different from *milites gloriosi*. Even Arnault, the irascible Gascon, the more developed of the two, can hardly be compared to Plautus' Pyrgopolynices. He says at one point:

> Mais j'en renie tous les cieux
> Si je ne fais tomber en bas
> Tant de jambes et tant de bras
> Que Paris en sera pavé.
>   (*L'Eugène*, III. i)

But all this is merely a part of a fuller character (he is a Gascon, a good soldier, a faithful follower of Florimond, and a scholar as well); we laugh, but only temporarily. In general, Jodelle uses these characters to praise, not to mock, the profession of arms, while there is no question of the boast being exposed as an empty boast, as in Plautus or in later French comedy. Although Messire Jean says of them:

> Sont de ceux, dont l'un vend sa terre,
> L'autre un moulin à vent chevauche,
>   (*L'Eugène*, IV. iv)

they are in fact taken quite seriously.

The next braggart, Panthaleone in Grévin's *Les Ébahis*, is also different from braggarts in any classical or modern source. As we have seen, he is not the equivalent of the Italian Pantalone. Dr. Perman calls him a 'young fop'. He sings, in Italian, to his lute;[1] he declares himself in love, but does nothing about it. Two passages link him with the braggart tradition:

> Vous le verrez tantost vanter,
> Tantost élever ses beaux faicts . . .
>   (II. iii)

and the scene in Act V, where he goes through the standard process of boasts, threats, and exposure when Julien calls his bluff and forces him to retreat. These two passages are scarcely

---

[1] Not macaronic French-Italian, as D. C. Boughner states (*The Braggart in Renaissance Comedy* (Minneapolis, 1954), p. 256).

sufficient to make him a full and successful character. His whole role, in fact, is handled with a certain clumsiness; he appears twice only, his role is peripheral to the main plot, he mixes confusingly the roles of Petrarchan lover and soldier, his very name is inappropriate to either role. In v. iv, his attempted intervention ('Messer Gérard, monstrez-vous sage') also seems inappropriate to either role. He is perhaps only a vehicle for Grévin's anti-Italian sentiments, a vehicle whom Grévin has failed to integrate into the play. He is interesting for his name: *Les Ébahis* dates from 1561, whereas the name Pantalone is not found in Italy until 1565.

The braggart soldier begins to be a recognizable type in French Renaissance comedy with 'Le capitaine' in Belleau's *La Reconnue*.[1] The others in the plays we are considering are Dom Dieghos in *Les Néapolitaines*, Rodomont in *Les Contents*, Prouventard in *Les Déguisés*, and Scanderbec in *Les Ramoneurs*.

One feature only is constant to all of them: the gap between what this braggart soldier boasts and what he is. This gap is usually made apparent by a threefold process of boasts, threats, and exposure. Thus, in *Les Déguisés*, ii. i, Prouventard boasts in a standard form of *gab*:

> J'ai fait connoistre ma vaillance
> Au pays de Flandre, où j'ay mis
> Cent fois à sac les ennemis.

He threatens Grégoire:

> Si vous ne me rendez le mien,
> Je le r'auray bien par justice.
> Il n'est chose que je ne puisse.
> Par le sang, le ventre et la mort!
> Vous vous repentirez du tort
> Que vous me faistes.
>
> (ii. iv)

---

[1] He is named in the dramatis personae as 'Le capitaine Rodomont'; but in fact his speeches merely bear the heading 'Le capitaine' and he is never actually named in the play. In v. iv, Maistre Jehan says he 'tranche là du Rodomont' as though this were *not* his name.

But a little later he sees a man with a sword:

> C'est de la part peut-estre aussi
> Du sire Gregoire . . .
> Mais je les empescheray bien
> De me tenir et me surprendre,
> Et deussé-je la fuite prendre.
> Mais s'ils viennent pour me frapper,
> Par où me pouray-je eschapper?
>
> (III. iv)

It may be fighting that is at stake (Prouventard) or it may be love (Dieghos). In any case the main dramatic function of these captains is to create a gap between what is claimed and what is performed.

Seen in this light, their significance in the dramatic structure emerges. The difference between what is claimed and what is performed is, after all, one of the main structural principles upon which Renaissance comedy is built. We might compare the moral situation: the actual lack of virtue in these plays coupled with concern for the outward appearance of it. The braggarts have their own application of it, sometimes simple, and sometimes more developed as in *Les Déguisés* where a valet (Maudolé) brags and is set against the braggart soldier proper.

It may be surprising, in view of the evident cowardliness of the captains, that they are readily accepted into society. The craven Prouventard is respected and indeed feared by Grégoire, and is twice offered an advantageous marriage. Rodomont in *Les Contents* is offered one as well, but refuses; Dieghos is summoned off to a good marriage at home; the Captain in *La Reconnue* is a highly respected member of the king's forces, who at the end of the play is given a spare niece and a job; and Scanderbec finds both a rich uncle and a wife. (Panthaleone is an exception in this respect as in others.) They may all be exposed as cowards, but instead of being chased off the stage at the end, they are all given a consolation prize of some sort. Dramatically, this

---

[1] *Ancien Théâtre français*, vii. 355, 367, 377–8.

procedure is odd: that a character should boast emptily and be mocked, and yet should be accepted in the end. Plautus' Pyrgopolynices is not accepted in this way, although Terence's Thraso is. It may be that the high esteem in which the profession of arms was held in the sixteenth century accounts for it: the braggart may personally be a fool and a coward, but his profession is an honourable one. Also, it may be acceptable as part of the required 'happy ending'. In *La Reconnue* at least it leads to a dramatic inconsistency: the captain's *gab*, considered as a verbal exercise and entertainment, is as good as any that will be found in these comedies, yet it is quite irrelevant both to the action of the play and to his known *really* valorous character. It is the first part of the 'boasts, threats, exposure' pattern, well executed but isolated and quite unintegrated.

The heroines, unlike the servants and captains, are nearly all of a type. Possibly played by boys and therefore by less experienced actors, their parts are generally small. In *Les Ébahis*, Madalène appears only in II. vi and IV. v, a timid, lamenting creature. In *La Reconnue*, Antoinette appears only in I. iii and IV. i–ii. She is a devout Huguenot, with little will of her own, and certainly not in control of the marital intrigues going on around her. The heroines of *Les Esprits* do not appear, or at least speak, at all, the only female parts being a mature wife and mother, and a maid.[1] In *Les Néapolitaines*, Angélique appears only in III. vi–viii and IV. ii. Nevertheless, she is certainly not timid; but then she is supposed to be a widow and is therefore not the typical young heroine. That role is filled by Virginie, whose one appearance in the play (III. viii–ix) shows her to be as timid as any. In *Les Déguisés*, Louise appears more often than is usual (II. iii; III. v and ix; IV. i and iii; V. iv and v), but she is extraordinarily timid. She breathes no word of protest at her father's command, either to him or to her maid; she leaves Olivier immediately when he reveals his disguise; her fear for her reputation is obsessive. In

---

[1] The absence of the three heroines, around whom the plot revolves, certainly creates an odd impression. But as the play is an adaptation from the Italian, their absence may be accounted for by Italian rather than French stage practice.

Les Corrivaux, Restitue appears only in I. i, while Fleurdelys does not appear at all. Most of the exposition is put into Restitue's mouth in this one early appearance, thus combining the demands of the exposition with a short appearance of the heroine.

The heroines, then, are very similar—more so perhaps than any other types to be found in these plays. Whereas the servants were different from play to play, these are usually exactly what one expects. A set piece that occurs again and again is the lament by the heroine on her unfortunate position, of which a typical example is this from *Les Ébahis*:

> MADALÈNE, *seule*
>
> Hé! la fleur de mes jeunes ans
> S'en ira-elle ainsi perdue,
> Et la joye tant attendue
> Mise à néant, par la contrainte
> D'une trop envieuse crainte?
> C'est or' que je sen la puissance
> D'amour; mais, las! mon impuissance,
> Les menaces et la promesse
> M'ont remis en telle destresse,
> Qu'ores que je veuille une chose,
> Toutesfois l'honneur s'y oppose.
>
> (II. vi)

One might suppose that this similarity is due to the lack of independence which unmarried daughters had, as a matter of historical fact, in the Renaissance. Only one heroine is more determined: Grassette in *Les Écoliers*, who, independent or not, aims to follow her choice by one means or another.

It would be tiresome to examine all the characters in all these plays. Besides the old man in love, the servant, the braggart, and the heroine, two of the most important are the young *innamorato* and the parent concerned for his child's welfare. Some few characters do not belong to a type. One is the Gentilhomme in *Les Ébahis*, a sensualist whose opinions contrast with his friend the Advocat's idealism and who reminds us of Tirsis in the first scene of *Mélite*; and Angélique in *Les Néapolitaines*, a supposed widow with a bigger part in the play than any young heroine in these comedies.

Character and plot are necessarily closely linked, and the more closely, the more coherent the whole play. *Les Contents* and *L'Eugène* achieve the closest synthesis of the two, in the sense that they depend only on the working out of the factors of situation and character given us in the exposition. In *L'Eugène*, the abbé's lack of practicality and Hélène's lack of response to Florimond led to all the trouble in the past, Guillaume's simplicity made it possible, and Florimond's anger brings it to a head. Every other French Renaissance comedy before *Mélite*, without exception, uses at least one *deus ex machina*.

Such a use of types is comparatively sophisticated. Admittedly it needs a finer dramatist than we are dealing with here to make out of a type a full character, but at the same time the inferior effect is avoided of mere recognition of the type and nothing more. In nearly every case, the author has indicated a type, so that the audience knows approximately what to expect; and then he has played upon this knowledge on their part by creating a variation upon that type. The technique is one more use of the theatrical relationship of the author and his audience. Among the most successful achievements are Josse in *Les Ébahis*, the braggart old man in love; Maudolé, the foolish valet in *Les Déguisés*; Françoise, the pious *entremetteuse* in *Les Contents*—in each case the success is due to the combination of something expected with something new.

4. SPEECH

The verbal style of comedy

When François d'Amboise, under his pseudonym Thierri de Timofile, praised his own comedy *Les Néapolitaines*, he emphasized the verbal style:

> En ceste-cy on trouvera un françois aussi pur et correct qu'il s'en soit veu depuis que nostre langue est montée à ce comble, à l'aide de tant de laborieux et subtils esprits qui y ont chacun

contribué de leur travail et diligence pour la rendre polie et par-
faicte. La lecture et la conferance en rendront seur tesmoignage,
outre la gentillesse de l'invention, le bel ordre, la diversité du
subject, les sages discours, les bons enseignemens, sentences,
exemples et proverbes, les faceties et sornettes dont elle est
semée de toutes parts.[1]

Except for the vague 'la gentillesse de l'invention, le bel ordre,
la diversité du subject', all these virtues refer to the verbal style.
Perhaps this is not surprising in a man who wrote a great deal and
published only one play. But it is a common emphasis in other
writers too: Larivey in his long *Épistre* to d'Amboise discusses
only the ethics of comedy and its language—not its plot, its
characterization, or its staging. Miss Bradbrook says that this
same emphasis is found in England too: 'The development of
Elizabethan comedy is very largely the development of its language'; and 'To examine the critical evolution of comic writing
is . . . to examine the general theory of rhetoric as applied to
poetry'.[2]

For verbal style as well as for characterization, ideas of decorum are again all-important. A character must speak, not only
behave, as his personality and situation demand. Vauquelin de la
Fresnaye's discussion of decorum in comedy is dominated by the
idea of speech:

> Un doux parler est propre aux hommes tels que toy [Ragot]:
> Aux hommes furieux paroles furieuses,
> Lascives aux lascifs, et aux joyeux joyeuses:
> Et le sage propos et le grave discours
> A quiconque a passé de jeunesse le cours:
> Car Nature premier dedans nous a formee
> L'impression de tout pour la rendre exprimee
> Par le parler aprés . . .
> Il faut que la personne à propos discourante,
> Suive sa passion pour estre bien disante.[3]

---

[1] *Les Néapolitaines*, preface to Charles, duc de Luxembourg, *Ancien Théâtre français*, vii. 239.
[2] M. C. Bradbrook, *Elizabethan Comedy*, pp. 49 and 32.
[3] *L'Art poétique*, i, ll. 838–45 and 851–2; ed. Pellissier, p. 50.

The plays do in fact follow these ideas. In *Les Contents*, III. ix, the servants Antoine and Perrette have a series of indecent exchanges suitable for the character of servants; while in the same play, V. iii, Basile and Geneviève have a 'love-duet' couched in the loftiest terms. The two take place at the same window of the same house, and are clearly meant to highlight each other. In such cases, the vocabulary, syntax, and imagery vary greatly, though there is no equivalent to Shakespeare's use of a mixture of verse and prose, or Bodel's use of different metres for different characters, for the poetic medium remains the same throughout each of these plays without exception. But within that medium, the braggarts, the older generation, the young lovers, all have their individual kinds of speech. The verbal difference between servant and master is one of the most important and clearly defined, since it is one of the clearest of social distinctions. Here are Olivier and Maudolé in *Les Déguisés*: the master in love expresses his misery with a typical invocation ('O petit dieutelet ailé'); Godard makes the servant first express his interest in food, as is quite conventional, but then plays with the master–servant convention by making Maudolé adopt the opposite view:

MAUDOLÉ. J'ai le foy et la rate esmue,
      Tant il m'a fallu cheminer
      Pour vous dire qu'on va disner,
      Et qu'on s'est desjà mis à table.

OLIVIER.   Helas!

MAUDOLÉ.   Quel mot espouvantable!
      Hé! se faut-il ainsi facher
      Quant c'est qu'on parle de mascher?
      Depuis un temps sans cesse il grogne
      Et contrefait toujours la trogne
      De quelque pourceau mau-bruslé.

OLIVIER.   O petit dieutelet ailé!

MAUDOLÉ. Il me faut en tristesse mettre:
      « Si joyeux ou triste est le maistre,
      « Le valet le doit estre aussi. »

> Ah! helas! que j'ay de souci,
> D'ennuy, de peine et fascherie!
> Que ma pressure en est marrie!

OLIVIER.   O petit dieutelet ailé!

MAUDOLÉ. Helas!

OLIVIER.   Hé! qu'a mon Maudolé? . . .

(I. iii)

The frequent proverbs and popular sayings, like Maudolé's 'Si joyeux ou triste est le maistre, / Le valet le doit estre aussi' above, correspond in a sense to the *sententiae* of Renaissance tragedy. These particular two lines even share the typographical convention of specially inserted guillemets to mark them. In tragedy, the *sententiae* are put into the mouths of kings and aristocrats, and express with remarkable constancy throughout the century some aspect of the Stoic philosophy supposed to be proper to people of that rank. In comedy, the proverbs and sayings express the wisdom supposed to be proper to the characters of comedy, namely the bourgeois and the serving class immediately beneath them. As d'Amboise says, *Les Néapolitaines* has a large number of them. So has *Les Contents*; curiously, when the play was re-issued as *Les Déguisés* in 1626, the title-page expressly stated that the new edition contained 'L'esplication des Proverbes et mots difficiles', as though proverbs as such presented great difficulty. Larivey, too, adapts into a very easy and natural French the Italian proverbs and sayings of his originals; while all the comedies of the earlier generation include them in plenty, as well. Many of the same phrases reappear in play after play, possibly sometimes as direct sources. They are a kind of popular storehouse providing material throughout all the Renaissance. Among the many parallels are: 'faire ses choux gras' in *Les Ébahis*, *Les Contents*, and *Les Déguisés*;[1] 'La fortune aide aux amoureux' in *Les Ébahis*, reappearing as 'Amour aide aux hardis' in *Les Déguisés*;[2] 'Mais qui est galleux qu'il se frotte' in *Les*

[1] V. iv; IV. v; V. iv (Maudolé: 'Ce n'est pas tout un que des choux, / Il y aura bien de la grasse').
[2] III. iii; III. viii.

Écoliers, corresponding to 'Vous me grattez ou il me demange' in *Les Corrivaux*;[1] 'Qu'il s'en torche la bouche' or some variant of the phrase in six plays at least.

The popular kind of imagery is the most frequent in the plays, though none of the plays is as deliberately or pointedly about the common people as, for instance, Dekker's *The Shoemaker's Holiday*. The distribution of different kinds of imagery in a play is significant of the author's conception of his subject, and of the audience it was intended for. French Renaissance comedies show four kinds of imagery: the popular imagery of proverbs and similar figures of speech; that of French history and literature; Petrarchan; and classical.[2] The references to native history and literature are, for instance, Rodomont's calling his sword Flamberge in *Les Contents*, or the frequent use of the word *patelinage*. In this breadth of imagery they differ from other works by the same authors. Grévin's *L'Olimpe* and *La Gélodacrye* use almost exclusively classical and Petrarchan imagery, but his two plays include a rich store of popular images and turns of phrase, and the same is true generally of French Renaissance comedy. We may compare Jodelle's *Amours* with *L'Eugène*, or d'Amboise's eclogues with *Les Néapolitaines*—just as we may compare Shakespeare's sonnets with his comedies—and find as great a difference between genres as between authors. The difference in imagery is due partly to theories of decorum (if your play includes valets, they must speak like valets), partly to the demands of the comic form. Tragedies too differ in this respect. Whereas plays like Grévin's *César* or Montchrestien's *L'Écossaise* were serious and elegiac, using Stoic imagery of one single and familiar kind, and therefore not so very different from some more solemn types of lyric poetry, comedies necessarily had to be livelier and lighter altogether and use a broader spectrum of images. It is indeed this liveliness,

---

[1] IV. ii; V. iii.

[2] It would, of course, be possible to list the images in the plays according to the type of the *comparé*, as Dr. Spector has done in his edition of *Les Contents*, pp. xlix–li (religion, the household, business, animals, the body, anti-clericalism, anti-feminism, war, games); but a list of this kind does not tell us much about the *function* of the images.

this lightness, this breadth of imagery that make French Renaissance comedies more acceptable to our modern taste than any of the tragedies of the same period.

An image typically makes only a momentary appearance. It is rare to find an extended image, or a succession of closely related images. Here is the procuress Dame Claude in *Les Ramoneurs*, IV. ii; in this passage, nine separate images follow at each other's heels:

Mais il n'y a Belistre si jaloux de sa besace que luy de sa nouvelle maîtresse, qui selon l'apparence tient ce pauvre fievreux aux alteres, et ne veut point choquer qu'à bonnes enseignes, s'apelle tant que le mariage tire son honneur du pair. Et elle fine, car ces jeunes Levrons n'ont pas sitost gousté d'un gibier, qu'ils ne courent à l'autre. Ces gueules fraisches entretiennent leur appetit dans la nouveauté, toujours prodigues d'une promesse de mariage, qui sert de leurre à faire venir ces oyseaux niais sur le poin. Mais, vienne qui plante, si quelque pluye de pistolles se présente, je suis bien resolüe de tendre mon giron et d'apprendre la leçon à cet Ecolier en cas de pucelles qui demandent vistement la presse, ainsy que les draps en la boutique du foulon. Mais j'entrevoy quelqu'homme d'Eglise qui s'approche du logis de ceans à pas de Loup, ce qui ne peut estre sans dessein. Ecoutons le parler.

Those rich forms of imagery, the emblem and device, find their way into the plays. D'Amboise, we know, was interested in them, translating and commenting on Paradin's book, and writing a *Discours ou traicté des devises* (Paris, 1620). And in his play—though it dates from many years earlier—the braggart Dom Dieghos has his *devises*:

DIEGHOS. Tu me vois bien à ceste heure paisible et amiable, tellement que je te semble un petit Ange, ou plustost un petit Cupidonneau; c'est pourquoy je porte en ma devise une Abeille, avec ces motz: *Frezia, y miel,* voulant donner à entendre par la fleche et le miel que je suis brave guerrier et amoureux tout ensemble; auparavant je portois une autre devise: *Mas honra que vida.*

GASTER. Proprement.

DIEGHOS. Je suis bien lors aussi furieux et terrible, de sorte
qu'il n'y a si brave qui ne tremble devant moy cent piedz
dans le corps. As-tu jamais veu painct le Dieu Mars? . . .

GASTER. Qui donc? Celuy qu'on dict le dieu des batailles?
N'est-ce pas cestuy là qui est pourtraict en une medaille que
vous portez au bonnet?

DIEGHOS. C'est luy mesme; voy me la tout faict.
                                    (*Les Néapolitaines*, I. iii)[1]

Another developed and frequent pictorial image is the Petrarchan one of the lover as a ship in a storm, seeking a refuge—it
is as it were a constant picture, the woodcut to which the play
supplies descriptive comments beneath. Here is Augustin in *Les
Néapolitaines*:

Apres une longue tempeste j'avois trouvé la mer calme et
tranquille pour l'esperance que je prins aux promesses de ceste
servante [Beta], et en un instant le vent furieux de jalousie m'a
remis en tourmente; puis le temps s'est rendu un peu plus serain,
le vent m'a donné en pouppe, qui me fait surgir au port tant desiré.
                                                        (II. iv)

Surprisingly absent is the use of jargon: the jargon of the
pedant, of the doctor, or of any such specialized types. Despite
their plentiful existence in the Italian models available to Larivey
and later playwrights, characters like these hardly appear in
French Renaissance comedy. Even Larivey, adaptor though he
was, is comparatively sparing in his use of them. Bruno in his
Il Candelaio uses an extreme pedant, Manfurio, but Turnèbe
and d'Amboise do not. The only pedant in the native comedy
is Bonarsius in *Les Ramoneurs*. So that although the speech certainly varies from character to character, this particular kind of
exaggeration is rare. The braggart seems to concentrate within
himself all the need for exaggeration in these plays, and even he
can hardly be said to use a jargon. Though his boasts may be

[1] *Les Néapolitaines* (Paris, 1584), ff. 23ᵛ–24.

grotesquely exaggerated, they are still couched in quite normal vocabulary.[1]

The kinds of language that I have described change abruptly with *Mélite*, more abruptly than either character or plot-structure. *Les Ramoneurs* was stylistically entirely in the sixteenth-century tradition, but *Mélite* begins something quite new for comedy: a style based on the *précieux* poetic language of the early seventeenth century, and in drama so far found only in some pastorals and tragi-comedies. The imagery is no longer colourful and down to earth, but abstract. There are no servants to bring their masters down from their fancies: only one nurse, whose entirely different function is that of a confidante. The language and imagery of every Renaissance comedy are related to a social situation and its practical problems; *Mélite*'s language and imagery are related to states of mind. The imagery is that of the *salons*, subtle but comparatively colourless, with the exception of Éraste's mad scene, in which the imagery of the underworld is developed at great length and with strong effect.

Verse and prose

The Pléiade comedies significantly used the vehicle of the native French farces, the octosyllable without alternate masculine and feminine rhymes. Apart from the translators Charles Estienne and Jean-Pierre de Mesmes, the first to change this is La Taille, a figure of transition in so many ways. His *Les Corrivaux* is in prose, perhaps following the model of Italy, where prose was already established as a medium for comedy. *Le Négromant* is also in prose, although Ariosto's *Il Negromante* was in verse. *Les Corrivaux* is written in an easy style, always flowing and colloquial, with very few passages in any kind of complex

[1] Robert Garapon, in his *La Fantaisie verbale dans le théâtre français* (Paris, 1957), ch. iii, comes to the similar conclusion that jargon and 'fantaisie verbale' are rare in French Renaissance comedy. He sees Le Loyer's *Néphélococugie* as an exception, where Le Loyer's model Aristophanes has prompted a number of overflowing torrents of words, recalling not only Aristophanes, but the farces of the time.

or elevated style. Even the lover's set speech is down to earth:

Mais quoy? qui est celuy qui ne connoit les forces d'amour? Qui ne connoit qu'il est aveugle, jeune et volage, sans loy et sans raison? C'est par luy que je n'aynon plus de repos que si j'avois le vif argent soubs les pieds. Et pour ceste cause, je n'ay fait que tracasser par toute la ville. (I. ii)

Compare Grévin's version of the same *topos*:

> Sera donque la récompense
> De ma longue persévérance
> Mise en oubly, et mon service
> Récompancé d'une injustice?
> C'est maintenant que j'aperçoy
> Combien est petite la foy,
> Et combien au double est traistresse
> La faincte voix d'une maistresse.
>
> (*Les Ébahis*, II. i)

—a lament fifty-four lines long, compared with La Taille's nine lines of prose before the lover turns to practical measures.

But La Taille is before his time in writing in prose. Baïf after him, and Chappuis, still use verse in their plays, and it is a whole new generation, dating exactly from the arrival in France of the Italian players, that turns to prose as a medium for comedy: first the minor figure de Vivre in the late 1570s, then Larivey, Turnèbe, and d'Amboise. Bruno's *Il Candelaio* is in prose, Fornaris's *Angelica* too, and its translation *Angélique*. *Les Ramoneurs*, though forty years later, shares the same medium, as well as sharing similar characterization and subject-matter.

Perrin and Godard both return to verse for their plays. Perrin of course is turning back to farce (and to Terence) for his models, and away from the Italians; Godard adapts a play of Ariosto's which existed in a version in verse as well as one in prose. Troterel, too, uses verse: the octosyllable for *Gillette*, and, surprisingly, the alexandrine for *Les Corrivaux*. Corneille turns to the alexandrine, doubtless because of its use in the tragi-comic and pastoral genres that preceded his play.

It would be true to say, then, that the farces provided a model for the octosyllabic metre of the Pléiade comedies, and the Italians one for the prose of the next generation. But these are historical reasons. Is there any intrinsic merit in one form rather than another, in the octosyllable, in the alexandrine, or in prose? Renaissance theorists and playwrights said that there was. One suggestion was that the more serious the subject-matter, the longer the line should be. Sébillet writes of the alexandrine:

> Ceste espece est moins frequente que les autres deus prece-dentes [eight- and ten-syllable lines] et ne se peut proprement appliquer qu'a choses fort graves, comme aussi au pois de l'aureille se trouve pesante.[1]

But this is of course an illusion. The test is an aural one, and in actual delivery the length of line makes very little difference. Gilbert Gadoffre writes in his *Ronsard par lui-même* about similar ideas of Paul Laumonier: 'On reste confondu devant une telle méconnaissance des structures poétiques', and shows how the shortest lines can have the heaviest effect:

> Ceux qui sont sous le resveil
>   Du soleil
> Ceux qui habitent Niphate,
> Ceux qui vont d'un bœuf suant
>   Remuant
> Les gras rivages d'Euphrate.[2]

Another suggestion was Larivey's, almost a naturalistic idea before its time: comedy deals with people of comparatively low rank, such people do not speak in an elevated way, therefore comedy should be in prose rather than verse:

> Or, si je n'ay voulu en ce peu, contre l'opinion de beaucoup, obliger la franchise de ma liberté de parler à la severité de la loy

---

[1] *Art poétique françois*, ed. Gaiffe, p. 41.

[2] *Ronsard par lui-même* (Paris, 1960), pp. 85–6. The verse is from Ronsard's *Ode au duc d'Orléans*.

de ces critiques qui veullent que la Comedie soit un poëme subject
au nombre et mesure des vers . . . je l'ay faict [i.e. he has written
in prose] parce qu'il m'a semblé que le commun peuple, qui
est le principal personnage de la scène, ne s'estudie tant à agencer
ses paroles qu'à publier son affection, qu'il a plutost dicte que
pensée.[1]

The very artificiality of drama, of course—particularly of the
un-naturalistic Renaissance drama—scotches this idea from the
start. And since such things as the coarse jests of the servants in
plays like *La Reconnue* do fit easily into verse, the theory cannot
be justified in practical terms either. However, in the Renaissance
context, it is evidently another attempt to achieve decorum, to
put the appropriate kind of speech into the mouth of the appropriate kind of person. Shakespeare indeed followed the same
principle of decorum in his use of verse and prose: in those
tragedies where comic passages appear in the mouth of lower-
class characters, those passages are in prose against a background
of verse for the rest of the play:

> MACBETH. To know my deed, 'twere best not know myself.
> > (*Knocking within*)
> Wake Duncan with thy knocking! I would thou
> > could'st!
> > (*Enter a porter. Knocking within*)
> PORTER. Here's a knocking indeed! If a man were porter of
> hell-gate, he should have old turning the key. (*Knocking*)
> Knock, knock, knock. Who's there, i' the name of Beelzebub?
> > (*Macbeth*, II. ii–iii)

Effective though these changes of poetic medium according to
speaker may be, they are of course not essential to the theatre:
Jonson's *The Alchemist* is entirely in verse whoever is speaking,
whether Sir Epicure Mammon with his complex rhetoric or the
officers and neighbours with their rapid exchanges in the fifth
Act.

Nevertheless, these theories, combined with the examples of
the various models, probably in fact determined the comic

---

[1] Preface to François d'Amboise, *Ancien Théâtre français*, v. 2–3.

practice in France. One may wonder only why the universally admired model, Terence, with his long senarii, was not imitated in this respect from the very beginning.

Monologues and asides

The monologues and asides in these plays, like the prologues and epilogues, provide a relationship with the audience. They may be compared with the chorus in tragedy, which inherited from the Greeks and Seneca the function of representing, to some extent, the audience's or the common people's point of view. The chorus, often composed of non-aristocrats, commenting on an action over which they had little or no power, provided a link between the characters in the play and the audience. A further link existed in the soliloquy. Both, however, remained on the further side of the boundary of illusion: in tragedy, neither chorus nor soliloquy would contain any direct allusion to the audience, or address it as 'vous'. Sédécie in *Les Juifves* may address Jehovah, but not the audience.

In comedy, monologues and asides have a comparable but more direct function. The aside, rare in tragedy, is common in the comedies, and by its very nature is a direct confidence made to the audience, unheard by the other characters. The soliloquy in tragedy by its nature admits the audience's presence, but the aside in comedy makes positive use of the audience and sometimes explicitly addresses it. Asides and monologues in, say, nineteenth-century melodrama are used to stir the audience's emotions; here the appeal is generally intellectual rather than emotional, but the procedure is the same.

In *Les Ébahis*, Grévin uses nineteen monologues and fifteen asides or groups of asides—a large number for a not particularly long play. Some are used for exposition, but not tiresomely so. Only once does a speaker ever address the audience directly (Julien in II. iii: 'Vous le [Panthaleone] verrez tantost vanter, / Tantost élever ses beaux faicts'), but there are questions and phrases such as 'Pensez que . . .' which are what we call rhetorical.

They are most remarkable for their quantity. There is not a single dialogue which is not flanked or interrupted by a monologue or an aside. A typical grouping is a monologue, followed by an aside, followed by a dialogue, thus:

LE GENTILHOMME. [monologue:]
      . . . Il faut sçavoir donner le tour
      A chacun: Et dieu sçait comment
      Ell' font espargne de serment,
      Pour mieux paslier leur deffaicte.
      [aside:]
      Mais voicy venir ma tendrette:
      Je croy qu'ell' est bien asseurée,
      A la voir tant délibérée;
      Il la fault avoir à la chaulde.

CLAUDE.   Dieu vous gard, Monsieur.

LE GENTILHOMME.   Dieu gard, Claude.
           (*Les Ébahis*, III. ii)

Many different combinations are possible; for instance, in the same play III. v begins with a monologue by Gérard, followed by a dialogue *aside* between Julien and Marion. The important point is that both monologue and asides are accepted as a more normal part of the dramatic structure than they generally are today.

Les Contents and *Les Néapolitaines* have typical groupings of the same kind, but in these plays it is more frequent to have a monologue followed by dialogue, without the aside. *Les Contents* as a whole includes only four asides or groups of them. Typically, a dialogue will not begin or end without being ushered in or out by a monologue, thus:

RODOMONT. Hé, mes amis, ayez pitié de moy!

SERGENT. Nous ne pouvons. C'est trop presché! Sus, sus, menons-le dessous les bras comme une mariée!

RODOMONT. Ha, Dieu, que je suis miserable! Au lieu d'aller fiancer ma maistresse, l'on me fait espouser une prison!

BASILE. [who, unobserved, has seen Rodomont carried off]
J'ay eu du plaisir pour plus de dix mille frans de voir ce
fendeur de naseaux si empesché au millieu de ces sergens . . .

(Les Contents, III. ii–iii)

In *Les Néapolitaines*, Gaster has six monologues and takes part in
six dialogues; Loys has five of each.

The fondness for asides and monologues is part of a whole
style of acting in the Renaissance: it was a style natural in some
ways, but exaggerated in others, and in it these easily over-acted
pieces of dramatic convention are not out of place. In theory,
they can be effective by their rarity. But in these comedies, they
are so frequent that they must be accepted as part of a fuller
convention: not a sudden effective exception, but part of the
essence of the play.

The monologues fall into recognizable patterns, by their form
and by their subject. Formally they stand at focal points of the
plot; at the beginning of acts or at points of tension or realiza-
tion. Thus in *Les Contents* again, Thomas's monologue about his
determination to make Rodomont pay begins Act III. And
Eustache's monologue about his detachment from Geneviève is
structurally important because it leaves the way clear for Basile.
Their subjects are regularly the same: to the lover's lament we
may add the young girl's lament, the valet's cynical comments,
and so on.

The asides represent one of the most exaggerated conventions
of these plays. They imply, of course, that the character speaking
is not heard by the others, and often indeed not even seen. Sometimes this leads to flat improbability. Here is the beginning of
the third scene of the third Act of *Les Corrivaux*, in which four
short monologues are followed by three asides:

CLAUDE. Puis que je ne voy plus personne en la rue il est
temps de faire le signe que j'ai promis à Filadelfe.

ALIZON. Puis que Claude et Fremin s'en sont allez, il faut
que j'aille bailler l'assignation à Euvertre.

CLAUDE. J'ay desja ouvert l'huis de derriere par où ils doyvent
entrer.

ALIZON. Je vien tout à point de trouver nostre huys de derriere deverouillé par je ne sçay qui.

CLAUDE. Qu'est-ce que j'oy parler derriere moy? Hà c'est Alizon, ceste vieille diablesse. Que le diable face maintenant une anatomie de sa cervelle: elle me gastera tout.

ALIZON. Ne voye-je pas là Claude? Hò bon gré en ait ma vie, il me destourbera.

CLAUDE. Si faut-il trouver façon de m'en depestrer vistement. Vien ça, que fais-tu icy?

The artificial convention implies an exaggerated kind of acting, associated today more with melodrama than with comedy.

The patterns of delivery, then, fall naturally into a small number of recognized kinds: prologues and epilogues, monologues, asides—and, of course, normal dialogue. The patterns form a convention. But there is more variety and less stiffness in their use, particularly in their many combinations, than there is in the corresponding conventions of French Renaissance tragedy: the opening monologues, the choruses, the stichomythia, the numbers of *sententiae*. Tragedy achieves a certain formality with them, but too often at the cost of stiffness, a fault which can seldom be laid at the door of the comic writers.

CONCLUSION

THE comedies of Jodelle, Grévin, Belleau, and La Taille are of a kind, sharing certain features of construction in such a way that they are unique in the history of comedy. All written by students of the University of Paris within some ten years, they have a family likeness. They blend the subject-matter of the native genres with the forms of classical comedy in a way which is not found in any other literature. Moral indignation is absent, so is profound characterization, but the peculiar blend that they have adopted gives them a liveliness that amply compensates. They are successful entertainment.

The later plays too are successful entertainment. But from Larivey onwards the Italian comedies are taken as a new model, and more wholeheartedly, so that the peculiarly French characteristics of *Les Contents* or *Les Néapolitaines* are fewer, found in varieties of speech and imagery rather than in characters or plot. *Les Ramoneurs*, as late as about 1624, is much more French in every way: in its lively style, its references to Paris where it takes place, its French characters, its use of French farce-actors—and it is regrettable that so lively a play should have been (as far as we know) the last of its kind, supplanted only some five years later by the new comic style of Corneille.

The décor for the plays seems to remain constant throughout the Renaissance, with some elaborations—but not basic changes—around the late 1570s. It consists, without exception, of a central area supposed to be a city street, flanked by a number of town houses provided with doors and windows and some of whose interiors are *praticable*. The *internal* evidence of the plays remains constant, and is supported by a certain amount of external, mostly pictorial evidence: the farces show a primitive neutral area; Serlio's 'comic scene' shows a décor of the kind needed (though more elaborate); the Italians vary, but in general support the pattern; while Mahelot, in a décor such as that for Rotrou's *Les Ménechmes*, corresponds entirely.

I have written at length about the conventions of the plays. These conventions, of plot-structure, of character, and of speech, remain generally constant through eighty years, despite the important arrival of the Italians and their adoption as models, and despite the forty-year gap between *Les Néapolitaines* and *Les Ramoneurs*. Troterel and Godard, within that gap, show that the same conventions continued to be accepted. During the whole of the period, a host of other writings of the most miscellaneous kinds show that the conventions were indeed continually known and used. They could be taken for granted by political and religious satirists, by literary theorists, by writers of dialogue, by artists, and by musicians. In the theatre, they are of course a means of relationship between author and audience: the author uses the technique of writing variations upon a norm. Braggarts and valets, for instance, are two accepted kinds of character: to mix the two, as Godard does in *Les Déguisés*, is to create a new effect. Another form of relationship with the audience is for a character to address us directly: when, for instance, Messire Jean tells us that Eugène is growing careless and will find himself in trouble—and the trouble then in fact arrives.

The constant recurrence of the conventions of course offends a certain twentieth-century idea of originality. But that idea is irrelevant. My aim here has been to show that in French Renaissance comedy, as in the lyric poetry of the time, variations upon a norm are used for the sake of the ways in which the variations are handled; to reveal not uniformity but variety. The principle has been well stated by Roland Barthes:

> Structuralement, le sens ne naît point par répétition mais par différence, en sorte qu'un terme rare, dès lors qu'il est saisi dans un système d'exclusions et de relations, signifie tout autant qu'un terme fréquent. . . . A partir de combien de tragédies aurais-je le droit de 'généraliser' une situation racinienne? Cinq, six, dix?[1]

[1] *Critique et vérité* (Paris, 1966), pp. 66-7.

Comedy in the French Renaissance is a self-conscious genre in that the elements of its speeches show a constant, and unusual, awareness of the audience. Prologues and epilogues lead the audience into and out of the play. Throughout the action, asides and monologues remind them that they are at the play. We find this self-consciousness less often in tragedy, in English Renaissance comedy, in Molière, or in modern comedy. Yet in another way, the French Renaissance genre stands aside from the audience, giving them comparatively few of the topical references that can be most effective in comedy—comparatively few, that is, compared with the farces and related genres, for instance the monologue *Le Franc-archer de Bagnolet*, which satirizes the corps created by Charles VII in 1448, or compared with English Renaissance comedy which is full of them. In France, the comic world is separate from the audience's world.[1] We may ask whether the comedies are relevant to their times in a more general way as many of the tragedies were claimed to be (Garnier said that his *Porcie* was 'propre pour y voir despeinctes les calamitez de ce temps'), but probably the relevance does lie only in details, as when Belleau refers to the sieges of Le Havre or Poitiers. Social criticism is rare, found only in a few situations and characters like Jodelle's hedonistic churchman or Belleau's dissatisfied men of law. The principal aim of French Renaissance comedy was not moral teaching of any kind, but delight.

In the same period, the genre of tragedy takes to itself not only fixed conventions of expression, but fixed philosophical ideas. They are the neo-Stoic ideas of the mid-sixteenth century, ideas about man's power over fate and death, and excessive declaration of strength, from which lyric poetry had moved on, from which Montaigne had moved on. Still in Garnier and

---

[1] A change may have occurred about the mid century. On 4 December 1550 Sir John Masone reported from Blois that proclamations had been issued to restrain freedom of speech touching the French king and the Council, and wished that there were a similar restriction in England. 'They were wont in their farces to spare no man; but now they are bridled for that point' (Calendar of State Papers, Foreign Series, 1547–53, p. 63; quoted from Frances Yates, 'Contribution to the Study of the French Social Drama in the Sixteenth Century', unpublished thesis for the degree of M.A. (London, 1926), p. 7).

Montchrestien we find these same ideas. But comedy, by aiming rather at delight and by combining modern elements with classical ones, achieved an awareness of the theatre and a liveliness which are its own special virtues and which are still capable of delighting us today.

APPENDIX A

Synopses of the plays

Jodelle, *L'Eugène*

I. Eugène (an abbé) and Messire Jean (his chaplain) discuss the luxury of a churchman's life. Eugène has married Alix off to Guillaume, *le bon lourdaut*, but is now worried lest Guillaume should realize why: namely, that Eugène might the more easily enjoy her favours. — Messire Jean, alone, reveals himself as Eugène's parasite, and confirms that Eugène is growing careless. — Guillaume and Alix display their respective simplicity and easy morals.

II. Florimond has returned to Paris from the wars; he is an old flame of Alix, and is anxious to renew the relationship. He and his follower Arnault discuss Paris, the wars, and learning, before Arnault goes off to find Alix. — Hélène, Eugène's sister, alone: she had herself been fond of Florimond, but he had been discouraged by her lack of apparent response. She tells Eugène of Florimond's arrival; he is, rightly, apprehensive.

III. Arnault returns with the news that Alix is married, and why. Florimond is furious; he has some furniture in Alix's house, and decides he will at least first reclaim this. — Messire Jean recovers from the tumultuous arrival of Arnault in Alix's house, which he reports to Eugène and Hélène. No solution occurs. — Florimond beats Alix, and with Arnault oversees the removal of his furniture.

IV. Guillaume, puzzled by the whole thing, goes to see Eugène. Matthieu, Guillaume's creditor, arrives and demands payment. They all, with Hélène, go into Eugène's house to discuss the matter. — Florimond decides to kill Eugène. Eugène realizes the danger and all the problems and retires alone to think.

V. Eugène has thought of the solutions. Hélène shall be reconciled with Florimond, and Matthieu is to be offered a benefice for one of his sons. Both of these are carried out, and Guillaume is content to share Alix with Eugène.

Grévin, *La Trésorière*

I. Loys (a gentleman) discusses with Richard (his valet) the progress of his love for Constante, wife of the Trésorier, a Government official. The Trésorier's impending absence may result in some success. Richard marvels at his master's folly in loving so inconstant a woman. — Richard on his master's behalf offers the Trésorier interest to obtain payment of a sum owed. — Marie, Constante's chambermaid, is overheard by Richard as she reflects that Loys takes second place to the Protenotaire in her mistress's affections.

II. The Protenotaire (probably a legal official[1]) discusses with Boniface (his valet) the progress of his love for Constante. The Protenotaire is short of money; Boniface promises to use his ingenuity to obtain some. — Boniface overhears Constante promising Richard a rendezvous for Loys; and then succeeds in borrowing 150 *écus* from Constante herself. — The Trésorier tries to borrow money from Sulpice. — Marie promises herself the pleasure of returning Boniface's advances.

III. Loys reflects on the profit motive for human actions, and on Constante. Richard informs him that the Trésorier will produce the money; then attempts, unsuccessfully, to seduce Marie. Constante scolds her for chattering to Richard, then herself reflects, strangely, on the inconstancy of men. — The Protenotaire appears, and Constante lets him into the house—but Richard sees this and vows that his master shall have vengeance.

IV. Richard has told Loys what he has seen. Loys reflects bitterly, and interrogates Richard to be sure. — The Trésorier and Sulpice arrive; they and Loys and Richard and an extra supporter Thomas all try to enter the house, and in the end break the door down. — Marie emerges and reports that the Protenotaire was caught *in flagrante delicto*; then Boniface, who had escaped by flight, joins her.

V. Sulpice and the Trésorier attempt to calm Loys and to prevent him from making the affair public; Loys agrees on condition that he receives back the money that he has given to Constante, and that the two quarters' money paid him by the

[1] Cf. Grévin, *Théâtre complet*, ed. L. Pinvert (Paris, 1922), p. 354.

Trésorier shall be null and void. — The Protenotaire and Boniface decide to keep the money lent them by Constante. — Marie also is content, and plans more *amours*.

Grévin, *Les Ébahis*

I. Josse alone: his wife Agnès left him three years ago for a lover, taking his money, and it seems that she has died. He is now engaged to Madelon, Gérard's daughter. Marion, *lavandière*, determines to prevent him; for although he claims to be vigorous enough for love, he wears a fur coat, has catarrh, a cold, and a cough. Antoine, his servant, allies himself with Marion.

II. L'Advocat, in love with Madelon, laments her engagement to Josse. He rejects his cousin the Gentilhomme's advice to turn to other women. With Julien his servant and the Gentilhomme, he plans to try to secure Madelon for himself. Panthaleone, yet another suitor, makes a brief appearance serenading her. Marion plans to borrow Josse's clothes from Antoine for L'Advocat so that he may easily enter Gérard's house. Madelon laments.

III. Claude, *maquerelle*: the trade is not what it was. She has Agnès in her house, and promises her to the Gentilhomme. L'Advocat, disguised as Josse, goes into Gérard's house; but immediately Gérard appears.

IV. L'Advocat emerges, full of joy at his success, and avoids Gérard (who had seen him through the keyhole without penetrating the disguise). Josse prepares to go to Madelon; Antoine returns with the clothes only just in time. He sets out; Gérard taxes him with his amorous exploits, which he indignantly denies, from which Gérard concludes that he now wishes to repudiate Madelon. Madelon fears for the future, and Marion consoles her. L'Advocat tells his cousin of his success; Julien goes off to find similar game.

V. Panthaleone is serenading again, until Julien interrupts. Josse arrives to fight Gérard, but Julien puts all the blame for the seduction on Panthaleone. Agnès arrives with the Gentilhomme; Josse recognizes her, while Panthaleone also has a claim on her, having kept her in Lyons for three years. Josse is forced to take her back, Panthaleone is chased off, while a marriage between L'Advocat and Madelon will be arranged.

Belleau, *La Reconnue*

I. Janne the maid, then Maistre Jehan the clerk, complain of their hard work and of the household. Madame appears; her sourness justifies some at least of their complaints. We learn that Monsieur, her husband, is courting Antoinette, a ward in their house, who, however, has an affection for a captain. Antoinette laments. Maistre Jehan, who had gone to the *palais de justice*, returns and inveighs against it.

II. L'Amoureux, an advocate like Monsieur, delivers a monologue on the torments of love. Potiron, his valet, arrives; we learn that Monsieur for his own ends is planning to marry Antoinette off to Maistre Jehan. Potiron and Janne tell Maistre Jehan of this.

III. Monsieur praises the virtues of love and laments his own wife's sourness. He tries to appease her; tells her that the captain is dead; and attempts to persuade her of the virtues of his plan — which L'Amoureux, Potiron, and Janne plan to thwart.

IV. Antoinette laments the captain's death and tries to reconcile herself to the idea of Maistre Jehan as a husband. Janne is ordered to buy food for the engagement dinner that evening. Madame and her neighbour discuss the proposed marriage. Monsieur hopes all will go off without mishap. L'Amoureux on love; Potiron tells him that the captain is dead.

V. The captain arrives with his valet Bernard, and they go into the house. Janne reports. Then the Gentilhomme de Poictou also arrives and goes in. Maistre Jehan comes out, then L'Amoureux; we learn that the Gentilhomme de Poictou is Antoinette's father, that a marriage has been arranged between Antoinette and L'Amoureux, that Monsieur is consequently thwarted, that L'Amoureux has been given a post as *conseiller* and the captain an option on a spare niece.

La Taille, *Les Corrivaux*

I. Restitue confides her woes to her nurse: not only is she pregnant by Filadelfe, but Filadelfe has transferred his affections to Fleurdelys. The nurse, taking a practical view, suggests that she try to go to the country to dispose of the child. — Filadelfe, waiting for news from Claude, a servant in Fleurdelys's house, justifies his infidelity by the irresistible power of love. Claude arrives; he has arranged for Filadelfe to enter the house within the hour, and he will signal with a torch when the time comes. Gillet, Filadelfe's valet, declares himself to be more down to earth than 'ces amoureux transis'. Filadelfe gives instructions for the coming adventure.

II. Euvertre, too, is planning an entry into Fleurdelys's house. Alizon, the other servant, arranges to signal to him with a distaff when the time comes. Her master Fremin, on his way to town on important business, urges her to take care of Fleurdelys. His own relationship with Alizon seems equivocal.

III. Jaqueline, Restitue's mother, agrees to let her go to the country, as she is unwell, but has meanwhile summoned a doctor. Claude and Alizon both appear at the same spot at the same moment to give their respective signals; they squabble, and Claude leaves. But now there are noises off in Fleurdelys's house, and the doctor has given the game away in Restitue's. Enter Gillet, then Felippes (Euvertre's father's servant), from whom we learn that the two young men both entered Fleurdelys's house, that there was fighting, and that the sergeants of the watch arrived and carried them and Claude off to prison.

IV. Benard, Filadelfe's father, arrives from Metz with his gluttonous valet Felix. Jaqueline heaps reproaches on him for his son's behaviour, and his son's attempt on Fleurdelys's honour is also revealed. Fremin and Benard meet; we learn that Fleurdelys is in fact Benard's daughter, lost at the siege of Metz ten years ago and taken in by Fremin.

V. Enter Gerard, Euvertre's father; with the two other men (Fremin and Benard) a solution is worked out: Euvertre shall marry Fleurdelys, and Filadelfe Restitue. They go off with Philandre, the master of the watch. The three valets, by now drunk, provide some light relief. After some frightening of the young men with the prospect of the law, the solutions are agreed and, moreover, Benard will marry Jaqueline.

Larivey, *Les Esprits*

I. Severin's brother Hilaire, since he and Elizabet his wife are childless, has brought up Fortuné, one of Severin's sons. Because of Severin's miserliness, his daughter Laurence cannot find a match, nor has Urbain his other son the allowance a young man should have. — Fortuné and his servant Frontin: Fortuné is in love with Apoline, a girl who is in a convent, though she has not made her profession. — Ruffin, *maquereau*, promises Urbain his Feliciane, on payment of ten *écus*. — Frontin can give Fortuné no good news of his Apoline. Meanwhile Ruffin has brought Feliciane.

II. Desiré is in love with Laurence; Frontin can offer him no good news either. Severin arrives; Frontin, to prevent his going in and discovering Urbain and Feliciane, persuades him that the house is full of ghosts. Severin goes off, first hiding his purse (with 2,000 *écus* in it) as he does not wish to carry it around. Desiré, who was hidden, sees him and takes the *écus*, putting pebbles in their place. Severin returns with Frontin, who promises to find a sorcerer to exorcize the ghosts; Severin checks that the purse is still in its hiding-place.

III. M. Josse the sorcerer, bribed by Frontin, conjures the ghosts: Frontin, pretending to be one of them, takes the ring from the blindfolded Severin's finger as a sign that they have left the house. Feliciane and Urbain go into Hilaire's house which is close by. Severin sends M. Josse away; Ruffin almost gives the plot away to Severin, but is prevented by Frontin. Severin discovers the theft of the coins.

IV. Hilaire tries to dissuade Fortuné from his affair with Apoline. Fortuné tells Hilaire of Feliciane's honourable parentage; and sends Pasquette, *servante*, to get news of Apoline. Gerard, Feliciane's father, arrives in town. Pasquette gives away to Hilaire the fact that Apoline has had a child.

V. Gerard has heard the news of Feliciane, but Ruffin assures him that a marriage with Urbain may be possible. They go to see Severin, who is interested in nothing but his purse; and then look for Feliciane at Hilaire's house. — Hilaire has been to the convent and arranged a marriage between Fortuné and Apoline.

Meanwhile, also by Hilaire's intervention, the marriages between Urbain and Feliciane and Desiré and Laurence need only Severin's consent. The purse is produced, financial arrangements made that satisfy Severin, and the marriages settled.

Turnèbe, *Les Contents*

I. Louise and her daughter Geneviève are on their way to church very early in order to avoid Basile and Rodomont, who in Louise's eyes are both unwelcome suitors for Geneviève. Nivelet, Rodomont's lackey, sees them go by, then Rodomont arrives. They overhear Basile, with his servant Antoine, planning to enter Geneviève's house disguised as Eustache. Basile persuades Françoise, *vieille femme*, to try to win Geneviève over to the idea and fix a definite time—which she does. Nivelet plans to see that his master seizes this chance to enter the house disguised as Eustache before Basile does.

II. Girard wishes to arrange the engagement of his son Eustache to Geneviève, but Eustache is reluctant because he knows that she favours Basile. Françoise succeeds in putting him off still further. Rodomont borrows a scarlet costume from him, identical to the one which Basile has already borrowed from him. Françoise tells Basile what she has done.

III. Rodomont, disguised, is seized by three *sergents* for debt to Thomas, a merchant, before he has a chance to enter Geneviève's house. Basile, also disguised, sees him hauled off. Saucisson, *maquereau*, bringing Alix for Eustache's pleasure, briefly mistakes Basile for Eustache. Basile goes in, leaving Antoine outside, who too late sees Louise returning home early. She goes in, looks through the keyhole, takes Basile for Eustache, locks them in, and goes off to look for Girard. Meanwhile, Antoine, with Perrette, Geneviève's maid, gets Basile out of the locked room through a window.

IV. Basile fetches Alix and puts her in his place in the borrowed costume to deceive Louise; on the way they pass Thomas (who is in fact Alix's husband). Rodomont has been freed. He is still dressed as Eustache (and is briefly taken for him by Girard), but decides it is too late to try to enter Geneviève's house. Louise taxes Girard with his son's supposed attack on Geneviève's honour; but Eustache explains to him that it was Basile. Eventually Louise unlocks the door, but finds only Alix with her daughter.

V. Françoise reports to Basile that Louise's latest idea is to marry her daughter to Rodomont. Geneviève at her window, and Basile below, exchange declarations of love. Rodomont, hearing that Basile has had Geneviève's virginity, consequently refuses her hand when it is offered to him. Louise realizes the truth, gives in, and consents to the marriage of Basile and Geneviève.

D'Amboise, *Les Néapolitaines*

I. Augustin is in love with the widow Angélique. He talks to Beta, her servant, who he hopes will help him to her favours. — Dom Dieghos, a Spanish braggart in exile from Naples, is in love with her too; in which Gaster, a parasite, encourages him. Gaster, alone, on his profession of parasite.

II. Gaster, too, attempts to employ Beta, for his master; she plays for time, giving him a promise for tomorrow. Augustin overhears, but she placates him with the promise of an immediate rendezvous. — Ambroise, Augustin's father, disapproves of the affair with the widow; though he fails to get definite confirmation of it out of Loys, his son's servant, he nevertheless decides to cut his son's allowance to the bare minimum. — Augustin is overjoyed at success with Angélique. To counter his father's decision, Loys suggests he turn to his friend Camille for money, and also for help if necessary against Dieghos.

III. Camille agrees, and they plan to go to Angélique's after lunch. Dieghos, rejected, goes off with Gaster to lunch. In the afternoon, Augustin and Camille arrive first at Angélique's; but Angélique is forced to invent a story for getting them out of the house when Dieghos and Gaster arrive too. She also succeeds in putting off Dieghos and Gaster until the next day. Virginie, her supposed daughter, laments: her father lost all his possessions through participating in the rebellion at Naples, and has died in Paris leaving her alone with Angélique, who is not in fact her mother. Meanwhile, Camille has fallen in love with Virginie, and plans how he may win her.

IV. Corneille, Virginie's servant, laments to Augustin and Angélique; Camille has succeeded in making his way into the house and seducing Virginie. Augustin suggests they try to persuade him to marry her, and goes off to find him. Meanwhile Loys has found his own pleasures.

V. Marc-Aurel, a jeweller from Naples, admires Paris. Meeting Camille, he is able to tell him what Virginie's family is, and moreover that by coincidence Camille has become heir to the lost fortunes of that family. Camille decides he will marry her, and with Augustin goes off to see her. Loys follows with Marc-Aurel. Dieghos is furious—until Louppes, a messenger, tells him that he is free to return to Naples, where a marriage has been arranged for him. Gaster decides he must look for a new *vache à lait*; a marriage will be arranged between Virginie and Camille; and Beta and Gaster go off to the engagement banquet.

Perrin, *Les Écoliers*

I. Maclou has heard that his son Sobrin, instead of studying, is spending time and money on a love-affair, and tries unsuccessfully to obtain the truth from his son's valet Finet. — Grassette, talking to her servant Babille, reveals that she is not interested in Sobrin, but in the less wealthy Corbon. — Friquet, a neighbour, reveals to Marin that his daugher Grassette is entertaining lovers.

II. Sobrin, against Friquet's advice, declares that he will pursue his love for Grassette. Finet, on his behalf, begins to win Babille over. — Corbon declares that he prefers learning, which can raise his social status, to amorous pursuits. — Maclou warns his son that he will not support him if he does not concentrate on his studies.

III. Babille speaks for Sobrin to Grassette, but without success; this she reports to Finet. Finet reports it to Sobrin, who is still determined; Finet promises to think again. — Marin suspects Babille of aiding her mistress's *amours*. — Finet meets Corbon and begins to plan in that direction.

IV. It is agreed between Sobrin, Corbon, and Finet that a rendezvous shall be arranged between Corbon and Grassette, but that it shall be Sobrin, disguised and at night, who shall keep it. In return, Corbon is to have the benefice that Sobrin controls. — Finet arranges the rendezvous with Babille. — Sobrin, disguised as a peasant and speaking in dialect, is admitted by Marin to the cellar. — Corbon expresses his pleasure. Sobrin emerges and recounts his success to Finet. — Friquet and Marin have discovered what has happened, and Maclou too learns it from Marin.

V. Sobrin and Finet gain Friquet to their side by threats and promises, and he persuades both Marin and Maclou to favour the marriage of Sobrin and Grassette. He reports this to Sobrin; and the marriage is arranged.

Godard, *Les Déguisés*

I. Grégoire laments: his wife has died, his household expenses are rising, while Prouventard is demanding a sum of money that Grégoire holds in trust for him. — Olivier alone, then with Maudolé, his servant: he is in love with Louise, Grégoire's daughter.

II. Prouventard boasts to his lackey Vadupié of his military exploits, and that he will soon recover the money. — Grégoire decides to offer him Louise's hand instead of the money; he tells Louise, then makes the offer—but Prouventard indignantly refuses it. — Maudolé discovers that Grégoire needs a new valet, and suggests that Olivier take the job.

III. Olivier and Maudolé exchange clothes. Olivier offers his services to Grégoire and is accepted. Maudolé brags in Olivier's clothes; Prouventard at first is terrified, but discovering he is merely a valet, with Vadupié's aid chases him off. — Nicole, Louise's servant, advises her that Prouventard would be a poor match; meanwhile Olivier is making a good impression. Maudolé in vain demands his clothes back. Olivier on love. He declares himself to Louise, who however registers only alarm.

IV. On Nicole's suggestion, Louise now encourages Olivier. — Grégoire sends Olivier to Prouventard, but Olivier suggests as a better match than Prouventard a rich young man whom he knows. Maudolé, impersonating Olivier, is to be that rich young man, a scheme which Louise approves. Maudolé carries out his part, but makes the slip of promising to fetch his father, Pierre

Galland, who does not in fact live in the town. Olivier and Maudolé, by blackmailing Passetrouvant, a passer-by, with attempted robbery, persuade him to impersonate Pierre Galland; this he successfully does.

V. Pierre Galland himself appears unexpectedly in town, and by coincidence meets Grégoire. Passetrouvant still maintains himself to be Pierre Galland, and tempers rise. Maudolé appears, still impersonating Olivier. The confusion increases, then is gradually cleared as Maudolé reveals the truth. The marriage of Olivier and Louise is eventually agreed, Prouventard is given an option on a spare sister of Olivier, and an engagement dinner is prepared.

Anon. (Hardy?), *Les Ramoneurs*

I. Le Capitaine Scanderbec boasts to his valet Galaffre; and instructs his sister Diane to stay quietly at home and see no one. — Philippes discusses with his valet Martin his love for Diane; then talks to the pedant Bonarsius; Martin wins to their side the fruit-seller Dame Bonne, who begins to win Diane over. The Captain returns. Philippes serenades Diane, but the Captain appears, and Philippes is forced to leave.

II. Madelon (*courtisane*) discusses with Dame Claude (*maquerelle*) the possibility of marrying the Captain. Negotiations are begun. — Philippes and Martin again turn to Dame Bonne, who takes a letter to Diane; but the Captain again interrupts, even though Philippes succeeds in chasing him into the house. Diane gives Martin a note for his master.

III. The Captain gives orders that the house is to be cleaned; Diane is to engage some chimney-sweeps. These are Philippes and Martin, who send Galaffre to fetch more wine and carry off Diane disguised as a sweep to Claude's house. The Captain returns to find her gone. Bonarsius, hidden, has seen them.

IV. Maistre Nicolas, Madelon's father, has arrived in Paris. — Bonarsius bribes Claude to smuggle him into Diane's room that night; but Martin overhears the arrangement. — The Captain is determined to recover Diane. Madelon is in the hands of justice for debt; she goes off with the Captain and the *sergents*. — Martin, unknown to Claude, has set a prostitute in Diane's place, and

Claude as agreed lets in Bonarsius. Martin's and Philippes's student friends, disguised as the watch, surprise him there, but for the promise of twelve *écus* let him go.

V. The Captain and Madelon are free and searching for Diane and Philippes. — The Captain's rich uncle Dubuisson has met Madelon's father Maistre Nicolas. — Claude gives Galaffre the word to follow Martin, thus setting the Captain on Diane's track. — Dubuisson and M. Nicolas find Madelon, who has by now married the Captain. — The Captain has found Philippes and Diane; eventually both the marriages are approved.

Corneille, *Mélite*

I. Eraste declares to his friend Tirsis his love for Mélite. Tirsis is sceptical about marriage, declaring that if he marries, it will be for financial advantage. Eraste, to change his friend's opinion, introduces him to Mélite—and succeeds only too well. — Tirsis finds his sister Cloris with her lover Philandre, and hints at his new love.

II. Eraste regrets that he ever introduced Tirsis to Mélite, the more so since Mélite herself now shows signs of her growing affection; and vows to take action. — Tirsis reads to his sister a sonnet in praise of Mélite which he has written, ostensibly for Eraste. Cloris sees the truth and encourages him. — Eraste has written a false love-letter, ostensibly from Mélite to Philandre, who however refuses to leave his Cloris, despite Eraste's encouragement. — Mélite indicates to Tirsis that she returns his love, and Tirsis gives her the sonnet.

III. The vain Philandre, flattered at Mélite's supposed affection for him, prepares to return it. He shows Tirsis two further false letters, these also supposedly from Mélite to Philandre. Tirsis, alone, laments. He shows the letters to Cloris, who tries to console him by pointing out Mélite's inconstant character; and herself determines to leave the inconstant Philandre. She shows Philandre that she has the letters, and says that she intends to show them to Mélite as a proof of Philandre's indiscretion.

IV. Mélite's nurse tries to persuade her to encourage the rich Eraste rather than Tirsis. — Cloris shows Mélite the letters, but she denounces them as forgeries. Lisis (a friend of Tirsis) announces Tirsis's death, at which Mélite immediately faints. — Eraste, rejoicing at Tirsis's death, hears that Mélite is dead also, and falls into a fit of madness, imagining that he too is dead. — Philandre, in search of his rival Tirsis, hears of his and Mélite's death, and of the falsity of the letters, from the mad Eraste. — Lisis reveals that his announcement was false, designed to test Mélite's affections.

V. Mélite's nurse brings Eraste back to sanity. — Philandre tries, and fails, to obtain Cloris's pardon. Tirsis and Mélite, now together, consider her excessively hard. Eraste confesses and is pardoned; and an attachment between him and Cloris is begun. The nurse speaks a closing monologue.

APPENDIX B

Grévin's La Maubertine

La Maubertine is possibly a third comedy by Grévin. Pinvert supposed it to be identical with *La Trésorière* (Grévin, *Théâter complet* (Paris, 1922), pp. 353–4; *Jacques Grévin* (Paris, 1899), pp. 172–3); M. Lebègue considers that it is probably rather a separate play (*Tableau*, p. 305). The evidence is as follows.

Grévin tells us that he wrote a comedy called *La Maubertine*, referring (in the preface 'Au lecteur' to *Les Ébahis* and *La Trésorière*) to 'ceux qui ont veu la Maubertine première Comédie que je mis en jeu, et que j'avoye bien délibéré te donner, si elle ne m'eust esté desrobée'. It is certainly possible that this was in fact an earlier version of *La Trésorière*, especially as the action of *La Trésorière* takes place 'non loing de la place Maubert' (*La Trésorière*, prologue).

It is true, also, that *La Trésorière* was first written for a performance in January 1559 (O.S. 1558) and not performed until February of that year, so that a *remaniement* in between is quite conceivable; a heading to the play reads:

Ceste comédie fut faicte par le commandement du roi Henry II pour servir aux nopces de madame Claude, duchesse de Lorraine, mais pour quelques empeschemens différée; et depuis mise en jeu à Paris au collège de Beauvais . . . le v. de fevrier M.D.LVIII.

It seems, too, that a complaint, perhaps the cause of such a *remaniement*, had been lodged by some ladies of the Maubert quarter:

> . . . ceste plaincte, qui fut faicte
> N'aguère encontre le Poëte,
> Pour la rancune et le soucy
> Des dames de ce quartier cy.
> (*Les Ébahis*, prologue)

These are the arguments in favour of identifying *La Maubertine* with *La Trésorière*. But they are none of them conclusive: for instance, the Maubert quarter was a student quarter, so that two separate plays could quite naturally both be set there. And they are outweighed by one argument: that the one reference to *La Maubertine* occurs in the preface to *both La Trésorière* and *Les Ébahis*, exactly as though it were in fact a third play. Grévin specifically says there that he is *not* publishing *La Maubertine*, 'que j'avoye bien délibéré te donner, si elle ne m'eust esté desrobée'. If *La Trésorière* and *La Maubertine* were identical, or even different versions of the same play, this would not make good sense. It is more likely, therefore, that *La Maubertine* was a third comedy by Grévin.

BIBLIOGRAPHY

Arranged as follows:

1. Manuscripts.
2. Books printed before 1636 (except secondary sources).
3. Comedies supposed to have been printed, but now lost.
4. Other comedies supposed to have existed in manuscript, but now lost.
5. Modern editions.
6. Modern adaptations.
7. Secondary sources.

1. MANUSCRIPTS

ANON. [possibly ALEXANDRE HARDY], *Les Ramonneurs*. Bibliothèque de l'Arsenal, Fonds Rondel, MS. 194. Eighteenth-century hand. In addition, a nineteenth-century copy from this manuscript is in the library of the Société des Auteurs Dramatiques. Cf. *Les Ramonneurs,* ed. A. Gill (Paris, 1957), pp. xiii–xviii.

BAÏF, JEAN-ANTOINE DE, *L'Eunuque*. Bibliothèque Nationale, MS. F. Fr. 867. The manuscript contains only *L'Eunuque*, in a sixteenth-century hand, not Baïf's own, according to M. Augé-Chiquet, *Jean-Antoine de Baïf*, p. 185. 52 ff. Vellum-bound. Headed 'L'Eunuque de Terance par Bayf'. A note at the end adds 'Achevée Lendemain de Noël devant jour 1565'.

BRUNO, GIORDANO, *Il Candelaio*. Bibliothèque Nationale, MS. F. Fr. n.a. 2879, ff. 226–48ᵛ. A translation into French of Bruno's *Il Candelaio*, which was originally published in Paris in 1582 (cf. section 2 below), bound in with other manuscript copies of plays of varying dates. Probably early seventeenth-century hand. Headed simply 'Candelaio'. Not the same translation as that published as *Boniface et le pédant* in 1633 (cf. section 2 below).

GRÉVIN, JACQUES. Some 300 alterations in Grévin's hand in a copy of *Le Theatre de Jaques Grevin* (Paris, 1567), in the Musée Plantin-Moretus, Antwerp. Alterations probably made for a projected new edition, to be printed by Plantin, which never appeared. They possibly date from October 1567 when Grévin was at Antwerp. Cf. Plate I and L. Pinvert, *Jacques Grévin* (Paris, 1899), p. 64.

LARIVEY, PIERRE DE. The British Museum copy of *Les six premieres comedies* (Paris, 1579) (shelf-mark 163. b. 24–6, 28, 62), has a manuscript list of actors written on the list of dramatis personae of *Le Morfondu*. Late sixteenth- or more probably early seventeenth-century hand.

PERRIN, FRANÇOIS, *Les Escoliers*. Bibliothèque Nationale, MS. F. Fr. 9299, ff. 220–62ᵛ. One of a number of copies of plays in a nineteenth-century hand; according to the catalogue of the Bibliothèque Nationale, made by M. de Soleinne. Copied from the printed version in *Sichem ravisseur* (Paris, Guillaume Chaudière, 1589).

2. BOOKS PRINTED BEFORE 1636

(except secondary sources)

Location of the copy used is given; a complete list of known copies is not attempted.

AMBOISE, FRANÇOIS D', *Les Neapolitaines, comedie françoise fort facecieuse. Sur le subject d'une Histoire d'un Parisien, un Espagnol, et un Italien* (Paris, Abel l'Angelier, 1584). Privilege 2 December 1583. (Bibliothèque de l'Arsenal.) The Bibliothèque de l'Arsenal possesses two copies: (1) Fonds Rondel, Rf. 1239, title as above, privilege ends 'Donné à Paris le 2. Decembre, 1583. Par le Conseil'; (2) Ancien Fonds, 8º B.L. 14.478, title omits the word 'fort', which has necessitated re-setting the word 'facecieuse'; privilege ends 'Donné à Paris le 2. Decembre, 1583. signé Par le Conseil DE NEUF-VILLE'. No other apparent alterations. These are probably small alterations introduced by l'Angelier in the course of printing, rather than indications of a second impression. No copies other than these two are known.

ANDREINI DA PISTOIA, FRANCESCO, *Le bravure del capitano Spavento. Divise in molti ragionamenti In forma di Dialogo. Di Francesco Andreini da Pistoia, Comico geloso. Les Bravacheries du capitaine Spavente, divisees en plusieurs discours en forme de Dialogue. De François Andreini de Pistoie,* Comedien de la Compagnie des Jaloux. Traduictes par I. D. F. P. [Jacques de Fonteny Parisien] (Paris, David le Clerc, 1608). Privilege 31 March 1608. (Bibliothèque de l'Arsenal.) A translation of the first six of fifty-five dialogues published by Andreini in 1607: *Le bravure del capitano Spavento, divise in molti ragionamenti In Forma di Dialogo, di Francesco Andreini da Pistoia Comico Geloso* (Venice, Giacomo Antonio Somasco, 1607). (Bibliothèque de l'Arsenal.)

ANON., *Compositions de rhetorique de Mr. Don Arlequin . . . Imprimé delà le bout du monde* [Lyons, 1600 or 1601]. (Bibliothèque Nationale.)

—— *La Comédie de proverbes, pièce comique* (Paris, François Targa, 1633). (Bibliothèque Nationale.)

BAÏF, JEAN-ANTOINE DE, *Le Brave, comedie de Jan Antoine de Baif* (Paris, Robert Estienne, 1567). No privilege. (Bibliothèque de l'Arsenal.) Acted, according to the title-page, on Tuesday 28 January 1567 [N.S. 1568] in the Hôtel de Guise in the presence of the King. Includes 'les chants recitez entre les actes de la comedie', by Ronsard, Baïf, Desportes, Filleul, and Belleau; as there are *five* of them and five acts in the play, they may either have preceded or followed each act. They are in praise of the Royal Family and have no connection with the content of the play.

—— *Les Jeux* (Paris, Lucas Breyer, 1572). (Bibliothèque de l'Arsenal.) [A manuscript note in the Arsenal copy has changed MDLXXII to MDLXXIII.] Includes *Le Brave*, ff. 89–160; and *L'Eunuque*, ff. 161–208. The 'chants' included in the 1567 edition of *Le Brave* are not given here.

BELLEAU, RÉMY, *Les Œuvres poetiques de Remy Belleau* (Paris, Gilles Gilles [or Mamert Patisson], 1578). (British Museum—a Gilles Gilles copy.) Contains, vol. ii, ff. 110–53, *La Reconnue, comedie. Par Remy Belleau.*

—— *Les Œuvres poetiques de Remy Belleau* (Paris, Mamert Patisson [or Gilles Gilles], 1585). (Bibliothèque de l'Arsenal—a Mamert Patisson copy.) Contains, vol. ii, ff. 111v–54, *La Reconnue, comedie. Par Remy Belleau.*

—— *Les Œuvres poetiques de Remy Belleau* (Lyons, Thomas Soubron, 1592). (British Museum.) Contains, vol. ii, ff. 111v–54, *La Reconnue, comedie. Par Remy Belleau.*

—— *Les Œuvres poetiques de Remy Belleau* (Rouen, Claude le Villain [or Jean Berthelin or Thomas Daré], 1604). (British Museum—a Le Villain copy. Bibliothèque de l'Arsenal—a Berthelin and a Daré.) Contains, ff. 393–434v, *La Reconnue, comedie. Par Remy Belleau.*

—— *La Reconnue.* A copy of *La Reconnue*, bound separately and foliated 111v–54, presumably a part of the 1585 or 1592 edition, is in the Bibliothèque de l'Arsenal.[1] Another copy, bound and foliated separately (Rouen, Thomas Daré, 1604), a part of the full 1604 edition, is also in the Bibliothèque de l'Arsenal. La Vallière, *Bibliothèque*, i. 218, Cioranescu, *Bibliographie*, p. 111, and Lebègue, *Tableau*, p. 285, give a 1577 edition of *La Reconnue*, which I have not traced.

BRUNO, GIORDANO, *Candelaio comedia del Bruno Nolano Achademico di nulla Achademia; detto il fastidito. In Tristitia hilaris: in Hilaritate tristis*

—————
[1] Its shelf-mark is that given by Mme Horn-Monval for a 1564 edition of *La Reconnue* (*Traductions et adaptations*, ii. 24) which is otherwise unknown and appears to be an error.

(Paris, Guillaume Julien, 1582). No privilege. (Bibliothèque de l'Arsenal.)

—— *Boniface et le pédant comedie en prose, Imitee de l'Italien de Bruno Nolano* (Paris, Pierre Menard, 1633). Privilege 2 April 1633. (Bibliothèque de 'Arsenal.) Based on *Il Candelaio*. According to the preface 'Au lecteur', cuts and changes have been made; in fact, rather cuts than changes; this version has lost much of the life of the original. Not the same as a translation of *Il Candelaio* in Bibliothèque Nationale, MS. F. Fr. n.a. 2879; cf. Ch. I, section 2, above.

CHAPPUIS, GABRIEL, *Les Mondes celestes, terrestres et infernaux . . . Tirez des œuvres de Doni Florentin, par Gabriel Chappuis Tourangeau. Depuis reveuz, corrigez et augmentez du Monde des Cornuz, par F. C. T.* (Lyons, Estienne Michel, 1580). (British Museum.)

CORNEILLE, PIERRE, *Melite, ou les fausses lettres. Piece comique* (Paris, François Targa, 1633). Privilege 31 January 1633. (Bibliothèque Nationale.)

D'AVES, *see* Troterel.

ELIOT, JOHN, *Ortho-epia Gallica* (London, 1593). A set of French–English dialogues. Cf. Ch. I, section 2, above.

ESTIENNE, CHARLES, *Comédie du Sacrifice, des professeurs de l'Academie vulgaire senoise, nommez Intronati, celebrée ès jeux d'un Karesme prenant à Senes, traduicte de Langue Tuscane par Charles Estienne* (Lyons, François Fradin and Pierre de Tours, 1543). (Bibliothèque de l'Arsenal.)

—— *Les Abusez* (Paris, Estienne Groulleau, 1548). (Bibliothèque Nationale.)

—— —— (Paris, Estienne Groulleau, 1556). (Bibliothèque Nationale.)

FONTENY, JACQUES DE, *see* Andreini.

FORNARIS, FABRIZIO DE, *Angelica, comedia de Fabritio de Fornaris Napolitano detto il Capitano Coccodrillo Comico Confidente* (Paris, Abel l'Angelier, 1585). No privilege. (British Museum; Bibliothèque de l'Arsenal.) The dedication to the Duc de Joyeuse refers to performance in the Duke's house.

—— *Angelique Comedie, de Fabrice de Fournaris Napolitain, dit le Capitaine Cocodrille Comique Confidant. Mis* [sic] *en François, des langues Italienne et Espagnolle, par le sieur L. C.* [= Larivey Champenois?] (Paris, Abel l'Angelier, 1599). Privilege 8 March 1599. (Bibliothèque de l'Arsenal, ex-libris Viollet-le-Duc.)

—— *L'Angelica, comedia di Fabritio de Fornaris Napolitano, Detto il Capitano Cocodrillo Comico Confidente* (Venice, Francesco Bariletti, 1607). (British Museum.) The dedication refers to 'l'Angelica Comedia del Capitan Cocodrillo, stampata già in Pariggi'.

GODARD, JEAN, *Les Œuvres de Jean Godard, Parisien. Divisees en deux Tomes. A Henry IIII, tres-Chrestien et tres-victorieux Roy de France et de Navarre* . . . (Lyons, Pierre Landry, 1594). 'Avec Privilege'; but none printed. (Bibliothèque de l'Arsenal.) Pagination irregular. Vol. ii contains *Les Desguises, comoedie de Jean Godard Parisien.* There are five pages of 'Argument sur la comoedie de Jean Godard, Par Claude le Brun jurisconsulte Beaujoulois', eight pages of a poem 'A Nicolas de Langes, premier president au Parlement de Dombes, et au Siege presidial à Lyon'; and the play, pp. 99–208.

—— *Meslanges poetiques: tragiques, comiques, et autres diverses. De l'invention de D. L. F. A la France* (Lyons, Ambroise Travers, 1624). (British Museum; Bibliothèque de l'Arsenal; Bibliothèque de Versailles.) Contains the 'Argument' by Le Brun, the poem to De Langes, and the play, pp. 99–208.

GRÉVIN, JACQUES, *Le Theatre de Jaques Grevin de Cler-mont en Beauvaisis* . . . *Ensemble, la seconde partie de l'Olimpe et de la Gelodacrye* (Paris, [Vincent Sertenas], 1561). Privilege, accorded to Sertenas, 16 June 1561. (Bibliothèque de l'Arsenal.) Contains, ff. *iii ff. [unfoliated, 11 sides in all], 'Brief discours pour l'intelligence de ce théatre'; ff. Ai–Aiii, an elegy by Ronsard to Grévin; pp. 43–5, 'Au lecteur'; pp. 46–111, *La Tresorière*; pp. 112–219, *Les Esbahis.* A copy in the Musée Plantin-Moretus, Antwerp, contains manuscript alterations in Grévin's hand.

—— *Le Theatre de Jaques Grevin de Cler-mont en Beauvaisis* (Paris, Vincent Sertenas and Guillaume Barbé, 1562). (British Museum.) Pp. 43–5, 'Au lecteur'; pp. 46–111, *La Tresorière*; pp. 112–219, *Les Esbahis.*[1]

JODELLE, ÉTIENNE, *Les Œuvres et Meslanges poetiques d'Estienne Jodelle sieur du Lymodin* (Paris, Nicolas Chesneau and Mamert Patisson, 1574). Privilege 24 September 1574. (Bibliothèque de l'Arsenal.) *L'Eugène*, ff. 188v–222v.

—— *Les Œuvres et Meslanges poetiques d'Estienne Jodelle, sieur du Lymodin, reveuës et augmentees* (Paris, Nicolas Chesneau and Mamert Patisson, 1583). (Bibliothèque de l'Arsenal.) *L'Eugène*, ff. 175v–207.

---

[1] La Vallière, *Bibliothèque*, i. 144–5, cites *Le Théâtre de Jacques Grévin* (Paris, Robert Étienne, 1560). L. Pinvert, in his *Jacques Grévin*, pp. 3–4, showed that this was an error.

JODELLE, ÉTIENNE, *Les Œuvres et Meslanges poetiques d'Estienne Jodelle, sieur du Lymodin, reveuës et augmentees* (Paris, R. le Fizelier, 1583). (Bibliothèque Nationale.) *L'Eugène*, ff. 175ᵛ–207.

—— *Œuvres et meslanges poetiques* (Lyons, Benoist Rigaud, 1597).

LARIVEY, PIERRE DE, *Les six premieres comedies facecieuses, de Pierre de Larivey, Champenois. A l'imitation des anciens Grecs, Latins, et modernes Italiens. A sçavoir, Le laquais. La vefve. Les esprits. Le morfondu. Les jaloux. Les escolliers* (Paris, Abel l'Angelier, 1579). Dedication dated 1 January 1579. Privilege 26 February 1579. (British Museum, imperfect; Bibliothèque de l'Arsenal.)

—— *Les Comedies facecieuses de Pierre de Larivey Champenois. A l'imitation des anciens Grecs, Latins, et modernes Italiens. A sçavoir, Le laquais. La vefve. Les Esprits. Le morfondu. Les Jaloux. Les Escolliers. Seconde edition* (Lyons, Benoist Rigaud, 1597). (British Museum.)

—— *Les Comedies facecieuses de Pierre de Larivey, Champenois. A l'imitation des anciens Grecs, Latins, et modernes Italiens. A sçavoir, Le Laquais. La vefve. Les Esprits. Le morfondu. Les Jaloux. Les Escolliers. Seconde edition* (Rouen, Raphaël du Petit Val, 1600).

———— (Rouen, Raphaël du Petit Val, 1601). (Bibliothèque de l'Arsenal.)

——— [. . . *La Vefve* . . . *Le Morfondu* . . .] (Rouen, Raphaël du Petit Val, 1611). (British Museum.)

—— *Trois Comedies des six dernieres de Pierre de Larivey Champenois. A l'imitation des ançiens* [sic] *Grecs, Latins et Modernes Italiens. A Sçavoir: La Constance. Le Fidelle. Et les Tromperies* (Troyes, Pierre Chevillot, 1611). No privilege. (Bibliothèque de l'Arsenal.) Also exists with a different title-page: *Trois nouvelles comedies de Pierre de Larivey, Champenois. A l'imitation des anciens Grecs, Latins, et modernes Italiens. A sçavoir La Constance, Le Fidelle, et Les Tromperies*. Imprimé à Troyes, Et se vendent à Paris. Chez La veufve Jean du Brayet, Jean de Bordeaux, et Claude de Roddes (1611).

—— *Les Esprits*. A copy of *Les Esprits*, bound separately, and foliated 111–65ᵛ, probably from the 1579 edition, is in the Bibliothèque de l'Arsenal. Conversely, the British Museum copy of the 1579 edition lacks *Les Esprits*; it may even be that the Arsenal copy is the missing section. A copy of *Les Esprits*, bound separately, and paginated 209–312, from the 1601 edition, is in the British Museum.

LASPHRISE, LE CAPITAINE, *see* Papillon.

LA TAILLE, JEAN DE, *La Famine, ou les Gabeonites . . . Ensemble plusieurs autres Œuvres poëtiques de Jehan de la Taille de Bondaroy . . . et de feu Jaques de la Taille son frere* . . . (Paris, Federic Morel, 1573).[1] (Bibliothèque de l'Arsenal.) On the reverse of the title-page, in the list of contents: 'Les Corrivaux, et le Negromant, Comedies tirees de l'Italien d'Arioste' [in fact, only *Le Negromant* is from Arioste; cf. I. 1 above]. Ff. 65–98ᵛ, *Les Corrivaus, comedie*; f. 99, a sonnet by Jacques de la Taille; ff. 99ᵛ–142, *Le Negromant, comedie de M. Louis Arioste, nouvellement mise en François, par Jehan de la Taille de Bondaroy.* Bound together, in the Arsenal copy, with other works by Jean and Jacques de la Taille, dated 1572 and 1573; privilege 18 October 1570.

—— —— (Rouen, Du Petit Val, 1602). (Bibliothèque de Versailles.) The same note on the reverse of the title-page; the same titles and foliation.

LAVARDIN, JACQUES DE, *La Celestine fidellement repurgee, et mise en meilleure forme par Jacques de Lavardin* . . . (Paris, Nicolas Bonfons, n.d. [1578]. No privilege. (Bibliothèque Nationale.)

—— *La Celestine tragicomedie, Traduit* [sic] *d'Espagnol en François* . . . *Derniere edition* (Rouen, Claude le Villain, 1598). (Bibliothèque Nationale.)

LE LOYER, PIERRE, *Erotopegnie, ou passetemps d'amour. Ensemble une Comedie du Muet insensé* (Paris, Abel l'Angelier, 1576). (British Museum.) Ff. 64–103ᵛ, *Le Muet insensé.*

—— *Les Œuvres et meslanges poetiques de Pierre le Loyer Angevin. Ensemble, La Comedie Nephelococugie, ou la Nuee des Cocus, non moins docte que facetieuse* (Paris, Jean Poupy, 1579). Privilege 1 August 1578. (Oxford, Bodleian Library; British Museum; Bibliothèque de l'Arsenal.) Ff. 122ᵛ–60ᵛ, *Le Muet insensé.* Ff. 161–238, *La Comedie Nephelococugie, ou la Nuee des Cocus. Nephelococugie* bears the date 1578, but to judge from the continuous pagination and the title-page of this edition, was probably not issued separately.

MAUPAS, CHARLES, *see* Turnèbe.

MESMES, JEAN-PIERRE DE, *La Comedie des Supposez de M. Louys Arioste, en Italien et Françoys* (Paris, Estienne Groulleau, 1552). Privilege 30 September 1549. (Bibliothèque de l'Arsenal.)

—— *Comedie des Supposez de M. Louys Arioste, Italien et François. Pour l'utilité de ceux qui desirent sçavoir la langue Italienne* (Paris, Hierosme de Marnef, et la veufve de Guillaume Gavellat, 1585). (Bibliothèque de l'Arsenal.) The same, re-issued with a new title-page.

PAPILLON, MARC DE (Le Capitaine Lasphrise), *Les Premieres Œuvres poetiques du Capitaine Lasphrise* (Paris, Jean Gesselin, 1597). Privilege 31

---

[1] According to De Maulde, *Œuvres de Jean de la Taille*, vol. iii, p. i, the two plays first appeared in 1574. No 1574 edition is known.

January 1597. (Bibliothèque Nationale.) *La Nouvelle Tragicomique*, pp. 565–91.

PAPILLON, MARC DE (Le Capitaine Lasphrise), *Les Premieres Œuvres poetiques du Capitaine Lasphrise* (Paris, Jean Gesselin,1599), 2 vols. (Bibliothèque de l'Arsenal.) *La Nouvelle Tragicomique*, vol. ii, pp. 635–57.

PERRIN, FRANÇOIS, *Sichem ravisseur, tragedie extraite du Genese trente quatriesme Chapitre. Par François Perrin Autunois* (Paris, Guillaume Chaudiere, 1589).[1] No privilege. (Bibliothèque de l'Arsenal; no other copy known.) No foliation before *Sichem* itself. The dedication of *Les Escoliers* to Jacques Arthault is on f. [10], that is, preceding *Sichem* but nevertheless not applicable to it. A sonnet by Arthault on f. [7] appears to suggest that Perrin had also translated the *Jephthes* of Buchanan. *Les Escoliers comedie*, ff. 41–73ᵛ, is not referred to on the title-page of this edition, nor has it a separate title-page. *Les Escoliers* is not included in the 1606 edition of *Sichem*: *Sichem ravisseur, ou la circoncision des incirconcis Tragedie. Par Françoys Perrin Autunois* (Rouen, Raphaël du Petit Val, 1606). (British Museum.)

TROTEREL, PIERRE, SIEUR D'AVES, *Les Corrivaux comedie facetieuse de l'invention de P. T. S. D.* [Pierre Troterel Sieur d'Aves] (Rouen, Raphaël du Petit Val, 1612). No privilege. (Bibliothèque de l'Arsenal.)

—— *Gillette, comedie facetieuse. Par le sieur D.* [D'Aves] (Rouen, David du Petit Val, 1620). No privilege. (Bibliothèque de l'Arsenal.)

TURNÈBE, ODET DE, *Les Contens comedie nouvelle en prose Françoise* (Paris, Felix le Mangnier, 1584). Privilege 16 September 1584. (Bibliothèque de l'Arsenal.)

—— *Les Desguisez. Comédie Françoise. Avec L'explication des Proverbes et mots difficiles. Par Charles Maupas* (Blois, Gauché Collas, 1626). A second edition of *Les Contens*, without mention of the name of Turnèbe. (Cited from Spector's edition of *Les Contens*, pp. xiii–xiv. Copies in the Bibliothèque Nationale and Bibliothèque de l'Arsenal.)

VIVRE, GÉRARD DE, *Comedie de la Fidelite nuptiale Composee par Gerard de Vivre Gantois, Maistre d'escole à Colongne* (Antwerp, Henry Heyndricx, 1577). No privilege. (British Museum.)

—— —— (Paris, Nicolas Bonfons, 1578). (Bibliothèque Nationale.)

[1] La Vallière, *Bibliothèque*, i. 286, gives 1586, not 1589; thus also Cioranescu, *Bibliographie*, p. 553; P. Lacroix in his 1866 edition of *Les Escoliers*; and Lebègue, *Tableau*, p. 331. Charmasse, *François Perrin*, showed that this was an error and that no 1586 edition is known; nor have I found such an edition.

—— *Comedie des Amours de Theseus et Dianira. Composé* [sic] *par Gerard de Vivre Gantois, Maistre d'escole à Colongne* (Paris, Nicolas Bonfons, 1577). No privilege. (Bibliothèque de l'Arsenal.) Dedicatory note dated 24 May 1577.

—— —— (Paris, Nicolas Bonfons, 1578). (Bibliothèque Nationale.)

—— *Trois Comedies françoises. De Gerard de Vivre Gantois. La premiere, Des Amours pudiques et loyales de Theseus et Dianita* [sic]. *La seconde, De la Fidelité nuptiale dune honeste Matrone envers son Mari et espoux. Et la troisieme, Du Patriarche Abraham et sa servante Agar. Le tout pour l'utilité de la jeunesse et usage des escoles françoises, reveu et corrige par Ant. Tyron* (Rotterdam, Jeab Waesbergue, 1589). No privilege. The dedication, slightly and clumsily altered to fit all three plays, is the same as that of the 1577 edition of the *Amours de Theseus et Dianira*, and is still dated 24 May 1577. (Bibliothèque de l'Arsenal.)

—— —— [slight orthographical difference in title] (Antwerp, Guislain Janssens, 1595). Privilege 15 November 1589. (Bibliothèque de l'Arsenal.)

—— —— —— (Antwerp, Guislain Janssens, 1602). (Bibliothèque de l'Arsenal.)

3. COMEDIES SUPPOSED TO HAVE BEEN PRINTED, BUT NOW LOST

BOURGEOIS, JACQUES, *Comédie très élegante, en laquelle sont contenues les amours recréatives d'Erostrate . . . et de la belle Polimneste . . .* (Paris, Veuve Jeannot, 1545). Title given by La Vallière, *Bibliothèque*, iii. 243. The very precision of the title gives an assurance that a copy was known to La Vallière, but none is known today. An adaptation or translation of Aristo's *I Suppositi*.

4. OTHER COMEDIES SUPPOSED TO HAVE EXISTED IN MANUSCRIPT, BUT NOW LOST[1]

AMBOISE, FRANÇOIS D': three comedies besides *Les Neapolitaines.* The preface to *Les Neapolitaines* refers to 'les comedies qu'il faisoit en la prime-vère de son adolescence' and which were acted: 'sur le theatre elles avoient esté veuës et receuës avec un plaisir indicible'; and to

---

[1] I have not included in this section references to plays called simply 'comédie' such as the 'plusieurs comédies en français' of Antoine Forestier (cf. Lebègue, *Tableau*, p. 292); the term is of such general application that it covers many kinds of dramatic production other than strict comedies. References of this kind are given in full in M. Lebègue's *Tableau*.

'plusieurs belles pieces' which might be published later. La Croix du Maine is more precise: in his list of works by d'Amboise, he cites 'Trois Tragedies, quatre Comedies' (*Bibliothèque* (Paris, 1584), p. 87).

AVOST, HIEROSME D': a comedy entitled *Les Deux Courtisanes*, translated or adapted from Loys Domenichi. This comedy, according to La Croix du Maine (*Bibliothèque*, p. 488) was ready for printing in 1584; but no copy of it is now known, so that it appears not to have been printed.

BAÏF, JEAN-ANTOINE DE: adaptations (on the lines of *Le Brave*?) or translations (on the lines of *L'Eunuque*?) of Terence's *Heautontimorumenos* and Aristophanes' *Plutus* (Du Verdier, *Bibliothèque*, p. 641; cf. Lebègue, *Tableau*, pp. 294 and 301). Claude Binet, in his *Vie de Ronsard*, states that Ronsard translated the *Plutus* while at the college de Coqueret, where it was acted; M. Lebègue suggests, very plausibly, that the two translations of the *Plutus* are one and the same, possibly made by Baïf and Ronsard in collaboration.

BOURRÉE, MICHEL, SIEUR DE LA PORTE: two or more comedies. According to La Croix du Maine, he wrote several tragedies and comedies in French (*Bibliothèque*, p. 323).

CHATEAUVIEUX (Cosme la Gambe): two comedies entitled *Le Capitaine Bouboufle* and *Jodés* (Du Verdier, *Bibliothèque*, p. 1196; cf. Lebègue, *Tableau*, p. 296).

GRÉVIN, JACQUES, *La Maubertine*: see Appendix B.

HARDY, ALEXANDRE, *Le Jaloux* and possibly other comedies. *Le Jaloux* was a comedy written by Hardy and sold by him to the troupe of Pierre Le Messier on 19 September 1625 for the sum of 100 *livres tournois*. For the evidence concerning this and possibly other comedies by Hardy, cf. S. W. Deierkauf-Holsboer, 'La vie d'Alexandre Hardy, Poète du Roi', *Proceedings of the American Philosophical Society*, 91 (1947), 328–404; *Les Ramonneurs*, ed. A. Gill (Paris, 1957), pp. lviii–xcviii.

JODELLE, ÉTIENNE, *La Rencontre*. E. Balmas, in his edition of *L'Eugène*, pp. 6–8, has shown that the identification of *L'Eugène* with *La Rencontre*, first made by the Frères Parfaict (*Histoire du théatre françois*, iii (Paris, 1745), 290), is an error. *La Rencontre* was a separate comedy, acted together with the tragedy *Cleopatre* in 1553, and now no longer extant.

LARIVEY, PIERRE DE: three comedies. The title-page of the 1611 edition of *La Constance*, *Le Fidelle*, and *Les Tromperies* implies that these are only three out of six further plays by Larivey: *Trois Comedies des six dernieres de Pierre de Larivey Champenois*. The dedication to François d'Amboise confirms this. Three others, therefore, may be presumed to have existed, but were never printed.

LA TAILLE, JACQUES DE: one or more comedies. Jean de la Taille, in his *Saül le furieux* (Paris, Federic Morel, 1572), f. 70, writes of his late brother Jacques that he wrote 'comme moy (selon le vray art, et la façon antique) Poëmes entiers, Tragedies et Comedies, en l'âge de 16, 17 et 18 ans', and that among his papers he found five tragedies and one comedy. In the same volume, a number of works by Jacques de la Taille are printed, with a title-page (f. 74) by Jacques de la Taille him-self where he says that he may afterwards publish his 'Tragedies, Comedies et autres poëmes nouveaus'.

LAUDUN D'AIGALIERS, PIERRE DE: one comedy. In his *Art poétique françois* (Paris, 1597), v. i, he writes: 'J'ay faict quelque comedie que l'on pourra voir, si je la mets chez l'imprimeur, toutesfois je n'en suis guere en deliberation. Plaute et Terence en ont faict en Latin lesquelles on pourra veoir et qui serviront de patron.' The mention of Plautus and Terence immediately after mention of his 'comedie' suggests that the play was a genuine comedy and that the word 'comedie' is not used in the more general sense of 'play'.

LE BRETON, GABRIEL: two or more comedies, one of which was entitled *Le Ramonneur*. La Croix du Maine, *Bibliothèque*, p. 143, writes of 'plusieurs autres tragedies et comedies Françoises' by him; Du Verdier, *Bibliothèque*, p. 429, mentions only one comedy and that entitled *Le Ramonneur*. Cf. *Les Ramonneurs*, ed. A. Gill (Paris, 1957), p. x.

PONTOUX, CLAUDE DE: three comedies. Du Verdier states that he left in manuscript 'deux tragedies et trois comedies accommodees sur les histoires de nostre temps' (*Bibliothèque*, p. 189; cf. Lebègue, *Tableau*, p. 294).

RONSARD, *see* Baïf.

TURNÈBE, ODET DE: manuscript copies of *Les Contens*, made from the 1584 edition. 'Plusieurs s'en sont fait avec grand labeur des copies à la main', writes Charles Maupas in his *Épître* to the 1626 edition of the play (see section 2 above).

VIVRE, GÉRARD DE: the dedication of the 1577 edition of *Les Amours de Theseus et Dianira* calls the play 'une Comedie des premieres de ma composition', suggesting that he may have written others besides this and *La Fidelité nuptiale* (also published in 1577).

5. MODERN EDITIONS

Collections:

Ancien Théâtre français, ou Collection des œuvres dramatiques les plus remarquables depuis les Mystères jusqu'à Corneille, ed. Viollet-le-Duc, vols. iv–viii

(Paris, P. Jannet, 1854–6). Jodelle, *L'Eugène*, iv. 5–81; Grévin, *Les Ébahis*, iv. 223–333; Belleau, *La Reconnue*, iv. 335–438; Larivey's nine plays, v. 1–vii. 105; Turnèbe, *Les Contents*, vii. 107–231; d'Amboise, *Les Néapolitaines*, vii. 233–333; Godard, *Les Déguisés*, vii. 335–462; Papillon (Le Capitaine Lasphrise), *La Nouvelle Tragicomique*, vii. 463–91; Troterel, *Les Corrivaux*, viii. 227–96.

French Renaissance Comedies, ed. B. Jeffery, an edition in preparation for the Athlone Press, London: to include Jodelle, *L'Eugène*; Belleau, *La Reconnue*; Grévin, *Les Ébahis*; d'Amboise, *Les Néapolitaines*.

Le Théâtre français au XVIe et au XVIIe siècle, ou Choix des comédies les plus curieuses antérieures à Molière, ed. É. Fournier (Paris, 1871), 8vo (reprinted in two 16mo volumes, Paris, 1872). Jodelle, *L'Eugène*, pp. 1–24; Belleau, *La Reconnue*, pp. 25–54; Larivey, *Les Esprits*, pp. 55–89; Turnèbe, *Les Contents*, pp. 90–131; d'Amboise, *Les Néapolitaines*, pp. 132–65; Perrin, *Les Écoliers*, pp. 166–91; Montluc, *La Comédie de proverbes*, pp. 192–227; Du Peschier, *La Comédie des comédies*, pp. 235–56; Du Ryer, *Les Vendanges de Suresnes*, pp. 319–47; Mairet, *Les Galanteries du Duc d'Ossonne*, pp. 373–99.

Separate editions:

ANON, *La Tasse*, ed. P.-L. Jacob, *Recueil de pièces rares et facétieuses*, vol. iii (Paris, 1873).

BAÏF, JEAN-ANTOINE DE, *Euvres en rime*, ed. Ch. Marty-Laveaux, 5 vols. (Paris, 1881–90) (*Le Brave*, iii. 183–373; *L'Eunuque*, iv. 1–138).

BELLEAU, RÉMY, *Œuvres poétiques*, ed. Ch. Marty-Laveaux, 2 vols. (Paris, 1878) (*La Reconnue*, ii. 355–451).

BRUNO, GIORDANO, *Il Candelaio*; reprinted, together with the 1633 adaptation *Boniface et le pédant*, in *Il Candelaio di Giordano Bruno; Boniface et le pédant comédie en prose imitée de l'Italien de Bruno Nolano*, ed. V. Imbriani (Naples, 1886).

CORNEILLE, PIERRE, *Mélite*, ed. Mario Roques and Marion Lièvre (Lille and Geneva, 1950).

GRÉVIN, JACQUES, *Théâtre complet et poésies choisies*, ed. L. Pinvert (Paris, 1922) (*La Trésorière*, pp. 51–113; *Les Ébahis*, pp. 115–217). Cf. also P. R. Auguis, *Les Poètes françois depuis le XIIIe siècle jusqu'à Malherbe* (Paris, 1824) (*La Trésorière*, v. 203–76).

JODELLE, ÉTIENNE, *L'Eugène*, ed. E. H. Balmas (Turin, 1955). Also in *Les Œuvres et Meslanges Poetiques d'Estienne Jodelle*, ed. Ch. Marty-Laveaux, vol. i (Paris, 1868), pp. 11–92.

LA TAILLE, JEAN DE, *Œuvres*, ed. R. de Maulde, 4 vols. (Paris, 1878–82) (*Les Corrivaux* and *Le Négromant* are in the volumes entitled *Comédies* (1879), iii–cvi and cvii–ccxxvii respectively).

LE LOYER, PIERRE, *La Néphélococugie ou la Nuée des cocus, comédie*, ed. G. B[runet] (Turin, 1869) (limited edition of 100 copies). Neither of Le Loyer's plays is in *Œuvres poétiques de Pierre le Loyer*, ed. M. J. Turquais (Angers, 1934).

PERRIN, FRANÇOIS, *Les Écoliers*, ed. P. L[acroix] (Brussels, 1866) (limited edition of 106 copies).

TURNÈBE, ODET DE, *Les Contents*, ed. N. B. Spector, 2nd ed. (Paris, Société des Textes français modernes, 1964).

6. MODERN ADAPTATIONS

CAMUS, ALBERT, *Les Esprits, comédie, adaptation en trois actes par Albert Camus* (Paris, Gallimard, 1953). Adapted from Larivey's *Les Esprits*; written in 1940, acted in 1946 in Algeria, remodelled for the Festival d'art dramatique d'Angers, 1953.

PHILIPPON, GUSTAVE, *La Trésorière* (*L'Idéale-Revue*, 25 November 1911). An adaptation in three acts of Grévin's *La Trésorière*.

7. SECONDARY SOURCES

ATKINS, J. W. H., *English Literary Criticism: The Renascence* (London, 1947).

ATTINGER, GUSTAVE, *L'Esprit de la commedia dell'arte dans le théâtre français* (Paris, 1950).

AUGÉ-CHIQUET, M., *Jean-Antoine de Baif* (Paris, 1909).

BALDWIN, T. W., *Shakespeare's Five-Act Structure* (Urbana, 1947).

BAPST, G., *Essai sur l'histoire du théâtre: la mise en scène, le décor, le costume, l'architecture, l'éclairage, l'hygiène* (Paris, 1893).

BASCHET, A., *Les Comédiens italiens à la cour de France sous Charles IX, Henri III, Henri IV et Louis XIII* (Paris, 1882).

BEARE, W. *The Roman Stage*, 3rd ed. (London, 1964).

BEIJER, A., and DUCHARTRE, P. L. (eds.), *Recueil de plusieurs fragments des premières comédies italiennes . . . Recueil dit de Fossard . . . suivi de Compositions de Rhétorique* (Paris, 1928).

BOTTASSO, E., 'Le commedie di Lodovico Ariosto nel teatro francese del Cinquecento', *Giornale storico della letteratura italiana*, cxxviii (1951), 41–80.

BOUGHNER, D. C., *The Braggart in Renaissance Comedy. A Study in Comparative Drama from Aristophanes to Shakespeare* (Minneapolis, 1954).

BOWEN, BARBARA C., *Les Caractéristiques essentielles de la Farce française et leur survivance dans les années 1550–1620* (Illinois Studies in Language and Literature, 53) (Urbana, 1964).

BRADBROOK, M. C., *The Growth and Structure of Elizabethan Comedy* (London, 1955).

BROWN, H. M., *Music in the French Secular Theatre, 1400–1550* (Cambridge (Mass.), 1963).

CANNINGS, BARBARA, 'Towards a Definition of Farce as a Literary Genre', *Modern Language Review*, lvi (1961), 558–60.

CASTOR, GRAHAME, *Pléiade Poetics* (Cambridge, 1964).

CHAMARD, HENRI, *Histoire de la Pléiade*, 4 vols. (Paris, 1939–40).

CHARMASSE, A. DE, *François Perrin, poète français du XVIe siècle*. Reprinted from *Mémoires de la Société Eduenne*, nouvelle série, xv (1887), 1–253.

CHASLES, E., *La Comédie en France au seizième siècle* (Paris, 1862).

CIORANESCU, A., *L'Arioste en France*, 2 vols. (Paris, 1939).

—— *Bibliographie de la littérature française du seizième siecle* (Paris, 1959).

CLUBB, LOUISE G., *Giambattista Della Porta Dramatist* (Princeton, 1965).

COHEN, G., 'Ronsard et le théâtre', *Mélanges offerts à Henri Chamard* (Paris, 1951), pp. 121–4.

—— *Le Théâtre en France au moyen âge*, vol. ii (Paris, 1931).

COUGNY, E., *Des représentations dramatiques et particulièrement de la comédie politique dans les collèges* (Paris, 1859).

DABNEY, L. E., *French Dramatic Literature in the Reign of Henri IV* (Austin, 1952).

DALEY, T. A., *Jean de la Taille (1533–1608), étude historique et littéraire* (Paris, 1934).

[DEIERKAUF-] HOLSBOER, S. WILMA, *Histoire de la mise en scène dans le théâtre français de 1600 à 1657* (Paris, 1933).

—— 'La vie d'Alexandre Hardy, Poète du Roi', *Proceedings of the American Philosophical Society*, 91 (1947), 328–404.

DELCOURT, MARIE, *La Tradition des comiques anciens en France avant Molière* (Liège, 1934).

DIETSCHY, CHARLOTTE, *Die 'Dame d'intrigue' in der französischen Originalkomödie des XVI. und XVII. Jahrhunderts* (Halle, 1916) (Beihefte zur Zeitschrift für romanische Philologie, 64).

DROZ, E., and LEWICKA, H. (eds.), *Le Recueil Trepperel: Les farces* (Geneva, 1961).

DU BELLAY, JOACHIM, *La Deffence et illustration de la langue françoyse* (Paris, 1549); ed. H. Chamard (Paris, 1948).

DUCHARTRE, P.-L. *La commedia dell'arte et ses enfants* (Paris, 1955).

DUCKWORTH, G. E., *The Nature of Roman Comedy. A Study in Popular Entertainment* (Princeton, 1952).

DU VERDIER, ANTOINE, *Bibliothèque* (Lyons, 1585).

ELLIS-FERMOR, UNA, *The Jacobean Drama* (London, 1961).

FEST, O., *Der Miles Gloriosus in der französischen Komödie von Beginn der Renaissance bis zu Molière* (Erlangen and Leipzig, 1897) (Münchener Beiträge zur romanischen und englischen Philologie, XIII).

FRANK, GRACE, *The Medieval French Drama* (Oxford, 1954).

GADOFFRE, GILBERT, 'L'université collégiale et la Pléiade', *French Studies*, xi (1957), 293–304.

—— *Ronsard par lui-même* (Paris, 1960).

GARAPON, ROBERT, *La Fantaisie verbale et le comique dans le théâtre français* (Paris, 1957).

GOFFLOT, L.-V., *Le Théâtre au collège* (Paris, 1907).

HAAG, H., *Der Gestaltwandel der Kupplerin in der französischen Literatur des 16. und 17. Jahrhunderts* (Marburg, 1936) (Marburger Beiträge zur romanischen Philologie, XVII).

HARASZTI, JULES, 'La littérature dramatique au temps de la Renaissance', *Revue d'histoire littéraire de la France*, xi (1904), 680–6.

—— 'La comédie française de la Renaissance et la scène', *Revue d'histoire littéraire de la France*, xvi (1909), 285–301.

HERRICK, M. T., *Comic Theory in the Sixteenth Century* (Illinois Studies in Language and Literature, 34) (Urbana, 1950; reprinted separately, Urbana, 1964).

—— *The Fusion of Horatian and Aristotelian Literary Criticism, 1531–1555* (Illinois Studies in Language and Literature, 32) (Urbana, 1946).

—— *Italian Comedy in the Renaissance* (Urbana, 1960).

HINDLEY, A., 'The Development and Diffusion of Farce in France towards the end of the Middle Ages' (unpublished dissertation for the degree of Ph.D., University of Hull, 1965).

HORN-MONVAL, M., *Traductions et adaptations françaises du théâtre étranger*, vols. i, ii, and iii (Paris, 1958, 1959, 1960).

HUGUET, E., *Dictionnaire de la langue française du seizième siècle* (Paris, 1925–67).

HYDE, M. C., *Playwriting for Elizabethans* (New York, 1949).

JACQUOT, JEAN (ed.), *Le Lieu théâtral à la Renaissance* (Paris, 1964).

—— (ed.), *La Vie théâtrale au temps de la Renaissance* [catalogue of an exhibition] (Paris, 1963).

JOSEPH, B. L., *Elizabethan Acting* (Oxford, 1951; second edition, considerably changed, Oxford, 1964).

KINDERMANN, H., *Theatergeschichte Europas*, vols. ii–iv (Salzburg, 1959, 1959, 1961).

KOHLER, P., *L'Esprit classique et la comédie* (Paris, 1925).

LA CROIX DU MAINE, FRANÇOIS GRUDÉ, SIEUR DE, *Bibliothèque* (Paris, 1584).

LANCASTER, H. C., *A History of French Dramatic Literature in the Seventeenth Century*, 5 parts (Baltimore, 1929–42).

—— (ed.), *Le Mémoire de Mahelot, Laurent et d'autres décorateurs de l'Hôtel de Bourgogne* (Paris, 1920).

LAUDUN D'AIGALIERS, PIERRE DE, *Art poëtique françois* (Paris, 1579).

LA VALLIÈRE, *Bibliothèque du théâtre françois depuis son origine*, 3 vols. (Dresden, 1768).

LAWRENSON, T. E., *The French Stage in the Seventeenth Century* (Manchester, 1957).

—— and PURKIS, HELEN, 'Les éditions illustrées de Térence dans l'histoire du théâtre', *Le Lieu théâtral à la Renaissance*, ed. Jean Jacquot (Paris, 1964), pp. 1–23.

LAWTON, H. W., 'Charles Estienne et le théâtre', *Revue du seizième siècle*, xiv (1927), 336–47.

—— *A Handbook of French Renaissance Dramatic Theory* (Manchester, 1949).

—— 'La survivance des personnages térentiens', *Bulletin de l'Association Guillaume Budé* (1964), pp. 85–94.

—— *Térence en France au XVIᵉ siècle* (Paris, 1926).

LEA, K. M., *Italian popular Comedy: a Study in the commedia dell'arte 1560–1620* (Oxford, 1934).

LEBÈGUE, RAYMOND, 'La comédie italienne en France au XVIᵉ siècle', *Revue de littérature comparée*, xxiv (1950), 5–24.

—— 'Les débuts de la commedia dell'arte en France', *Rivista di studi teatrali*, 9/10 (1954), 71–7.

—— 'Premières infiltrations de la commedia dell'arte dans le théâtre français', *Cahiers de l'Association des études françaises*, xv (1963), 165–76.

—— 'Tableau de la comédie française de la Renaissance', *Bibliothèque d'Humanisme et Renaissance*, viii (1946), 278–344.

LEROUX DE LINCY, A. J. V., and MICHEL, F., *Recueil de farces, moralités, et sermons joyeux*, 6 vols. (Paris, 1837).

LIDA DE MALKIEL, M. R., 'El fanfarrón en el teatro del Renacimiento', *Romance Philology*, xi (1957–8), 268–91.

LINTILHAC, EUGÈNE, *La Comédie: Moyen Âge et Renaissance* (Paris, n.d. [1905]).

MAXWELL, IAN, *French Farce and John Heywood* (Melbourne, 1946).

MIGNON, MAURICE, 'Les influences italiennes dans la comédie française de la Renaissance', *Revue des cours et conférences*, xx (1911–12), 354–60.

MONGRÉDIEN, G., *Dictionnaire biographique des comédiens français du XVIIe siècle* (Paris, 1961).

MORIN, LOUIS, *Les Trois Pierre de Larivey* (Troyes, 1937).

MOUSSINAC, LÉON, *Le Théâtre* (Paris, 1957).

NICOLL, ALLARDYCE, *Masks, Mimes and Miracles* [1931] (New York, 1963).

—— *The World of Harlequin* (Cambridge, 1963).

PASQUIER, ÉTIENNE, *Les Recherches de la France* (Paris, 1611).

PATTERSON, W. F., *Three Centuries of French Poetic Theory, a Critical History of the Chief Arts of Poetry in France (1328–1630)* (University of Michigan Publications in Language and Literature, xiv–xv), 2 vols. (Ann Arbor, 1935).

PELETIER DU MANS, JACQUES, *L'Art poëtique* (Lyons, 1555), ed. A. Boulanger (Paris, 1930).

PERMAN, R. C. D., 'The Influence of the commedia dell'arte on the French Theatre before 1640', *French Studies*, ix (1955), 293–303.

PETIT DE JULLEVILLE, L., *Répertoire du théâtre comique en France au moyen âge* (Paris, 1886).

PICOT, ÉMILE, *Les Français italianisants*, 2 vols. (Paris, 1906–7).

PINVERT, L., *Jacques Grévin* (Paris, 1899).

PURKIS, HELEN, 'Les intermèdes à la cour de France au XVIe siècle', *Bibliothèque d'Humanisme et Renaissance*, xx (1958), 296–309.

RATERMANIS, J. B., and IRWIN, W. R., *The Comic Style of Beaumarchais* (Seattle, 1961).

RIGAL, E., *Alexandre Hardy et le théâtre français à la fin du XVIe et au commencement du XVIIe siècle* (Paris, 1889).

—— *De Jodelle à Molière* (Paris, 1911).

—— 'Les personnages conventionnels de la comédie au XVIe siècle', *Revue d'histoire littéraire de la France*, iv (1897), 161–79.

—— *Le Théâtre français avant la période classique* (Paris, 1901).

RIVAILLE, LOUIS, *Les Débuts de P. Corneille* (Paris, n.d.) [1936].

ROBBINS, E. W., *Dramatic Characterization in Printed Commentaries on Terence, 1473–1600* (Illinois Studies in Language and Literature, 35) (Urbana, 1951).

ROY, DONALD, 'Conditions and Conventions of the early Seventeenth-Century Theatre in France' (unpublished dissertation for the degree of M.A., University of Wales, 1954).

ROY, ÉMILE, '*L'Avare* de Doni et *L'Avare* de Molière', *Revue d'histoire littéraire de la France*, i (1894), 38–48.

SAULNIER, F., *Le Parlement de Bretagne 1554–1790* (Rennes, 1909).

SCALIGER, J.-C., *Poetices libri septem* [Lyons, 1561] (Heidelberg, 1607).

SCHERER, JACQUES, *La Dramaturgie classique en France* (Paris, 1950).

—— *La Dramaturgie de Beaumarchais* (Paris, 1954).

SCHWARTZ, I. A., *The Commedia dell'arte and its Influence on French Comedy in the 17th Century* (New York, 1933).

SÉBILLET, THOMAS, *Art poetique françoys* (Paris, 1548), ed. F. Gaiffe (Paris, 1932).

SERLIO, SEBASTIANO, *Il primo libro d'architettura* [*Il secondo libro di perpettura*] *di Sebastiano Serlio* . . . *Le premier livre d'architecture* [*Le second livre de perspective*] *de Sebastiano Serlio* . . . *mis en langue françoyse par Jehan Martin* (Paris, 1545).

SPECTOR, N. B., 'Odet de Turnèbe's *Les Contents* and the Italian Comedy', *French Studies*, xiii (1959), 304–13.

STERLING, C., 'Early Paintings of the Commedia dell'arte in France', *Bulletin of the Metropolitan Museum of Art* (New York, 1943), pp. 11–32.

SYDOW, P., *Die französische Originalkomödie des 16. Jahrhunderts* (Halle, 1908).

TILLYARD, E. M. W., *The Nature of Comedy and Shakespeare* (London, 1958) (The English Association, Presidential Address, 1958).

TOLDO, PIETRO, 'La comédie française de la Renaissance', *Revue d'histoire littéraire de la France*, iv–vii (1897–1900).

VAUQUELIN DE LA FRESNAYE, JEAN, *L'art poetique* (Paris, 1605), ed. G. Pellissier (Paris, 1885).

VIGNIER, N., *Histoire de la maison de Luxembourg* (Paris, 1617).

VYVYAN, JOHN, *Shakespeare and the Rose of Love* (London, 1960).

WEINBERG, BERNARD, *Critical Prefaces of the French Renaissance* (Evanston (Illinois), 1950).

WILEY, W. L., *The Early Public Theater in France* (Cambridge (Mass.), 1960).

YATES, FRANCES, 'Contribution to the Study of the French Social Drama in the Sixteenth Century' (unpublished thesis for the degree of M.A., London, 1926).

—— *Giordano Bruno and the Hermetic Tradition* (London, 1964).

——*A Study of Love's Labour's Lost* (Cambridge, 1936).

YOUNG, MARGARET L. M., *Guillaume Des Autelz* (Travaux d'Humanisme et Renaissance, xlviii) (Geneva, 1961).

INDEX

PRINTED IN GREAT BRITAIN
AT THE UNIVERSITY PRESS, OXFORD
BY VIVIAN RIDLER
PRINTER TO THE UNIVERSITY